Ministerial Ethics

Ministerial Ethics

Moral Formation for Church Leaders

Second Edition

Joe E. Trull
and
James E. Carter

 **Baker Academic**
Grand Rapids, Michigan

© 2004 by Joe E. Trull and James E. Carter

Published by Baker Academic
a division of Baker Publishing Group
P.O. Box 6287, Grand Rapids, MI 49516-6287
www.bakeracademic.com

Sixth printing, April 2008

Printed in the United States of America

Library of Congress Cataloging-in-Publication Data
Trull, Joe E.
  Ministerial ethics : moral formation for church leaders / Joe E. Trull and James E. Carter.—2nd ed.
      p.   cm.
  Includes bibliographical references and index.
  ISBN 10: 0-8010-2755-1 (pbk.)
  ISBN 978-0-8010-2755-0 (pbk.)
  1. Clergy—Professional ethics. 2. Clergy—Conduct of life. I. Carter, James E., 1935– II. Title.
BV4011.5.T78 2004
241'.641—dc22   2003055916

To
all good ministers
who faithfully serve
Jesus Christ and his church
with integrity

Wide was his parish, houses far asunder,
But never did he fail, for rain or thunder,
In sickness, or in sin, or any state,
To visit to the farthest, small and great,
Going afoot, and in his hand a stave.
This fine example to his flock he gave,
That first he wrought and afterwards he taught;
Out of the gospel then that text he caught,
And this figure he added thereunto—
That, if gold rust, what shall poor iron do?
For if the priest be foul, in whom we trust,
What wonder if a layman yield to lust?

Geoffrey Chaucer, *The Canterbury Tales*

Contents

Preface to the Second Edition

The first edition of this book appeared in 1993 under the title *Ministerial Ethics: Being a Good Minister in a Not-So-Good World*. Due to a growing recognition of ethical dilemmas faced by ministers, concern for professional ethics in ministry has increased in all denominations. During the past decade, this interest has moved beyond the religious institutions to the community at large.

In 2002, clergy sexual misconduct by Roman Catholic priests, coupled with an apparent cover-up by church officials, shocked a nation and captured the news. Lawsuits threatened to bankrupt several dioceses. Leaders in all religious groups reassessed the need for ethics in ministry among their own clergy.

Parallel to this increasing awareness, religious schools and seminaries have accepted greater responsibility to develop moral character in their students. New studies in spiritual formation now appear in the curriculum of almost every Christian school. A plethora of textbooks on the subject supports this new interest in personal spiritual growth and ethical character development.

The need for an updated and expanded edition of our text is obvious. It is our hope that this second edition will support this renewed awareness of the importance of ministerial ethics. In addition, we believe churches as well as educational institutions will benefit from understanding and addressing the issues outlined in these pages.

To this end, we have added a new chapter (chap. 7) that focuses specifically on clergy sexual abuse. We hope this addition will help counteract the disturbing incidences of ministers crossing into the "forbidden zone," as well as guide churches in prevention and response strategies.

Many reviews of the first edition expressed appreciation for the appendices, which contained a number of ministerial codes of ethics, past and present. We have strengthened this section by revising the list, as well as adding several contemporary codes developed in the last few years.

Preparing the second edition has reminded us of the book's limitations, namely, the brevity with which we address many significant subjects. Some of the chapters could easily be the subject of an entire book. Nevertheless, we believe a general overview of the entire scope of ministerial ethics in the form of an introductory text is justified.

Finally, we wish to express gratitude to Baker Book House for their willingness to publish this revised and expanded second edition and to acquisitions editor Robert N. Hosack, whose patience and second-mile efforts made this new edition a reality.

Preface to the First Edition

After half a century of relative silence on the subject, the last decade has witnessed a renewed interest in ministerial ethics. One reason for this attention is our rapidly changing culture; clergy ethics are more complex in today's society. Another factor is the seeming increase in moral failures in the ministry.

Rightly or wrongly, churches formerly assumed that Christian ministers were persons of integrity who could be counted on to be ethical. No longer is this presumption possible. As a result, theological seminaries and church-related colleges are reexamining their responsibilities for spiritual formation and rethinking their curricula. The teaching of ministerial ethics to ministerial students is a new priority in many schools.

The purpose of this book is twofold. First, this study intends to teach Christian ministry students the unique moral role of the minister and the ethical responsibilities of that vocation. A second purpose is more practical: to provide new and established ministers with a clear statement of the ethical obligations contemporary clergy should assume in their personal and professional lives.

This work is the joint effort of two people who have been friends since seminary days and who feel uniquely bonded by their Christian faith, their love of ministry, and their like-mindedness. We have spent most of our adult lives as pastors, an aggregate of more than fifty-five years of ministry in rural, small-town, suburban, university, and downtown churches. The two of us now serve by guiding and training other ministers in the vocation.

Although the seminary teacher authored the more foundational chapters of the book (1, 2, 6, 7) and the denominational worker the more practical ones (3, 4, 5), the entire work is the product of both of our minds, as we have labored together throughout the project.

We have also worked very hard at inclusiveness. Aware of our own white-male-Baptist-pastor perspective, we have intentionally tried to address all ministers: male and female, pastors and associate ministers, generalists and specialists, various ethnic groups and Christian traditions. Although our theological approach is based in the evangelical tradition, we hope clergypersons of every persuasion will find in this book encouragement and assistance for their own ministry.

Like all good ethical choices, this book is the result of the broad influence of many people. Numerous colleagues, friends, and ministers have made significant contributions. Each topic brings to mind many "good ministers" we have known throughout the years. We wish to thank each of them.

In particular, Joe E. Trull is grateful to New Orleans Baptist Theological Seminary for sabbatical leave in 1991–92 to complete this book, to Union Theological Seminary in Virginia for inviting him to be a research fellow on their campus during that time, to the T. B. Maston Foundation for providing a grant to assist in this project, and to the late T. B. Maston himself, beloved mentor and teacher whose life and lessons are often reflected in this work.

James E. Carter is particularly grateful to the churches he has served as pastor through the years, to the executive board of the Louisiana Baptist Convention for its encouragement to write, to the Southern Baptist churches and ministers in Louisiana with whom it is his privilege to work, and to T. B. Maston, who though not his primary professor was also a major influence in the formation of his ethical thinking.

Both of us wish to give special recognition to the laypersons, teachers, and ministers who read our manuscript and gave invaluable advice along the way: John Alley, Larry Baker, Wayne Barnes, Cheryl Burns, Cynthia Greenleaf, Robert Parham, Allen Reasons, and Nell Summerlin.

For that unique support and counsel that only a spouse can give, our personal gratitude to Audra and Carole.

Introduction

Ours is an age of ethical uncertainty. In Walker Percy's novel *The Thanatos Syndrome*, a minister faces an ethical dilemma. Percy capsules his moral confusion and ours in one line: "This is not the Age of Enlightenment, but the Age of Not Knowing What To Do."[1] One writer calls this quote an apt aphorism for our age and adds:

> Politicians, scientists, physicians, business leaders, everyday citizens, and our clergy increasingly find themselves in situations where they really do not know what to do. As a result, ethics has become a boom industry, and moral failure a regular front-page phenomenon. Conventional wisdom seems glaringly inadequate in the face of our environmental, technological, political, economic, and social situations.[2]

Ministerial ethics can no longer be assumed, if ever they were. In a city not far from where one of us lives, the pastor of one of the fastest growing churches in the South was arrested for drug smuggling. He confessed to flying cocaine from Colombia for $50,000. The minister, whose church had led the state in the number of baptisms for several years, was sentenced to three years in prison and fined $10,000.

A regional magazine in a metropolitan area in the Southwest featured a cover story titled "Thy Neighbors' Wives," which chronicled the sexual affairs of a megachurch's pastor. The article claimed that the charismatic leader was obsessed with wealth, power, and status. "One beautiful woman was not enough," said a deacon, referring to the minister's wife. "He was set up as an ideal man. He was adored and he ate it up."[3]

The saddest chapter in these two tragic stories was the final one. Neither fallen minister seemed remorseful when exposed, nor did he appear repentant when sanctioned. After a brief absence, they both established new independent congregations in the same cities where they had previously pastored.

Moral failures in the ministry are all too common today. Chaucer asked, "If gold rust, what shall poor iron do?" Obviously, it too rusts, perhaps more rapidly. "For if the priest be foul, in whom we trust," continued the author of *The Canterbury Tales*, "what wonder if a layman yield to lust?"

The present crisis in ministerial ethics is both a reflection of our times and an influence on our society. Ethical failure in the pulpit affects the pew. At the same time, clergy morals seem to mirror the general decline in morality among the laity. Our day is fraught with political cover-ups, insider trading on the stock exchange, corporate scandals, and media manipulation. Numbed by it all, people are seldom shocked when they hear of an immoral minister.

Several years ago the academic dean of a seminary asked one of us to develop a course in ministerial ethics. Although this ethics professor was a freshman faculty member, he did understand the subject after twenty-five years in pastoral ministry. The congregations served by this new teacher were varied: a rural mission church in Oklahoma, a small-town church in north Texas, a fast-growing congregation in a suburb of Dallas, and a downtown church in the international city of El Paso. (The coauthor of this text served similar congregations in Louisiana and Texas for over thirty years before becoming the director of the Church Minister Relations Division of the Louisiana Baptist Convention.) From our own experiences, both of us knew that ministers needed help in personal and professional ethics.

The dean of the seminary had concerns beyond the need he saw for students to study pastoral ethics. Moral scandals involving televangelists and prominent religious leaders had recently made the pages of *USA Today, Time,* and *Newsweek*. These embarrassing stories had created an atmosphere of distrust toward all ministers. Even more alarming to the dean was that almost every week another Shakespearean moral tragedy came to his attention, as the curtain rose to reveal a new tale of a fallen minister and a forced termination.

A study of the dismissals of Southern Baptist pastors by Norris Smith, a specialist in the area of forced terminations, revealed that "immorality" was a leading cause of dismissals, second only to a "lack or abuse of communication." The survey defined "immorality" as "sexual misconduct, substantive lying, and the misuse or embezzlement of church funds." Smith pointed to a lack of accountability and of clear professional guidelines among pastors as contributors to their ethical failure.[4]

These events, as critical as they were, did not in and of themselves fully justify a new course in the seminary curriculum. Three significant facts verified the crucial need to teach professional ethics to today's clergy.

The first actually became the basic rationale for the ministerial ethics course and for this book: *The Christian minister occupies a unique role among all vocations.* This is true in relation not only to other occupations but also among the traditional service professions. No vocation is as ethically demanding as the

Christian ministry. No professional is expected to model morality as much as a minister.

Today's ministers walk an ethical tightrope. At one moment they may serve as prophets, priests, or educators; in the next, they may be administrators, counselors, or worship leaders. Each of these roles raises ethical dilemmas and exposes moral vulnerability not faced by doctors, lawyers, or other professionals.

For example, most church members trust their minister without hesitation. Yet this intimate relationship often involves a parishioner sharing her soul, which makes a church minister vulnerable to many subtle temptations. The most obvious danger is sexual misconduct. Many clergy catastrophes involve romantic affairs, sexual liaisons, pedophilic acts, and other sexual transgressions.

Equally immoral, though often overlooked, are certain ministerial habits that may be considered part of the "job description." Pulpit exaggeration is accepted as a normal trait of preachers. How often does a church member say, "Oh, he's just preaching!"

More serious is the unethical conduct of an autocratic leader who misuses power, manipulates people, and practices deception and dishonesty. Pascal warned that people "never do evil so completely and cheerfully as when they do it from religious convictions." The American culture stimulates in many clerics the desire to succeed. To be called as a pastor of a large, prestigious church is the goal that has led many good ministers to sacrifice their integrity on the altar of success.

The first fact led to the second: *Literature on the subject of ministerial ethics was rare.* Two decades ago in his classic *Survey of Recent Christian Ethics,* Edward Leroy Long Jr. noted that "practically no attention has been given to the ethical problems arising from the practice of ministry, though the role of the church with respect to social issues has been hotly debated."[5] Other than Bishop Nolan Harmon's *Ministerial Ethics and Etiquette* (a 1928 publication now in its twelfth reprinting) and J. Clark Hensley's booklet *Preacher Behave![6] little was available as a resource for ministers. One notable exception was Karen Lebacqz's *Professional Ethics,*[7] an excellent academic text dealing with basic concepts in pastoral ethics. Two works dealing with professional ethics in general completed the list of early clergy ethics resources.[8]

In the years just before the first edition of this text was published in 1993, three new books on clergy ethics appeared,[9] along with a few articles in journals.[10] Although helpful in many ways, the new books seemed hesitant to give specific guidance and failed to discuss many practical issues in ministerial ethics. A compilation of essays written by members of the Chicago Area Ethics Study Group also appeared in the early 1990s. The authors intentionally chose a "terrain-mapping model," explaining that specific issues facing modern clergy "are simply too numerous and too varied."[11] Regrettably, most of these books are now out of print.

Recently, three significant texts addressing the ethical life of the minister have appeared.[12] Richard Gula's *Ethics in Pastoral Ministry* is written from a Roman Catholic perspective, and the strength of the book lies in his development of theological foundations and his discussion of two issues: sexuality and confidentiality.[13] The most recent clergy ethics text is *Calling and Character: Virtues of the Ordained Life,* written by William Willimon of Duke University.[14] Both books intentionally avoid analysis of specific issues, proposing that character or virtue is the basis for ministerial ethics; "Who am I to be?" rather than "What am I to do?" is for them the crucial question.[15] About the same time Willimon's work appeared, twenty-two Roman Catholic and Protestant contributors published *Practice What You Preach,* a third text focusing on character ethics.[16] Though the case study format enhances the work, the use of multiple authors, the broadness of topics, and the lack of pastoral experience among the writers (only one of twenty-two) seriously limits the presentation.[17]

Fifteen years after we first surveyed the resources on ministerial ethics, our conclusions remain the same: Literature on the subject is scarce, and most of the few texts that are in print have serious limitations.

A third fact became apparent in 1988 when "Professional Ethics for Ministers" was first offered at the seminary where one of us taught: *Ministerial ethics was not taught in most seminaries.* As we surveyed a large number of colleagues and studied seminary catalogues, we found that few ministers had ever studied ministerial ethics and only a few divinity schools listed a course on the subject. Only one out of six Southern Baptist seminaries offered such a study.[18] A representative sampling of twenty other Protestant seminaries revealed that only three of them offered a course in pastoral ethics (two were courses taught by authors of recent texts in this field).[19] Ironically, this occurred at a time when graduate schools of law, medicine, and business were reinstituting courses in professional ethics.[20]

Now add to these three facts a disturbing trend evident at the beginning of the twenty-first century: *The teaching of Christian ethics in seminaries and universities seems to be declining.* Ron Sider once observed that theological scholarship is forever leaving ethics until last, and then leaving it out. Many theological schools make this mistake when they attempt to include the teaching of ethics in other disciplines. The result is the omission of important areas of Christian ethics.

The largest seminary in the United States (from which both of us graduated) recently announced that it was suspending doctoral degree programs in Christian ethics "due to the retirement or resignation of faculty." Two decades ago this school had five ethics professors; today it has only one! Another example is a new seminary that has recorded phenomenal growth since it began nine years ago on the campus of a major university. Just recently this divinity school announced a record enrollment of 353 students—yet the first course in Christian ethics has yet to be taught in this graduate school.[21]

Little wonder, then, that this is a critical day for pastoral ethics. With seminary training in ministerial morality seldom available and with a minimal amount of adequate literature on the shelf, church ministers are left to flounder with little aid in an ethical sea churning with moral storms. Young ministers soon discover that they face many difficult ethical questions in their professional life. For example: What ethical standards are required of a minister? What does confidentiality mean, and is it always expected? How is pastoral authority abused? When is preaching plagiarized? Is there a code of ethics that all ministers should follow? These and many other queries from clerics deserve an answer.

This, then, is the rationale behind our book: We wanted to create a text that would strengthen moral formation in ministers and help them resolve the complex professional problems they face daily. This volume is by no means exhaustive, nor is it an "answer book" for all of the tough questions the ordained face. However, it is an attempt to provide basic ethical guidance for persons involved in Christian ministry—not only pastors but also ministers of education, music, and youth, as well as church counselors, chaplains, and other similar church professionals.

New Orleans is built on swampy, spongy, and unstable marshlands. The city lies below sea level. Whenever a building of any size is erected, the contractor must first bring in a large pile-driving machine to pound long telephone poles into the ground. These treated pillars become the foundation on which the structure sits. Otherwise, the edifice would slowly disappear into the Delta mud, having no adequate support.

Since ethics is about "oughtness," this book discusses what people called to be ministers of Jesus Christ ought to be and do in their professional lives. But certain basic assumptions, foundation pillars on which the structure of this book is built, undergird that discussion. The following six statements reveal our fundamental convictions about ethics in ministry.

1. *Most ministers want to be persons of integrity, persons whose professional lives uphold the highest ethical ideals.* Christ's moral imperative in the Sermon on the Mount, "Be perfect, therefore, as your heavenly Father is perfect" (Matt. 5:48), is a call to all disciples for Christian maturity. This "impossible possibility," as Reinhold Niebuhr described it, is especially pertinent for the Christian minister. One goal of this book is to assist clergy in fulfilling this command of Christ to attain moral maturity in both their personal and professional lives.

2. *Developing moral character and ethical conduct is a difficult process.* Neither a salvation experience nor a call to ministry ensures ethical uprightness. All major books on ethics in ministry echo a common theme: the necessity for trustworthiness, prudence, truthfulness, and integrity in the life and vocation of the ordained. Developing these character traits is a daily discipline.

3. *Every cleric needs training in ethics and spiritual formation.*[22] If personal character and conduct have a place in ministerial ethics, vocational training

should at least address these issues. In the 1970s, the Association of Theological Schools became convinced that "the spiritual development of persons preparing for ministry" is "a priority issue of major dimensions."[23] The association initiated two studies designed to meet this need. The result was the development of a new holistic model of theological education that integrated spiritual formation into the seminary curriculum and community. Since then spiritual formation has become a topic of major concern among religious institutions of higher education.[24]

All of this does not mean that adequate theological education will automatically produce moral ministers. Walker Percy, physician and novelist, had one of his characters say, "I made straight A's and flunked ordinary living."[25] Nevertheless, ethical training can help.

A wise prophet taught both of us years ago that most pastors do not fail in ministry because of faulty doctrine or poor preaching. Success in the ministry, he said, depends on how well you get along with people and how Christlike you are in behavior. Both of these qualities are not natural endowments; rather, they are traits developed over time.

4. *There is an art to doing ethics, one that can also be learned.* Before entering the gospel ministry, every ordained church leader must be examined by a responsible group to determine moral and spiritual fitness.

Christians rightly assume that a person set apart by a church or denomination measures up to the biblical standards outlined in 1 Timothy 3:1–7. The term translated "bishop" or "pastor" in this passage is *episkopos* (v. 1), a Greek word meaning "overseer." The title stresses the administrative role of the church leader. This pastoral function is not limited to skillful management of church business affairs; it also includes the ability to analyze facts, discern judgments, and make wise moral decisions. Doing ethics is, in part, a skill that can be learned and one that must be practiced by a capable minister.

5. *The central moral choice facing the Christian minister is the same one facing all professionals: Will I be an enabler or an exploiter?*[26] As explained fully in the first chapter, it is the nature of a professional to render services that pose serious possibilities: life or death (doctor), poverty or wealth (lawyer), and salvation or damnation (minister). The client/parishioner is in a dependent position and is vulnerable to exploitation by the professional who holds "dangerous knowledge," knowledge that can be used for benefit or for exploitation. Ministers, like doctors and lawyers, must be sure that the service they render is given to enable, not to exploit financially, sexually, or in any other way.

6. *A ministerial code of ethics, if used appropriately, is beneficial to ministers and to the communities they serve.* If a life of moral integrity is the goal of every ordained cleric, and if the Christian community desires to encourage and support that intent, a written ethical covenant can help.

There are risks involved in an established code of ethics for ministers, but there are also hazards associated with having no clearly stated standards of conduct. A written code of conduct is not meant to be a moral creed set in concrete. Rather, it is a personal, dynamic document that challenges ministers to uphold an ethical lifestyle. A code of ethics will also inform the community of the moral boundaries within which the minister will serve. The final chapter discusses these issues and proposes that every minister write his or her own code of ethics (see the worksheet following chap. 8).

From biblical times to the present, the moral character of the minister of the gospel was expected to be exemplary and "above reproach" (1 Tim. 3:2). Being a good pastor has always meant more than just maintaining minimal standards. It is a calling to maximum discipleship. "Follow my example, as I follow the example of Christ," asserted Paul (1 Cor. 11:1).

Ministerial ethics does not end when a pastor walks out the office door. In many ways it just begins. Ethics in ministry includes personal lifestyle, financial decisions, family commitments, pastoral responsibilities, congregational relationships, community involvement, and much more. We will look at these worlds of the contemporary minister and try to explain how Christian ethical ideals apply.

Let us say, finally, that our approach to these questions has been influenced by our own experiences and traditions. We are well aware of the "rock" from which we were hewn and the "quarry" from which we were dug (Isa. 51:1). Hopefully, the wisdom we have gained from our traditions and experiences will aid you in your ministry.

To give ethical meaning to the ministerial pilgrimage, we have drawn a few maps. As cartographers know well, maps need constant updating, as do our limited observations (which is one of the reasons for this second edition). However, the stars by which we set our sextant have been fixed in the heavens since creation. In addition to consulting these ministerial maps, if you take regular bearings using the Creator's divine compass, keeping your eyes fixed on "the bright Morning Star" (Rev. 22:16), you will arrive at your appointed destination without destruction or detour.

Suggested Reading

Marty, Martin E. "Clergy Ethics in America: The Ministers on Their Own." In *Clergy Ethics in a Changing Society: Mapping the Terrain,* edited by James P. Wind, Russell Burck, Paul F. Camenisch, and Dennis P. McCann, 23–36. Louisville: Westminster John Knox, 1991.

"Ministry Ethics." *Review and Expositor* (fall 1989): 505–73.

Noyce, Gaylord. *Pastoral Ethics: Professional Responsibilities of the Clergy.* Nashville: Abingdon, 1988.

Willimon, William H. *Pastor: The Theology and Practice of Ordained Ministry.* Nashville: Abingdon, 2002.

1

The Minister's Vocation

Career or Profession?

Oliver Sacks began his book *The Man Who Mistook His Wife for a Hat* with the fascinating story of a person suffering from agnosia.[1] Dr. P. (the patient) was a distinguished musician and teacher in Berlin. His students first recognized his strange behavior when he was unable to identify people he knew well. In addition, he often mistook objects such as parking meters and fire hydrants for young children. At the close of one session with Dr. Sacks, Dr. P. started looking for his hat. Finally, he reached toward his wife's head and tried to put it on his own.

Agnosia is the psychiatric term for the loss of the ability to recognize familiar objects. Although Dr. P. retained a highly abstract cognitive ability, his illness prevented him from recognizing people, for he saw faces only in bits and pieces. Incredible as it seems, Dr. P. got along quite well despite his disability and was able to work until the end of his life.

Amusing and yet tragic, the case of Dr. P. is a metaphor for the practice of ministry and for ministerial ethics.[2] Every seminarian knows that a call to become a minister of a church is a call to various tasks. Preaching, teaching, counseling, visiting, administrating, promoting, recruiting, leading worship, and doing community service are just a few of those tasks. Today's minister must wear many hats. The unseen danger for the busy religious worker is "clerical agnosia," becoming a minister who mistakes a parishioner for one of his or her hats! In short, people can get lost in the midst of an active ministry.

What caused this multiplication of roles that increases the risk of contracting clerical agnosia and overlooking persons? James Gustafson observed three primary developments during the past century that precipitated this role change for ministers:

> The first is the voluntary character of religion in the United States, which in its various dimensions makes the clergy unusually responsive to the desires and needs of the laity and to changes in the culture. The second is the breakdown of a sense of independent authority in the clergy; in the absence of wide acceptance of the traditional bases of their authority, clergymen seek substitute ways to make themselves legitimate. The third is the effort of the clergy to find new ways to make religious faith relevant to changing social and cultural patterns.[3]

These changes have led to clergy confusion and a condition Gustafson calls *anomie,* a lack of clear delineation of authority.[4] The typical minister is bewildered, not only about what to do but also about whom to serve. Who has the final word: the individual member, the congregation, the denomination, or God?

The Dr. P. story is a parable of what can happen to any church overseer. Without realizing it, pastors and other ministers can slip into believing that as long as the "bits and pieces" of people are visible, all is well. Ministry can become very impersonal. Church members begin to look like consumer-oriented clients, and the church itself takes on the appearance of a corporation, whose chief executive must work to keep "profits" high and "customers" happy. In the midst of this busyness, the real purpose of ministry can be lost.

Recently, one of us was reading a state denominational paper that featured a seminary student we both know. The student identified himself as pastor of "one of the fastest growing churches in Louisiana." Both of us knew very well the small mission church where he served. The caption did not seem to fit. A check of denominational records for the previous three years verified our suspicions. The church membership numbered only a few more than one hundred. During one year, church records reported a large decrease in numbers, followed by a similar increase the next year. While this was "growth," overall attendance was roughly the same as it had been for several years. There is nothing wrong with numerical increases in a church. If ministers become so obsessed with growth that statistics are manipulated, however, they worship their own success rather than God.

As we propose in the next chapter, the moral ideal for a minister is integrity, a life of ethical wholeness and moral maturity. How does the person called of God to serve the church achieve integrity of character and conduct? The most naive believe that since a minister is set apart by God, ethics will take care of itself, for God calls only good people. Others assume that those who preach the gospel must surely live by the Bible's precepts and principles. Most laypersons admire the dedication of those who devote their lives to a Christian vocation and suppose that this commitment ensures a Christian lifestyle.

Ministerial integrity is neither simple nor automatic. Clergy ethics, however, does begin with a proper understanding of the minister's vocation. Therefore, the purpose of this chapter is to reexamine the vocational role of the clergy. This begins with the minister's understanding of "calling." Is it to a career or to a profession? To answer this basic question, we must also define *profession*. A brief review of the history of professions, which originated in religious orders (whose members "professed" something), will aid an understanding of the term. This chapter also explores a significant change in cultural values that precipitated a crisis for professionals. Many believe that because of a change in professionalization in American society, the professional ethics model is fundamentally inappropriate for today's clergy. Finally, we will attempt to determine whether the minister is indeed a true professional, and if so, how the professional ethics model can be a tool for "doing" clergy ethics.

The Call to Ministry

A basic prerequisite for an ethical ministry is a clear understanding of the minister's calling. How does a person enter vocational Christian service? Does a candidate receive a divine calling from God or simply choose a career? Is the ministry an occupation or a profession? What does the office itself require of the ordained: an inspiring moral life, effective church leadership, polished ministry skills, sound theological beliefs, unerring professional conduct, or some combination of these ministerial attributes?

H. Richard Niebuhr called the ministry of his generation a "perplexed profession." The situation today has not improved, for contemporary clerics are equally puzzled. Like butterflies newly hatched, seminary graduates flutter away from ivy-covered campuses planning to fly high, only to crash into the brick wall of "Old First Church." Young ministers quickly discover that pastoral ministry, rather than the spiritual enterprise they expected, is more like running a secular business. The weekly calendar is crammed with financial meetings, publicity decisions, personnel problems, and laity complaints. When will there be time for theological discussions, spiritual disciplines, or the real mission of the church?

A survey of recent graduates conducted by two seminary faculty members revealed that the major concern of these first-time ministers was coping with uncertainties regarding their roles in ministry. "We found beginning clergypersons almost completely at the mercy of the expectations of their first parish without counterbalancing claims from denomination or profession. Formation of clerical identity depended on satisfying the first congregation."[5]

If this is true, it is important for first-time clergy to have a clear understanding of their role. Every church has an unwritten list of expectations for its ordained, and similarly, each new church shepherd arrives with a notebook filled with plans and priorities. The two sets seldom match. Much disappointment and many tensions arise during the first years because of such misunderstandings. The result can be catastrophic: increasing conflict, ministerial fatigue, and even forced termination. Yale professor Gaylord Noyce asserts, "Clergy 'burnout,' so publicized, results more from a blurred pastoral identity than from overwork. Professional ethics well taught counteracts that kind of haziness."[6]

So the question arises again: To what is a minister called, a career or a profession? An occupation or a unique vocation? Each cleric must also ask, "Whom do I serve, Christ or the congregation?" Or to put it another way, "Am I serving Christ as I serve the congregation?" Building a ministry based on integrity requires that a minister's sense of calling and concept of service be biblical, ethical, and Christlike.

Most evangelical ministers would identify with Jeremiah's account of his calling: "The word of the LORD came to me, saying, 'Before I formed you in the womb I knew you, before you were born I set you apart; I appointed you as a prophet to the nations'" (Jer. 1:4–5). This messenger to Israel believed that the sovereign Lord had graciously planned for him to be a spokesman for God from the beginning of his existence. Christian ministers should likewise be confident of God's plan for their lives as revealed in their call to Christian ministry. This conviction about the will of God is more than a choice of career based on personality inventories; it is an acknowledgment of a divine appointment. As Yahweh chose Abraham to lead a new people (Gen. 12:1–3) and sent Moses on a redemptive mission (Exod. 3:10), so God calls and sends ministers today. Their response to God's calling must be like that of Isaiah: "Here am I. Send me!" (Isa. 6:8).

Jehovah's prophets are not only called but also given a message and a mission. Such was the case with Deborah (Judges 4–5), Isaiah (6:8–9), Amos (7:15), and John the Baptist (John 1:6–8). The apostle from Tarsus was so convinced that God had appointed him as a missionary to the Gentile world that he wrote, "I am compelled to preach. Woe to me if I do not preach the gospel!" (1 Cor. 9:16). There can be no doubt that the minister of the gospel of Jesus Christ is set apart and sent forth by God to fulfill a divine mission. The ministry is a *vocatio,* a calling from God.

At the same time, the minister usually fulfills this calling through service to a congregation of God's people. This body of believers pays the salary of the church leader and expects some type of ministerial service in return. How should a person set apart by God to minister to the Christian community interpret his or her relationship to the church?

An early church leader, Simon Peter, wrote a clear word about pastoral responsibility to the *ekklēsia* of Christ:

> Be shepherds of God's flock that is under your care, serving as overseers—not because you must, but because you are willing, as God wants you to be; not greedy for money, but eager to serve; not lording it over those entrusted to you, but being examples to the flock.

> 1 Peter 5:2–3

It is impossible to discuss ministers and what they do apart from the church, for what the clergy most needs is a function of what the church most needs.[7]

> [A]t a very early date, from among the ranks of the baptized, the church found it good to call some of its members to lead, to help the congregation nurture within itself those virtues needed for the life and work of the colony. Call these leaders preachers, priests, pastors, prophets, or just plain Jane—this is their particular vocation: building up a congregation.[8]

Although a minister's primary loyalty is to God, this devotion must never be an excuse for avoiding pastoral duties. Ministry involves both privilege and responsibility. A minister's calling always must be fleshed out in some kind of community, usually a local congregation. One cannot serve Christ without serving people, for to serve people is to serve Christ (Matt. 25:31–46).

As we seek a clear understanding of the minister's calling, we should note that the terms *vocation, profession,* and *career* have multiple meanings. William May of Southern Methodist University has suggested that this confusion of terminology has created tensions. He points out that every Christian has a vocation, which traditionally has meant a commitment to God and neighbor. A career, however, is a more selfish thing; it is a means to pursue one's own private aims and purposes. Instead of asking what the need of the community is, a career person asks, "What do I want to be, and where do I want to go?"[9] If these two questions are uppermost in your mind, does that not mean you are pursuing a career rather than answering a call?

In the biblical sense, as Martin Luther and John Calvin both emphasized, all Christians are "called" to serve God in and through their vocation. The minister stands somewhere between this generalized concept of vocation for all Christians and a specific career. He or she is fulfilling a calling and not just choosing a career. Yet something more is involved. The unique calling to be a Christian minister has features that result in unusual obligations.

Historically, the word *profess* meant "to testify on behalf of" or "to stand for something." Being a professional person carried implications about knowledge and moral responsibility. "The professional knows something that will benefit the wider community, and he or she has a responsibility to use that knowledge to serve the wider human community."[10] Let us now explore how this traditional concept of a professional relates to the vocation of the minister.

The History of Professions

John Piper wants his fellow pastors to know, "We are *not* professionals," which is the title of his latest book.[11] The work is a collection of essays that urges his preaching colleagues "to quit looking at their jobs through the eyes of secular society." He believes professionalism leads to spiritual decline and has nothing to do with the essence and heart of Christian ministry.[12]

This misunderstanding is common. The term *professional* is often considered a secular title reserved for reverends who are more concerned with status and prestige than spiritual ministry. In fact, the very opposite should be true. Indeed, only if a minister is truly a professional will that person's ministry be truly biblical and Christian.

To understand the true meaning of the word *professional,* it is necessary to review briefly the history of professions, how professionalization began, and what changes have occurred over the years. This is especially crucial for comprehending the present-day crisis facing all professionals, including ministers.

Darrell Reeck believes that the roots of contemporary professions can be traced back to those early priests, healers, and chiefs who promoted human values in primitive societies. Unlike the modern version, these "prototypical professionals" were unspecialized and usually perpetuated themselves through inheritance rather than through achievement. Nevertheless, these traditionalists did use their basic skills to meet basic human needs in their cultural groups.[13]

In early Israel, a special class of religious professionals developed, namely, priests and prophets. They became the supreme authorities in law and religion and also performed some medical functions. The wealthy commercial and political "professionals" were castigated by prophets such as Amos for crushing the poor through dishonest and unethical business practices. The concept of the prophet in ancient Israel was a "religious-cultural creation of the highest order" because this religious profession "presuppose[d] the very source and meaning of the life of the individual and of the covenanted community."[14]

By the time of Jesus, a variety of professions had emerged: priests, teachers, lawyers, physicians, and soldiers. Although Christ often denounced the clerics and legal experts of his day as hypocritical and legalistic, Jesus himself became known as a rabbi from Galilee, a member of the teaching profession. In the Gospels and the Book of Acts, we meet another professional, the "beloved physician" Luke, who ministered to Paul and wrote two books of the New Testament.

During the Middle Ages, particularly in Northern Europe, little change occurred. With the established church in control, the clergy became the dominant professional group. The religious leaders of the medieval period also controlled education, allowing them to write the rules governing the practice of all other professions. There were some benefits of this control. Medicine, law, business, and teaching all existed within a common framework of shared values and beliefs.

During this time and afterward, many occupations and commercial groups organized into guilds. The guilds served to maintain standards, train recruits, and discipline the wayward. After the Industrial Revolution, some guilds evolved into professions.

Important to an understanding of modern professions and the ministry is the revival of a key biblical doctrine during the Reformation. Before the Reformation it was generally believed that the only people who received a divine calling were those chosen by God to enter the spiritually superior monastic way. This calling *(vocatio)* was reserved for religious professionals alone. Martin Luther and John Calvin challenged this tradition, basing their argument on the biblical teaching of calling prominent in the Pauline epistles (Rom. 12:6–8; 1 Cor. 7:20–24; 12:28; Eph. 4:11). Both Reformers asserted that every worthwhile form of work was a divine calling. The farmer, the merchant, and the cobbler, not just the priest, had a call from God to serve the world in their work.

Luther, being a bit more conservative, felt that each person should labor in the occupation of his forebears. Calvin disagreed. He taught that the call to serve God and people was through whatever vocation best suited that person. According to his view, admittance to a profession should be based not on inheritance but on achievement. The importance of this teaching for professional life is difficult to overestimate.

> [T]he Judaeo-Christian culture from Biblical times through the Reformation imbued the concept of profession with the moral principle of service grounded in a religious vision of God working together with people for the improvement of all creation. The doctrine of the vocation or calling became the religious and moral theme that most illuminated the meaning of the professions and professional work.[15]

After 1500, most professions stagnated, remaining small in number and exclusive. Members of the professions led the "good life" of leisurely gentlemen, gaining high social status through attachment to the king and his court. Work that required labor was for the trades; professionals lived the life of refinement among the upper classes.

Even as late as the eighteenth century, the education and competence of professionals were deplorable. Physicians knew Latin and the Greek classics but very little about science or how to treat sick people. The law profession had actually deteriorated since medieval times, as barristers primarily served the gentry.

The clergy was not unaffected by these social trends. In eighteenth-century England, the minister's role was mainly "an occupational appendage of gentry status."[16] By the nineteenth century, many of the clergy were anxious to be regarded as professionals with specific functions and duties. Regrettably, this desire was difficult to achieve, for a minister's role included many functions more related to his social position as patriarch of his rural parish than to his ordination. Often the local English pastor was also judge, doctor, lawyer, magistrate, and teacher.[17]

The professions in colonial America, however, took on a new character. Unhampered by the social class restrictions and institutional inheritance so rigid in England, the American professional "blithely ignored such hallowed distinctions as that between barrister and attorneys, or between apothecary and physician. Professionals were judged by the competency of their performance and not by the impressiveness of their credentials."[18]

This unique development of the professions in America also had a significant impact on religion. At first there were relatively few professions, the major ones being medicine, law, and ministry. As in rural England, in many towns in the new colonies, the minister was the only professional, the one called on to help in matters of law and medicine as well as religion. At this time, all professionals felt a sense of service to the entire community, but they also believed their service was to God. For the minister, this sense of calling, of being chosen by God for this work, was even more intense. Yet Protestants, with their Reformation tradition, also insisted that every occupation was a holy calling. This generalization of the idea of calling led many in America to adopt an attitude of antiprofessionalism.

> Lay preachers who were truly called by God could be seen as superior to an educated but spiritually tepid ordained ministry. The growth of the Baptist churches, which began to outnumber the older established Protestant denominations . . . offers an indication of this trend.[19]

The social situation in America created a new history for professionals. Because there was no noble class, doctors, lawyers, and ministers attached to the middle class and offered to the young an avenue of expression and achievement.

The twentieth century witnessed an explosion of the professions in the United States. One of the positive results has been a high degree of specialized knowledge and skills. Orthodontists straighten teeth, neurosurgeons correct spinal injuries, and ministers of music direct church choirs. However, because of the market orientation of American capitalism, the services of professionals have sometimes been seen as one more commodity for sale to the highest bidder. Lawyers often feel like hired guns; doctors appear more preoccupied with technology and economics than patients; ministers view themselves as slaves to laity expectations.

A large Southern Baptist seminary surveyed laity and clergy in eight southeastern states concerning the role of pastors. About thirty-two hundred people responded. The results indicated unreasonably high expectations for pastors by laity, as well as wide differences of opinion between the two groups.

> Lay respondents showed a strong preference for a direct, aggressive, program-oriented leadership style, whereas professional ministers said they valued "shared, caring relational styles." . . . [P]eople in the pews expect pastors to be equally competent in virtually all aspects of ministry. . . . [W]hen laypeople were asked 108 questions about qualities for pastoral ministry, "they basically said all 108 are important. So there is nothing unimportant, which is in a way quite unrealistic."[20]

This is part of the crisis that ministers face today as they seek to clarify their role and define their ministry in the modern world.

What conclusions can be drawn from this brief history of the professions? The earliest use of the word *profession* was in relation to those who "professed" vows in a religious order. The essential services provided to society by these religious communities included both the sacred and the secular, as monasteries became centers of culture and education. Thus, these religious orders provided society with artists and educators, experts in law and medicine, political advisors and leaders, as well as theologians, priests, and ministers.[21] Gradually, the three vocations of medicine, law, and divinity came to be regarded as unique. The term *laity* originally referred to those untrained in these three professions. By the late Middle Ages, physicians and lawyers who took no religious vows were practicing their crafts. However, the original qualities the clergy "professed" continued to define the true professional.[22]

One ideal that emerges from this moral heritage of professional life is a theme that Darrell Reeck calls *enablement,* "the devotion of professional skills to meeting the needs of client groups and ultimately, to the common good."[23] The opposite of enablement is exploitation. Reeck believes that a critical question for all contemporary professionals, and especially for the modern minister, is, Am I in my professional life an enabler or an exploiter? Before that question can be fully addressed, however, we must first understand what it means today to be a professional and if that term really fits the minister's role.

The Meaning of Professional

In popular language, the word *professional* is used in careless ways that confuse. Athletes call themselves "pros," and people in occupations such as exterminator and beautician advertise their work as "professional." This common usage of the term is intended to elicit from the public both respect and confidence, but it actually conceals the true meaning of the word.

Sociologists have written extensively about the true nature of professions, professionalization, and professionalism. Two major schools have developed: the "Harvard school" exemplified by Talcott Parsons and the "Chicago school" represented by Eliot Friedson. The Harvard school is functionalist in approach, seeing a profession as a distinct occupation characterized by complex knowledge, social importance, and a high degree of responsibility. The Chicago school sees the category of professional as a "semi-mythic construct" created by members of an occupation to obtain social and economic advantage.[24]

The functional definition of a profession has been accepted by most researchers, and it is conceptually more substantial. Using Talcott Parsons's definition as a basis, James Adams characterizes a profession this way:

> [I]t performs a unique and essential social service; it requires a long period of general and specialized training, usually in connection with a university; it presupposes skills that are subjected to rational analysis; service to the community rather than economic gain is supposed to be the dominant motive; standards of competence are defined by a comprehensive self-governing organization of practitioners; a high degree of autonomy . . . ; some code of ethics.[25]

Sociologist Parsons also argues for certain moral obligations, such as competence and a lack of self-interest, as essential to performance of the social function of a profession.

Concerned about the moral drift in medicine, a health practitioner contends that there are four unchangeable characteristics of the helping professions:

> The four features that are fundamental to a true profession are: (1) the nature of the human needs it addresses, (2) the vulnerable state of those it serves, (3) the expectations of trust it generates, and (4) the social contract it implies. Taken together, these features set the traditional ideal of a profession apart from other occupations that lay claim to the title.[26]

In a contemporary text on professional ethics, Michael Bayles outlines three central features that are necessary for an occupation to be a profession: (1) extensive training, (2) a significant intellectual component in the training, and (3) a trained ability that provides an important service in society. He also notes other features common to many professions, namely, credentialing, an organization of members, and autonomy in the professional's work.[27]

Other functional definitions of a professional devised by sociologists are similar, emphasizing four traits: (1) specialized training, (2) a sense of calling to serve the public, (3) self-regulation including a code of ethics, and (4) autonomy.[28] Reduced to the simplest terms, "a profession is intended to be a combination of *techne* and *ethos*—of technical knowledge and practice combined with responsible behavior . . . the joining of knowledge and character."[29]

A comparison of these professional characteristics with the vocation of minister reveals many points of identity. The role of minister matches all of these characteristics except two, a code of ethics and autonomy, both of which are partially met in some denominations.[30]

Concerning the first, a code of ethics, some Christian groups have developed this document for their ministers, while others have not. The reasons for this inconsistency and the difficulty a code of ethics poses for ministers are explored in chapter 8. The second characteristic, autonomy, is the most critical dimension in an analysis of professions and one especially plaguing for the clergy. Professional autonomy is rooted in an authority based on superior competence. It is assumed, for example, that an orthopedic surgeon is competent in his or her area of specialized knowledge and therefore will assume responsibility for professional decisions. This issue of professional autonomy has become a major area of conflict between professionals and the organizations to which they belong.[31]

The autonomy of Protestant ministers is much more limited than other professionals because in most churches the clients (members) are also the directors and owners of the organization in which the ministers practice. There has been no small amount of church conflict over pastoral authority and congregational control.

One of the reasons many sociologists are reluctant to include clergypersons in the category of professional is that the pastoral role has become an occupational conglomerate. There are not only various specializations, such as education minister, church counselor, church administrator, and youth minister, but also a multiplicity of tasks in each category.

> The job means different things to different people, depending upon who these people are and what they do. In fact, the overall image of the clergy appears confused, and to many, both in and outside the ministry, unattractive.[32]

Another research team, A. M. Carr-Saunders and P. A. Wilson, in a standard volume on the professions, excludes the church from consideration because "all those functions related to the ordinary business of life . . . which used to fall to the Church, have been taken over by other vocations. The functions remaining to the Church are spiritual."[33]

An adequate definition of professions is critical because "one of the most revealing ways of grasping the character of any civilization is precisely through discerning the ultimate orientation and the types of leadership which the civilization adopts."[34] Our culture could be judged by the nature of professional life today. A widening gap is developing between the traditional definition of a profession and the way professions function at the beginning of the twenty-first century.

Before we attempt to determine whether the minister is a true professional, then, one other task remains: to understand the cultural crisis that threatens professional life today. It may well be, as a result of the shift of values in modern American society, that the possibility for a minister to be a professional is no longer an option.

The Crisis in Professional Life Today

Michael Bayles began both editions of his contemporary and much quoted book *Professional Ethics* with this paragraph:

> The ethics of professional conduct is being questioned as never before in history. Lawyers, physicians, engineers, accountants, and other professionals are being criticized for disregarding the rights of clients and the public interest. Perhaps society is reconsidering the role of professions and professionals. In any event, many difficult ethical challenges are being faced by both professionals and the public. Given the important roles professionals are playing in society during the last decade of the twentieth century, everyone is concerned with professional ethics.[35]

The Alban Institute sponsored a study in 2001 on the status of leadership in American religion. The study concluded that professional ministry today evidences two basic pictures: crisis and ferment.[36] What has happened?

Between the Reformation and modern professionalization, the twin Christian doctrines of vocation and covenant changed decisively. The sense of calling was broadened to the "priesthood of all believers" and eventually included every individual. The doctrine of covenant encouraged the formation of religious communities whose members believed they served the purposes of God by serving others.

> In recent years, however, the idea of vocation has been replaced by the idea of career as the governing notion of professional life. And the idea of covenant has been replaced by the idea of contract. "Career" comes from a word that referred to the race course in the ancient Roman world. It is a word that refers to achievement by competitive combat, getting ahead, and triumphing over others—even if such achievement involves merely going around in circles. . . . The word "contract" refers to the utilitarian agreements between parties whereby we establish a give-and-take relationship in which goods or services are exchanged on a tit-for-tat basis.[37]

This secularization of vocation and covenant into career and contract has seriously threatened the recovery of the traditional virtues of professionalism. A physician, Edmund Pellegrino, is alarmed that the central ideas of a profession, altruistic service and effacement of personal reward, are today downplayed. The shift is in the direction of self-interest and away from moral commitments. Pellegrino believes that the present moral character defects of many doctors, lawyers, scientists, and even ministers constitute a grave danger to professional life and to our present society.[38]

The crisis has both a personal and a social dimension. On the personal side, contemporary professional life poses certain risks. A researcher who has studied the professions in American history has recently warned that teachers, doctors, lawyers, and pastors face three present dangers: to become more self-reliant, more success oriented, and more convinced of how deserving they are. This Notre Dame professor concluded:

> The church of Christ does not need smug professionals, preoccupied with managing their own careers. The church does not need success-oriented members who reach out only to other winners. The church does not need those who expect the good life because of how hard they work. Instead, Christians are to live out the original ideal of the professions: to serve rather than to be served.[39]

On the other hand, Dennis Campbell has analyzed some new realities in American society that threaten a Christian approach to professional practice. Three major movements in Western culture that are wearing away the underpinnings of professionalism are secularization, pluralism, and relativism.[40]

The United States, like most other nations in the Western world, is predominantly secular. Life is no longer informed by a vision of God or the church. There are many competing views of reality in the marketplace of ideas, and thus, no one view commands the ultimate loyalty of a majority of Americans.

During the Middle Ages, when the professions were emerging, a Christian worldview prevailed. All aspects of personal and social life were defined by the church and a religious interpretation of life. Society was unified by common religious beliefs and shared values. Concepts of professionalism developed during a time when Christian moral values were widely accepted.

Secularization, like weeds in an unmanaged garden, gradually outgrew the Christian monopoly of Western civilization. As new views challenged the traditions of the past, a plurality of ideas about the meaning and value of life emerged. This pluralism created many problems for the common life of Americans because it bred another cultural monster, relativism. Relativism contends that there is no one absolute view of reality; therefore, all perspectives are equal in value.

With nothing of ultimate meaning to believe in, the average American must turn to material reality for salvation. Religious affirmations make no sense for people who believe that only "what is, is now, and there is no more." When it comes to values and virtues, modern Americans are diverse, divided, and often disinterested.

This absence of shared values is a serious problem for the professions. Since the devastating attack by radical Islamic terrorists on September 11, 2001, the American public has become acutely aware of multiculturalism in our society. Tolerance of all views and values is the new order of the day. Yet if America encourages a pluralism of worldviews and if all these views and their ethical teachings are of equal value, how can anyone make judgments about moral actions?

> Unless judgments can be made about moral decisions, they are not *moral* decisions, but simply decisions of individual idiosyncrasy. Ethical reflection requires clearly stated assumptions to which one can appeal when reasons for action are examined.[41]

Developing guidelines for ethical conduct among professionals requires some consensus about values. The social crisis facing all professionals today is the increasing lack of shared values in American society.

Professional ethics also faces a crisis that has other personal and social dimensions. In many ways, it is an outgrowth and reflection of the social changes discussed above. The authority and identity of the professional person is in jeopardy as never before. Traditionally, the authority of doctors, lawyers, and ministers was never questioned because of their vocational competence and their dedication to serve. In the contemporary world, however, the lay public is challenging the professionals at both points. As laypeople have become more knowledgeable, they have become more critical of professional practice. Public disclosures of malpracticing physicians, incompetent lawyers, and misguided ministers have increased society's skepticism. Lawsuits have escalated dramatically.

A lack of public confidence in professional competence has paralleled the charge of diminishing professional dedication. Historically, those practicing medicine, law, and religion were trusted because people assumed their only interest was the welfare of those they served. Today, people are not so sure a professional practitioner can be trusted. "Reports abound of unnecessary surgery, unreliable dental practice, questionable legal advice, and poor-quality teaching."[42]

The Gallup Index of Leading Religious Indicators in 2002 reached its lowest level ever, the most negative overall rating for organized religion since the index began in 1940. The 2002 figure was 641, a thirty-point drop from the 2001 figure of 671.[43]

Since 1977, the Gallup organization has asked the public to rate the honesty and standards of the various professions and occupations. In 1985, the clergy had its highest positive rating of 67 percent. In the 1989 poll, 12 percent of the public said the clergy rated "very high" on ethical standards, and 43 percent gave a rating of "high"—a 55 percent favorable rating, second to pharmacists and druggists (62 percent), followed by physicians and dentists (52 percent). The clergy have ranked first or second among the professions since testing began.[44] In 2002, 52 percent of Americans gave "very high" or "high" ratings to clergy, compared to 64 percent in 2001. Researchers attributed the decline in large part to the highly publicized sex scandals that plagued the Roman Catholic Church in 2002, but religious leaders believed there was more to it.[45]

The point is obvious. Doctors, lawyers, teachers, and even ministers do not command the aura of respect and admiration they once did. Professionals themselves do not share common values, which has no doubt contributed to this question of competence and dedication. Ministers in particular are confused about their identity. James Glasse reported over three decades ago what seems to be true even today: "The image of the ministry is cloudy, confused, and unattractive."[46] In particular, he noted that three images of ministry create an identity crisis for the clergy: the ministry as (1) a calling for a particular kind of person, (2) a calling from a particular kind of institution, and (3) a calling to a particular kind of work.[47] In an analysis of the role of the minister, James Gustafson further pointed out:

> The problem the minister faces in any social context is that of determining *who he is* and *what he is doing* within the complexity of his functions. He frequently lacks, more than anything else, an awareness of what he is about, and therefore he has no central focus for the integration of his various activities.[48]

The crisis faced by ministers is similar to that of other professionals because both have been significantly affected by the shifts in cultural values in America. Perhaps the situation is best summed up by Martin Marty in a recent text on clergy ethics in America. The highly respected historian contends that the context for clergy ethics has changed to "a more privately contracted entrepreneurial understanding."[49] Five elements have intensified this centuries-long trend: (1) a secular view of the clergy, (2) the legal subordination of religion to the state, (3) modernity and modernization, (4) the moral specialization of the clergy, and (5) theological accommodation. Using show business lingo, Marty explains that in days past a minister's identity was determined by being part of a church establishment or denomination, but now "you are only as good as your last act."[50]

After extensive research, an Alban Institute leader concluded:

> If professional ministry is to take its new place in our postmodern world, it need not compete with other professional jurisdictions. . . . The new jurisdiction that awaits professional ministry depends upon a return to the theological vocation of interpretation—a prophetic role filled by the professional minister.[51]

An exploration of the factors that have contributed to a crisis in the professions has revealed that Americans lack a shared moral tradition. This cultural change has created a social and personal crisis for professionals. An absence of shared values has contributed to skepticism from without and an identity crisis from within. In a secularized, materialistic culture in which moral values are relative, what is a minister to be and to do?

This brings us then to the crux of the matter: Is the minister a true professional? If the minister does "profess" something, what is it he or she professes and in what way does this "profession" affect ministerial ethics?

The Minister as a Professional

To summarize, then, we can now define a professional as a broadly educated person with highly developed skills and knowledge who works autonomously under the discipline of an ethic developed and enforced by peers, who renders a social service that is essential and unique, and who makes complex judgments involving potentially dangerous consequences.[52] A professional is more concerned with communal interest than with self and with services rendered than with financial rewards.[53] The question we must now answer is this: Does the minister's vocation fit this general characterization of a profession?

First of all, the concept of a professional does not neatly describe the minister. Many ordained ministers do not have a higher education, and even more lack professional (theological) training. Although the clergy was the historical setting to which the modern professions owe their origin, intellectual training among modern ministers varies greatly.[54]

Another sphere of difference is the social role of the minister, which today includes not only pastoral responsibilities but also many other parish skills. The contemporary minister, for example, must be adept in business administration and public relations, tasks for which most ministers do not have technical competence.[55] At the same time, theological education has moved away from the study of divinity to provide "a cafeterialike offering of studies in specialized disciplines and an accumulation of professional skills."[56] Too often this effort to prepare ministers for the multiplicity of vocational demands they will face is incomplete and superficial.

Peter Jarvis has raised another question: Is the ministry an occupation, a profession, or a status? He notes two major difficulties: The concept of profession has undergone a transformation from status to occupation, and second, there are no universally accepted criteria for a profession. Jarvis concludes that the minister is something less than a professional because (1) the ministry is so heterogeneous that it is impossible to argue that it is either an occupation or profession, and (2) the ministry has become a status profession with no high social position and thus is anachronistic in a world emphasizing achievement and specialization.[57]

Although a lack of autonomy and specialization may prevent ministers from being considered professionals, Jarvis believes this "neither denies the possibility of individual ministers being professionals nor that they may develop expertise which makes them highly skilled practitioners."[58]

There is also an opposite sense in which the minister of a Christian church is something more than or other than a professional. Similar to Søren Kierkegaard's distinction between the apostle and the genius, there is a "nonprofessional" ingredient in the vocation of the religious calling. The minister's *vocatio* is not of this world.[59] This distinction underscores the minister's unique authority, which is not ultimately grounded in technical competence but in religious and moral tradition. This means the clerical office is legitimized by its charismatic witness, which does not maintain cultural tradition as much as reject self-sufficient culture, bringing it under the judgment of the One who transforms both church and culture.[60] Perhaps for this reason Jacques Ellul contrasted vocation and profession, seeing them as a "total divorce between what society unceasingly asks of us and God's will. Service to God cannot be written into a profession."[61]

Two Duke University professors, Stanley Hauerwas and William Willimon, also believe the ministry is something more than one of the "helping professions." They resist placing the minister in this category because of the implied presumption that ministry is simply a matter of meeting the needs of people. This "sentimentality" makes a ministry of integrity impossible, for people "not trained to want the right things rightly" will shape ministry more than the gospel narrative. "Being a minister (like a pastor) is not a vocation merely to help people. We are called to help people 'in the name of Jesus.'"[62]

Having admitted these ways in which the modern minister of the gospel is unlike the traditional professional, let us also note some ways in which the ministerial vocation fits that designation. Unlike the typical specialist today, the minister is usually concerned with the total person; he or she is a generalist with a broad educational background, traditionally a trait of the professional. As the status of professionals depends on technical competence in their field, so the status of the clergyperson depends on competence in certain theological disciplines, both theoretical and practical.[63] Church clerics, for example, must be able to explain the meaning of Christian marriage, as well as perform a wedding service.

As leaders in the colony that exists as God's redemptive community in the world, pastors and other ministers render service that is both unique and essential. The message they preach and teach is "dangerous knowledge," for it reveals the real meaning and purpose of life, as well as knowledge of the One who is "the way and the truth and the life" (John 14:6).

As a professional, the minister of the gospel is dedicated to serving others. Financial reward and social status are not primary motivations; the minister puts the needs of others before his or her own, for this is what it means to be a called minister and a follower of Jesus.

Many ministerial bodies have developed codes of ethics for their clergy. As explained in chapter 8, these codes are usually developed by peers for the purpose of guiding ministerial conduct, particularly in areas of unusual vulnerability. At the same time, there is a conspicuous absence of codes of ethics for large groups of ministers, particularly those of the "free church" tradition (which is a partial explanation).

The classic defense of the minister as a professional is set forth by James Glasse in *Profession: Minister*. Urging church leaders to reaffirm their vocational identity as professionals, Glasse suggests that a religious professional should embody five important characteristics. The Christian minister is:

1. an *educated* person, the master of some body of knowledge. This knowledge is neither esoteric nor mundane but essential to ministry and available through accredited educational institutions.
2. an *expert* person, the master of a specific group of vocational skills. These abilities, while requiring some talent, can be learned and refined through practice and with supervision.
3. an *institutional* person, relating to society and serving persons through a social institution, of which the minister is partly servant and partly master. Ministers are also part of an association of clergy, usually a denomination, to which they are uniquely responsible.
4. a *responsible* person who "professes" to act competently in any situation that requires the minister's service. This includes the highest standards of ethical conduct.
5. a *dedicated* person who also "professes" to provide something of great value for society. The minister's dedication to the values of Christian ministry is the ultimate basis for evaluating ministerial service.[64]

Glasse builds his concept of "the professional perspective" on these five points, which all professions have in common. To identify the minister as a professional, Glasse traces the relationship of doctor, lawyer, teacher, and clergy to these factors.[65]

Adapting this model, Gaylord Noyce develops a grid that compares five professions (he adds business manager) in like manner. Though his list of elements is similar, he adds several new characteristics. For him a professional (1) is educated in a body of knowledge, (2) makes a commitment of service, (3) is part of a peer group that sets standards of practice, (4) is in an institutional matrix that claims allegience, and (5) serves immediate goals in the name of certain ultimate values that are (6) specific to that profession.[66] Noyce graphically illustrates how these aspects of obligations apply to the religious professional. Reflecting on the grid, Noyce concludes that the minister belongs in the category of a professional.

> The ordained minister learns theology, and steps into service in relation not only to a denomination and through it to the whole church, but also to peers in the ordained ministry. Entry into the colleagueship is celebrated as the ordinand pledges churchly participation and loyalty. All of this is clearly designated for the mission of Christ and the extension of Christian faith, by means of the proximate goals of pastoral care and the building up of the church.[67]

In an article in the *Christian Century* titled "The Pastor Is (Also) a Professional," Noyce adds, "Thus, rightly understood, the professional tag is not destructive. Quite the contrary. It can firm up our sense of purpose and our understanding of how to go about the work of ministry."[68]

What then can we honestly conclude? Should the minister today accept the title "professional," or should it be rejected? It is our conviction that there is more to be gained than lost by a minister assuming the designation of a professional. This is not to say that this title fits neatly or that there are not some drawbacks to the proposal. Nevertheless, as Glasse and many others observe, there are two main reasons for seeing ministers as professionals: traditional identification and rational definition.[69]

On the one hand, many clergy today fit the traditional description in the historical sense: university educated, full-time, resident, tenured, and salaried. On the other hand, even among denominations that allow less than these standards, expectations for ministers continue to rise toward professional standards in all categories. Most Protestant churches view their ministers as professional, whether they use the title or not.[70]

If we who are ministers call ourselves professionals, what significance does this have for ministerial ethics? Acknowledging the danger of being redundant, let us one more time affirm that if the Christian minister is a professional, he or she is committed to certain ideals. The standards of professional practice that apply to the Christian ministry include these six ethical obligations:

1. *Education.* The minister will prepare for Christian service by experiencing a broad liberal arts education, followed by specialized training in theology and ministry. Ministers will also be committed to a lifelong process of study and growth that prepares them for continued service (2 Tim. 2:15).
2. *Competency.* The church shepherd will develop and refine pastoral gifts and vocational skills in order to act competently in any situation that requires his or her services (1 Cor. 12:7–11; Eph. 4:11–12).

3. *Autonomy.* The minister is called to a life of responsible decision making involving potentially dangerous consequences. As a
   spiritual leader, the minister will make decisions and exert pastoral
   authority in light of the servant-leader model exemplified by Christ
   (John 13:1–16).
4. *Service.* The minister's motivation for ministry will be neither social
   status nor financial reward but rather *agapē* love, to serve others in
   Christ's name (1 Corinthians 13).
5. *Dedication.* The minister will "profess" to provide something of
   great value, the good news of God's salvation and the demonstration
   of God's love through Christian ministry. To these values the called of
   God is dedicated (Rom. 1:11–17).
6. *Ethics.* In relation to congregation, colleagues, and community,
   as well as in personal life, the ordained will live under the discipline
   of an ethic that upholds the highest standards of Christian morality
   (1 Tim. 3:1–7).

One intangible factor is the honor all professionals seek: the esteem of
others in their profession.[71] Anyone familiar with Harper Lee's novel, later an
Academy Award–winning movie, *To Kill a Mockingbird,* will remember the
climax of the story. Atticus Finch fails to gain an acquittal for Tom Robinson,
the black man who had been falsely accused of raping a white woman in a
small Alabama town. As the white lawyer leaves the courtroom, the Negroes
who had been segregated in the balcony all rise. One of them says to the young
narrator of the book, "Miss Jean Louise, stand up. Your father's passin'." Justice
has failed, but the pursuit of it brought professional honor.

In conclusion, vocation, in the sense of a calling by God, is the essential
element that prevents the concept of a professional minister from degenerating
into an enterprise for personal success. While not demanding that a minister
exemplify the notion of the professional in every way, we are convinced that
there are good historical and theological reasons for asserting that the Christian
minister is a professional. If this is the case, then the recovery of the religious
and social meaning of the clergy vocation and profession can revitalize the
church as well as build a foundation for an ethical ministry. Perhaps Paul
Camenisch sums it up best:

> I would argue that the professional ethics model is useful and appropriate for the
> clergy as far as it goes. Seen positively as the standards that guide professionals
> in their relations to clients and the larger society in light of the special skills and
> knowledge they claim to have, the distinctive goal they pursue in their profes-
> sional activity, and the atypical moral commitment they aspire to, professional
> ethics sets a floor below which the clergy ought not fall.[72]

The heart of this book is an attempt to explain what this commitment to an ethical ministry means in these various arenas of the minister's life. Without being legalistic, we will attempt to apply and illustrate the ethical demands the gospel makes on the professional life of the Christian minister. It is our hope that by the time we reach the last chapter, you will be prepared to write a personal code of ethics as a guide for your ministry.

The task of the next chapter is to review the art of ethics. To evaluate the ethical life of the minister, a clergyperson must first have a clear understanding of the role of character, conduct, and moral vision in the process of making good moral choices.

Suggested Reading

Bayles, Michael. *Professional Ethics.* 2d ed. Belmont, Calif.: Wadsworth Publishing, 1989.

Glasse, James D. *Profession: Minister.* Nashville: Abingdon, 1968.

May, William F. *Beleaguered Rulers: The Public Obligation of the Professional.* Louisville: Westminster John Knox, 2003.

Reeck, Darrell. *Ethics for the Professions: A Christian Perspective.* Minneapolis: Augsburg, 1982.

Theology Today 59 (October 2002), 349–420.

Wind, James P., Russell Burck, Paul F. Camenisch, and Dennis P. McCann, eds. *Clergy Ethics in a Changing Society: Mapping the Terrain.* Louisville: Westminster John Knox, 1991.

2

The Minister's Moral Choices

Endowed or Acquired?

On January 31, 1872, the renowned minister Henry Ward Beecher traveled to Yale to deliver the first of the Beecher Lectures on preaching. His biographer noted:

> He had a bad night, not feeling well. Went to his hotel, got his dinner, lay down to take a nap. About two o'clock he got up and began to shave without having been able to get at any plan of the lecture to be delivered within the hour. Just as he had his face lathered and was beginning to strop his razor, the whole thing came out of the clouds and dawned on him. He dropped his razor, seized his pencil, and dashed off the memoranda for it and afterwards cut himself badly, he said, thinking it out.[1]

A century later another renowned minister, Frederick Buechner, commented, "And well the old pulpiteer might have cut himself with his razor because part of the inner world his lecture came from . . . was the deep trouble that he was in or the deep trouble that was in him."[2] Rumors about Beecher's relationship with the wife of a parishioner had gone beyond the gossip stage. Embarrassing letters and tearful confessions had surfaced. A public trial for adultery was not far away. So as Beecher stood gazing into the hotel mirror, with soap on his face and a razor in his hand, what he saw was not himself, for everything he believed in and stood for and had come to Yale to talk about was not reflected in that mirror.

> Henry Ward Beecher cut himself with his razor and wrote out notes for that first Beecher Lecture in blood because, whatever else he was or aspired to be or was famous for being, he was a man of flesh and blood, and so were all the men over the years who traveled to New Haven after him to deliver the same lectures.[3]

All ministers who stand behind pulpits less prominent than the one at Yale can also "cut themselves badly." How do ministers keep their lives unscarred by ethical misconduct? Is there a single formula for learning to do the right thing? Are "good ministers" born with moral character, or do they acquire the ability to make right moral decisions?

Some moral choices are fairly ordinary, such as choosing between recreation with the family or sermon preparation. Others are quite complex. A teenager reveals in counseling that she is pregnant but asks you not to tell her parents. What do you do? Every day ministers must make decisions that touch other people's lives, as well as their own. In the process, they often ask, "Did I do the right thing? How does one know? Can I improve my ability to make the right choices?"

A hotly debated topic in ethics studies today is whether ethics can be taught. In a *New York Times* article, Michael Levin asserted that "ethics courses are an utterly pointless exercise. . . . [A]bstract knowledge of right and wrong no more contributes to character than knowledge of physics contributes to bicycling."[4] Teachers of ethics responded vigorously. Acknowledging Levin's contention that right living is mainly a matter of instilling good habits of the heart, they nevertheless asked, "Is there no place for reason?" A decent ethics class, they claimed, accomplishes three things: It stimulates moral imagination, hones moral analysis, and elicits a sense of moral obligation.[5] Indeed, these three goals spotlight the aims of this chapter.

In religious circles, the argument against learning ethics takes a different form. There is a popular myth that ministers automatically know the right thing to do. As noted in chapter 1, most ministers believe their vocation is a calling from God. In addition, the laity often assumes that God calls only persons of good moral character to begin with.

Some believe that a minister develops moral sensitivity through education and experience so that by the time of ordination, an articulate ethical expert walks forth with credentials in one hand and a resume in the other. However, no one knows better than persons called parsons that Solomonic wisdom is rare, even among the clergy. For a minister to develop skills in moral decision making, he or she must understand the role of virtues in character, the place of values in conduct, and the way to develop integrity through moral vision.[6]

In light of the continuing moral failures of prominent preachers, it is surprising that anyone believes ministers are innately endowed with moral character or discernment. Nevertheless, it is not uncommon (especially in seminary classrooms) to hear a young theolog say, "Why do I have to take ethics? I know what's right. I believe the Bible, and I am committed to do the will of God." Many experienced ministers also believe they need no special training in moral decision making. Somehow they feel that their enlightened conscience, Scripture, or common sense will carry them through.

This last statement raises a basic ethical question, that of authority. Who, or what, determines right or wrong for the minister? Is the answer found within the person? Has God given a trustworthy "inner light" to ministers—a moral gyroscope that always points northward toward God's perfect will? Thomas Aquinas saw reason as an infallible teacher. Joseph Butler, on the other hand, elevated the conscience to the role of unerring guide. Quakers such as George Fox listened for the voice from the "inner light" in order to decide what was right or wrong.

Most Christian ministers look beyond themselves for a dependable ethical compass to help them navigate through moral storms. Evangelical clerics normally turn first to the Bible. Worshipers often hear their ministers proclaim, "Look to the Bible. It has the answer for every question." Certainly, most Protestant clergy accept Scripture as the "main tangible, objective source for a knowledge of the will of God."[7] Yet sometimes our understanding of Scripture is so limited that we view the Old Testament simply as a book of moral rules and the New Testament simply as an advanced ethic of principles. Closer examination, however, reveals that the entire Bible includes a diversity of ways to do moral reasoning.[8]

Two contemporary ethicists have appealed to their colleagues to reconsider the role of the Bible in Christian ethics. In *Bible and Ethics in the Christian Life,* Bruce Birch and Larry Rasmussen build a strong case for seeing the Bible as the major "formative and normative" authority for Christian character development and moral decision making.[9] Yet simply saying "follow the Bible" does not solve all our moral questions. Some ethical issues, such as divorce and war, seem both to be condoned and condemned in Scripture. Also, a number of modern moral concerns, such as artificial insemination and media morality, did not exist in biblical times. Properly applying the ethical teachings of Scripture to these and other issues requires skillful exegesis and sound hermeneutics.[10] The Bible has a rich vein of ethical gold to be mined by the minister "who correctly handles the word of truth" (2 Tim. 2:15).

Taken as a whole, then, the Bible is the primary resource for doing ethics. "The Biblical writers do offer a helpful lead. They suggest what sort of ethical approach is appropriate for the Christian—even if a lot of the details remains to be filled in."[11] One way the "details are filled in" is through the work of the Holy Spirit, the subjective means of revelation. As Christ is the pattern for morality, the Spirit is the power that makes Christian living possible (Rom. 8:13–14). The apostle John wrote, "When he, the Spirit of truth, comes, he will guide you into all truth" (John 16:13). The word *truth* presumably includes moral truth, the Spirit's help and guidance in moral choices. The apostle Paul reminds us that the *paraclete* of God is our abiding moral guide (Rom. 8:9–14; 1 Cor. 6:19–20). Sometimes we limit the Spirit's work to sudden inspiration or direct prompting regarding a certain action. While the Spirit can certainly guide in this way, he also gives insight to Christians in the midst of serious reflection on moral decisions.

What about the Christian tradition—the documents of early Christianity as well as the thoughts of present-day writers? Some of the best insights about Christian living are found in the writings of Augustine and Aquinas, Teresa of Avila and Catherine of Siena, Luther and Calvin, along with those of modern communicators such as Karen Lebacqz, Lewis Smedes, and Stanley Hauerwas. Ethically serious ministers should read widely from the great books that inform and inspire.

Reflection and the ability to analyze situations are also extremely important aids in moral decision making. Prayer is a vital link to the mind of God and often the final way of confirming God's will; this was true in Jesus' life (Matt. 26:42; Luke 6:12; John 17). In sum, the Christian minister must utilize every means at his or her command in order to discover and do the right thing.

This list of resources brings to mind an important distinction. Is ethics a matter of character or conduct? Which is more important, virtues or values? Does what *I am* determine what I do, or does what *I do* shape who I am? The answer to these last two questions is yes. Being affects doing, and doing shapes being.

Although some ethicists believe the key to morality is character development, an equal number would argue that the secret to correct conduct is how one does ethics. In fact, both "being good" (character) and "doing good" (conduct) are necessary. The two elements are interdependent. Like the bow and the violin, they work together to produce the harmonious music that we call moral vision—a lifestyle of "living good." The best word to describe the minister's moral life is *integrity,* a term that is the theme of this book and the "integrating" element that unifies character, conduct, and moral vision into a "life worthy of the calling you have received" (Eph. 4:1).

Discovering the will of God and discerning the right thing to do are not always easy; doing the right thing is equally difficult. In Dante's *Inferno,* the first group in hell whom the poet meets are those who could not make a moral decision. The process of learning what is moral for the Christian minister, as well as developing the fortitude to do the right thing, is a lifelong challenge. Growing in the ability to analyze each situation correctly, applying Christian principles and perspectives wisely, and walking in the pathway that leads toward the ultimate will of God are the goals of moral decision making.

As we begin the larger discussion of ministerial ethics, let us be sure that we understand the basics of moral decision making. There are three major components in this task: character, conduct, and moral vision or integrity. Sometimes ethicists use the terms *virtues, values,* and *vision* to define these three dynamics in the moral life.[12] Being a good minister is obviously a matter of *being;* however, it is also a matter of *doing* and a matter of *living.* As with each leg of a three-legged stool, each of these ethical supports is needed to keep us from falling and failing in our moral choices.

Being Good—The Ethics of Character

Henry Ward Beecher saw two images in his hotel mirror the night before the Yale lectures. He gazed at both the man he wanted to be and the person he had become. Although Rev. Beecher had an ideal image of himself in his mind, the face he viewed as he shaved troubled him. He was ashamed to look himself in the eye, for that meant facing his own failure and folly. Perhaps that is why he "cut himself badly."

Beecher is certainly not the only preacher who bleeds, "for all have sinned" (Rom. 3:23). In one way or another, every person of the cloth has felt the weight of his or her own humanity. We have all cut ourselves—if not in the flesh, then in the spirit. But the question is not, "Have I ever failed?" Rather, it is, "How do I live as a human being in the world and not be controlled by my human appetites?"

A large part of the answer is found in the merging of those two images in the mirror, synthesizing the ideal person we ought to be with the real person we are capable of becoming. It all begins with the development of the inner life—something called *character.*

The Meaning of Character

Character is basic to all ethical decisions. Who we are determines what we do. Jesus stressed that truth in his teachings, especially in the Sermon on the Mount (Matthew 5–7). Scholars agree that this monumental message contains the essence of Christ's ethic. Jesus emphasized again and again that character precedes conduct and that morality is a matter of the heart (5:3–48). It is futile to pray or give gifts to the poor in order "to be seen by others," said Jesus, for wrong motives nullify good deeds (6:1–8). Christ condemned the superficial righteousness of many scribes and Pharisees, not because the act was wrong but because the actor played the role of hypocrite (5:20; 6:5). Albert Knudson notes that Jesus upheld two principles that all Christians accept: the principle of love and the principle of moral inwardness.[13] The first is the supreme Christian virtue (1 Cor. 13:13); the second is the key to Christian morality—character.

Though we all have an idea of what is meant by the term *character,* it is not that easy to define. Character refers to the kind of person who acts in a certain way. It is the inner realities of the self. Theologian-ethicist Stanley Hauerwas describes character as "the qualification or determination of our self-agency, formed by our having certain intentions rather than others."[14] William Willimon calls it the

> basic moral orientation that gives unity, definition, and direction to our lives by forming our habits and intentions into meaningful and predictable patterns that have been determined by our dominant convictions.[15]

According to Willimon, character is formed consciously and unconsciously in a community or a social setting.

Sondra Ely Wheeler praises character and virtue ethics as those "skills, dispositions, and habits that enable us to behave rightly under pressure," stating the paradoxical classical insight that "you cannot act virtuously without possessing virtue, and you cannot develop virtue without acting virtuously."[16]

No one-sentence definition or paragraph description can begin to do justice to the complexity of the concept of character. More important to the task at hand, however, is the need to understand how moral character is formed and how it functions in a Christian's ethical life.

In recent years, the focus of decision making has shifted to the role of character and the place of its source, community. Perhaps no modern writer has emphasized the place of character in Christian ethics more than Stanley Hauerwas. In his view, what we *are* is the ultimate determinative of what we *do.* Individuals do not approach a moral choice objectively; "rather, each person brings the dispositions, experience, traditions, heritage, and virtues that he or she has cultivated."[17] We develop these "habits of the heart" within the communities to which we belong: family, church, schools, and society.

If character is that inner "moral orientation" that shapes our lives into "meaningful and predictable patterns," then the Christian minister must internalize "both the demands and limits of professional life to the point of behaving ethically most of the time as though by instinct."[18] This reality, that being shapes doing, influences an approach to personal and social ethics. "The first task of Christian social ethics, therefore, is not to make the 'world' better or more just, but to help Christian people form their community consistent with their conviction."[19]

Like Beecher, we look into the mirror each morning, gazing at two images. One is clear and distinct; it is the real person we are. The other is a hazy projection from our inner being; it is the person we hope to be. Rather than always asking, "What should I do?" we should also ask, "What should I be?"

The Role of Virtues in Character

Darrell Reeck describes character ethics as "expressive ethics." The question he poses is, "What moral values do you wish to manifest through your life and practice?"[20] As traditional Catholic moral theology states it, *agere sequitur esse:* "We act out of who we are." "Character refers to the *kind of person* who acts in a certain way. It focuses on inner realities of the self: motives, intention, attitudes, dispositions. We do not see character directly. We see it in its fruits."[21] Character consists of those personality traits that are moral and traditionally have been called *virtues*. Historically, character ethics has encouraged the cultivation of moral excellences considered essential to the "good life."

Ancient Greek philosophers saw four traits as cardinal virtues: prudence, justice, temperance, and courage. Prudence is practical wisdom—not to be confused with intelligence. Such wisdom always leads to good choices. Justice centers on fairness, honesty, and the rule of law. Temperance is self-discipline, the capacity to control one's impulses to gratify immediate desires that are harmful in the long run. Courage, also called fortitude, is the capacity to do what is right or necessary, even in the face of adversity.

> It is not good enough to get two out of three or three out of four. That might be great for baseball, but it is bad for society. The core virtues make each other possible. A sense of justice is ineffectual if one lacks the courage to stand against injustice. Courage without wisdom is simply foolhardiness. And all the other virtues are undercut when one lacks self-control.[22]

Christian theologians such as Augustine and Aquinas accepted these ideal traits as the very best natural humans could discover through reason. To these cardinal virtues they added the theological virtues of faith, hope, and love, virtues received through revelation.

> For the Greeks, as well as the Christians, virtue was the central concept for moral reflection. Although there was no complete consensus about what constitutes virtue or which virtues should be considered primary, it was accepted that consideration of morality began with descriptions of the virtuous life.[23]

For many centuries, the Christian moral life was mainly a matter of pursuing the right virtues. In a general sense, once the virtuous life was achieved, one was believed to be a "good person."

While virtue has had an important place in Christian ethics from the beginning, there has also been some suspicion of it. Reformers such as Luther saw the inherent danger in such a quest. Much evil is the corruption of good, and much vice the perversion of virtue. The very pursuit of morality, felt Luther, inevitably led to self-righteousness. Rejecting the Aristotelian idea that ethics was a movement from vice to virtue, the German Reformer said that if there be a "movement," it is from vice *and* virtue to grace.[24]

Modern theologian Reinhold Niebuhr has also reminded us that human nature has a tremendous capacity for self-deception and evil in the guise of good.[25] In our zeal to defend orthodoxy and uphold righteousness, we may sometimes manipulate the truth to suit our purposes, read data with a bias, or use people to achieve our grand goals.

In spite of these built-in dangers, character remains the single most important factor in ethical decision making. A person must *be* something before he or she can *do* anything. A person of integrity not only tells the truth but is also truthful.

Writing to ministers, Karen Lebacqz pleads for two basic character traits: trustworthiness and prudence. Ministerial character absolutely requires trustworthiness. A clergyperson must be "a person of integrity who not only does the 'right' thing, but is an *honorable person*."[26] Trustworthiness, writes Lebacqz, means that a minister is a "trustworthy trustee," one who can be trusted to be honest, fair, helpful, and not hurtful. He must be not like Judas, but like Jesus.[27]

No real Christian ministry can exist without the ability to discern the truth. *Prudence* is Lebacqz's word for it. This virtue helps a minister perceive what is required in any situation. Prudence, or discernment, is the ability to make right decisions and thus is central to ethical decision making.[28] Lewis Smedes agrees. A key element in Christian decision making, declared the late Fuller Seminary professor, is "the ability to see what is really going on, the small things . . . the difference between things . . . what is new and what is bizarre . . . what is excellent and what is only good."[29]

Yale professor Gaylord Noyce has addressed the professional responsibilities of the clergy in his book *Pastoral Ethics*. The basic character trait necessary in ministers, Noyce contends, is "faithful integrity." A responsible shepherd of God strives to be "a person of religious integrity, a person of faith and spiritual wisdom."[30]

Seminary professors Walter Wiest and Elwyn Smith have written a basic ministerial ethics text in which they center ethical ministry around the nucleus of truth, "which includes both truthfulness and being true."[31] These Presbyterian ministers believe that a primary requirement of clerical ministry is being honest about one's self, the gospel preached and taught, and the conduct of ministry.[32]

In a contemporary text produced by the Chicago Area Clergy Ethics Study Group, Dennis McCann proposes a unique character trait as the distinctive of clergy ethics.

> I will argue that a capacity for self-sacrifice is and ought to be the indispensable first principle for clergy ethics, regardless of specific denominational traditions,

precisely because the role of the clergy in any society is to be the institutional bearers of whatever learning and teaching about sacrifice inevitably goes on in that society.[33]

Although these various writers have differing opinions regarding the most important clergy virtue, they unanimously agree that ministerial morality always begins with character.

Lewis Smedes's book *A Pretty Good Person* explains the necessity of a cluster of significant virtues for a moral life. Living the "good life" and becoming a "pretty good person" require living with qualities such as "gratitude, guts, simple integrity, self-control, discernment, and fair love."[34] Individual virtues not only help us to be better persons but when taken together produce a whole person. To achieve good character, wholeness is needed. Smedes concludes that character is a living network that links all virtues, each depending on the other.

> Without gratitude there can be no integrity; ingratitude falsifies life at the start. But integrity needs courage when honesty runs the risk of trouble. And courage needs discernment so that we can see what is going on and know when bravery calls us to act and when it calls us to stay where we are. But discernment needs self-control because when we fly off the handle we cannot see what is going on; and when we cannot see what is going on we usually *end* up making a mess of things.[35]

The Centrality of Character

Character ethics, then, are basic to ministerial ethics. William Willimon warns:

> The great ethical danger for clergy is not that we might "burn out," . . . not that we might lose the energy required to do ministry. Our danger is that we might "black out," that is lose consciousness as to why we are here and who we are called to be for Christ and his church.[36]

The clerical collar does not guarantee ethical conduct; rather, what exists under that collar significantly affects every moral choice. In fact, character is the link between a person's past and future. A minister who has proven to be trustworthy in previous church relationships usually can be counted on to continue that pattern in the future.

There is an overwhelming consensus that character is central to the clergy role. Bishop Nolan Harmon put it succinctly years ago: "The Christian minister must *be* something before he can *do* anything. . . . His work depends on his personal character."[37] Numerous writers throughout the years have sounded that same note of conviction: "What the minister *is* will be his greatest sermon";[38] "What he does is sometimes not nearly so important as what he is";[39] "I do not just *perform* a ministry, I *am* a minister."[40] Although ministry has changed over the years, this theme of *being,* not merely *doing,* has remained at the forefront of ministerial ethics.

A three-year study by the Association of Theological Schools identified qualities church people look for in young ministers. Of the five leading characteristics, four focused on the minister as a person. Similarly, the three images ranked least desirable also dealt with issues of character. All forty-eight denominations agreed that "service in humility" was most important. Lebacqz believes the phrase stresses humility rather than service and thereby affirms that character, not just function, is central to the clergy role.[41]

Character ethics enables ministers and other professionals to fulfill their roles by providing "a certain sense of calmness in doing the right thing and courage in resisting the wrong," and "a measure of discretion" that leaves "final judgment up to the individual."[42] However, in this individuality lies one of the weaknesses of character ethics. Social and institutional moral values are not often based on personal ethics; they are usually based on social survival goals such as economic profit. Wise ministers, while retaining their inner convictions, must learn to deal with social structures inside and outside the church. The correct way to express ministerial virtues in real-life dilemmas is not always clear.

Thus, acting ethically always involves more than just having a sterling moral character. That is certainly basic, but the moral life is more than simply being a good person or playing out our character in society.[43] Along with a healthy wholeness of *being,* a consistent method of *doing* is needed. To character and its virtues must be added conduct and its values: the perspectives, obligations, and aspirations that guide the Christian minister in making right choices.

Doing Good—The Ethics of Conduct

Traditionally, books addressed to pastors have focused on certain areas that seem to tempt ministers more than others. Because of the nature of the profession and the unique vulnerability of the minister, clergy ethical misconduct seems to concern sex, money, and power. These topics are discussed fully in chapter 3.

Quaker theologian Richard Foster has called attention to these triple temptations. To help Christians reconsider the monastic quest for spirituality, he reviews the early struggle of the religious hermit with worldliness. To renounce the material values of society, the monk took a vow of poverty. To flee the follies of the flesh, the celibate pledged chastity. To conquer the inner will, the recluse pledged obedience to ecclesiastical authority. Warning our generation not to misjudge the monastics, Foster calls us to reexamine the monastic dilemma. He does not accept the monastic ideal uncritically, however. Instead, he bases his concept of the disciplined Christian life on the monastic pursuit and makes it relevant for today. "We are faced with the necessity for framing a contemporary response to the issues of money, sex and power."[44] Modern ministers are especially vulnerable to this trilogy of temptation, and the three are uniquely related. "Money manifests itself as power. Sex is used to acquire both money and power. And power is often called 'the best aphrodisiac.'"[45] The minister's world often seems like the ancient Roman Colosseum, where lurk three voracious lions—greed, lust, and power.

Earlier we noted that Wiest and Smith identified truthfulness as the central issue of ethics in ministry. For these seminary professors, the principle of truthfulness applies to the ordained in five areas of ministry: letters of recommendation, plagiarism, theological differences with the laity, theological growth, and confidentiality.[46] The point made by these authors is this: Ministerial behavior is a crucial ingredient in the performance of ministry. Acting in ways both unethical and indiscreet can seriously jeopardize a person's ability to serve the church of Jesus Christ.

A prominent pastor of one of the largest churches in the South led a campus revival at a seminary in New Orleans. He encouraged the students to bring their wives on Friday to hear his famous sermon on the family. The auditorium was filled with over fifteen hundred people who marveled at his message. The very next day the deacons of his church confronted him with evidence of his many sexual affairs with women in the congregation. Whatever gifts he possessed were overshadowed by his moral failure.

The Meaning of Values

Just as *being* centers on virtues, *doing* revolves around values. What are values? Values are "moral goods to be realized in society."[47] They are the ideals and concepts considered by a group of people to be of great worth. In the United States, for example, freedom and justice are important values. One function of a value is to highlight the consequences of behavior in society. When someone acts in a way that violates an accepted value, the unifying beliefs of that community are weakened and threatened.

The people of faith, the Christian church, have been called forth to be an alternate community, "a society shaped and informed by the truthful character of the God we find revealed in the stories of Israel and Jesus."[48] The biblical writers often use the word *good* to identify moral and spiritual values.

> He has told you, O mortal, what is good;
> and what does the LORD require of you
> but to do justice, and to love kindness,
> and to walk humbly with your God?

Micah 6:8 NRSV

Over the centuries, certain values kept appearing as reminders to God's people that they were "resident aliens . . . a colony, an island of one culture in the middle of another."[49] These essential "goods" revealed the nature and character of God, especially in the story of Jesus in the Gospels. From these values come the theological perspectives that ground us, the obligations that bind us, the norms that guide us, and the goals that motivate us.

The Theological Question

Just as virtue emphasizes moral character within, values stress moral ideals realized without. As the minister considers the role of values in his or her ethical life, the first question raised is a theological one: What moral values stabilize the clergy?

Basic to an understanding of ministerial ethics is comprehension of the moral nature of God. Leviticus 19:2 is the *shema* of ethical belief: "Be holy because I, the LORD your God, am holy." Biblical faith is an ethical faith because the one and only true God is inherently holy, righteous, and just. Throughout the canon the moral character of God is revealed, both in God's actions and God's expectations.

The climax of God's revelation was the incarnation—the life, death, and resurrection of Jesus Christ of Nazareth. "The Word became flesh and made his dwelling among us. We have seen his glory, the glory of the One and Only, who came from the Father, full of grace and truth" (John 1:14). Jesus' entire life was in perfect harmony with the ethical ideals he taught. There is no other religion whose founder was himself the norm and the illustration of the values he professed.

One statement captures the essence of Jesus' ethics. When asked, "Teacher, which is the greatest commandment in the Law?" (Matt. 22:36), Jesus replied using two key Old Testament passages, Deuteronomy 6:5 and Leviticus 19:18: "'Love the Lord your God with all your heart and with all your soul and with all your mind.' This is the first and greatest commandment. And the second is like it: 'Love your neighbor as yourself'" (Matt. 22:37–39). These two commandments of love, one vertical and one horizontal, are the fulfillment of the entire Old Testament revelation (v. 40). In other words, the Christian faith is an ethical one because Yahweh, the God whose nature is steadfast love (Hosea 11:1–4), expects his covenant people to love as God loves.

The theologian Reinhold Niebuhr has reminded contemporary believers, however, that self-sacrificial love generally does not work in society because of different sets of values in social groups. As Niebuhr put it, individuals and groups have different moral possibilities (as the title of his book *Moral Man and Immoral Society* suggests).[50] Although love is the ideal for personal relationships, in social organizations, justice is often the best humans can achieve.[51] For ministers of the church, this is a reminder that social groups (committees, churches, denominations) usually operate by a different set of values. Christian love may seem to be absent from decisions concerning, for example, who pays for medical benefits for the minister; fairness is probably a more realistic goal.

Moral values, such as love and justice, are guides for ministerial ethics. One of the ways we discern the "good" we are to follow is through our understanding of God and his will. This is the theological basis for an ethical ministry.

The Question of Obligations

After determining the theological perspectives that ground us, we face additional inquiries: What obligations bind the minister? Are there moral imperatives the clergy must always follow? The deontological question is, What duties are necessary for the minister?

The ethics of obligation seeks to define the moral principles or laws that must be obeyed. Darrell Reeck points out that "if one of the weaknesses of character ethics is to specify with clarity what a person ought to do," then "that deficiency is satisfied to some extent by . . . the ethics of obligation."[52]

Biblical examples of deontological duties are numerous. The two tables of the law Moses brought down from the mountain were neither ten suggestions nor ten multiple-choice options. The Ten Commandments were moral absolutes for Israel to follow (Exod. 20:1–17). New Testament moral imperatives, such as the Golden Rule (Matt. 7:12) and the call for nonretaliation (Matt. 5:38–39), are "ethical ideals and principles which are implicit in that new relationship to God into which a man enters when the Kingdom is established within him."[53]

The philosopher Immanuel Kant is sometimes called the "dean of the deontologists." Kant concluded that universal moral absolutes, which he called "categorical imperatives," must be followed without exception. One is the maxim always to treat persons as an end, never as a means.[54]

A more recent ethicist, W. D. Ross, developed his own list of absolutes, which he called prima facie ("on first appearance") duties. Examples of prima facie duties are fidelity, gratitude, justice, duties of beneficence (helping those who cannot help themselves), and duties of nonmaleficence (no injury to others).[55]

Applying this to ministers, Lebacqz writes that "certain acts tend to be right because of the nature of the act that they are."[56] This ethics professor sees the following responsibilities as compulsory for the clergy, all other things being equal: promise keeping, truth telling, beneficence, nonmaleficence, and justice.[57]

Obligations also include rules. Just how should biblical norms, church codes, and governmental edicts be understood by the minister? Laws are written to be obeyed. The Bible gives specific guidance on many subjects and admonishes, "Fear God and keep his commandments, for this is the whole duty of man" (Eccles. 12:13). Both Testaments define in detail behavior that is considered moral and immoral. Can a prophet of God take these commandments seriously without becoming a legalistic Pharisee?

First, let us affirm that rules have value. Biblical norms give guidance for ordinary, everyday decisions. This is especially true for new Christians, who are moral and spiritual infants as they begin their new life in Christ (1 Cor. 3:1–2). Several lists of vices and virtues appear in the Pauline letters; new Gentile converts in a pagan, immoral Roman world needed immediate guidance for their daily lives.

Rules also describe the kind of people Christians ought to be. They spell out in specific ways how those who have been captured by Jesus Christ act in certain situations. Biblical norms also show the unbelieving world what they can expect from disciples of Jesus.

What about a code of ethics for the church professional? Many professional roles carry obligations specific to them, often expressed in an ethical code. Doctors, lawyers, and scientists practice within self-imposed limits that are usually expressed in a code of ethics sanctioned by an oversight committee. The professional nature of the minister's work would seem to suggest that a similar set of mutually accepted rules of conduct is needed. Chapter 8 addresses that need and poses the possibility of developing a code of ethics for ministers.

At this point, however, the question of ministerial codes relates to the value of rules and the dangers of prescriptive ethics. Legalism has always been a virus of religion. In Jesus' day, Sabbath laws had become burdensome restrictions. In their zeal to keep the letter of the Torah perfectly, orthodox rabbis missed the spirit of the law, even accusing Jesus of breaking the law of Moses (Mark 2:23–24). Jewish casuistry, with its meticulous regulations, continues to transform the faith of Abraham into a book of rules.

Christian ministers are also tempted to fall into legalism. Most evangelical pastors resist papal pronouncements, church dogmas, and authoritative creeds of conduct, which eliminate the priesthood of every believer. Yet how easy it is for ministers to turn the Bible into a rule book, to rely on the judgments of a religious hero, or to allow a church tradition to become a rule of faith. Ministers ought to know better, yet many are guilty on occasion of regressing to an ancient list of dos and don'ts rather than seeking the will of God.

Legalism is an inadequate approach to decision making for several reasons. First, any list of laws is never long enough. A code can never cover every possible circumstance. Also, keeping some laws requires breaking others. To save a life, it may be necessary to tell a lie (Exod. 1:19). Finally, perhaps the greatest weakness of legalism is that it almost always hinders moral maturity and stimulates egoistic pride.

To guard against even subconscious legalism, the minister must understand the relationship between rules and values. Every biblical rule expresses a value, which is the reason behind the rule. For example, the seventh commandment, "You shall not commit adultery" (Exod. 20:14), does not condemn sexual desire. The value expressed in this rule is the sanctity of marriage and family life. Stated as a principle, this commandment declares, "Marriage is an intimate sexual union that excludes all sexual partners except husband and wife." The ethical emphasis of the Bible, as T. B. Maston often stressed to his students, is on principles rather than rules.[58]

The Question of Consequences

Values also have to do with teleology, the ethics of aspiration. *Telos* is the Greek word for "end" or "goal," and such ethics ask, What is the purpose or end result of an action? This focus on consequences raises another ethical issue, how to act in such a way as to bring about a better state of affairs.

The nineteenth-century social philosopher and reformer John Stuart Mill articulated a policy called utilitarianism. In short, his goal was to bring the greatest good to the greatest number of people. The value of utilitarianism is that it forces a person to consider all the relevant factors in a decision and their consequences. Its weakness, of course, is that one can never know for sure what a consequence may be. A minister may believe that if she reveals a teenager's drug problem to a parent, the family will respond positively. Just the opposite may occur.

Consequentialism is present in both the Old and New Testaments.[59] Wisdom literature seldom takes the imperative form but usually gives practical advice about how to achieve the good life (Prov. 9:10). Hebrew midwives who "feared God" made their decision to deceive Pharaoh on the basis of consequences: to save the male babies. God apparently approved of their decision (Exod. 1:15–20).

Jesus had numerous conflicts with religious leaders over the observance of Sabbath laws. The Lord of the Sabbath was concerned that the purpose of the day of rest not be lost in Jewish casuistry: "The sabbath was made for humankind, and not humankind for the sabbath" (Mark 2:27 NRSV). In the Sermon on the Mount, Christ stressed motives, noting that good deeds may be corrupted by wrong reasons. The apostle Paul often evaluated consequences before making a final decision. Once he took a vow and shaved his head, not because of religious obligation but probably to conciliate Jewish Christian leaders (Acts 18:18), a practice of accommodation he followed on other occasions (Acts 15:29; 16:3). The end result of any moral choice must be taken into account as part of the final decision.

The teleological question is usually raised when two values seem to be in conflict. When Nazis came knocking on Corrie ten Boom's door during World War II, the heroine of the historical story *The Hiding Place* faced a dilemma. Should she tell the truth and reveal the Jews hiding in her house, or should she lie to the Gestapo to protect them? Her decision involved consequences; to tell the truth meant Auschwitz and the "final solution." With much courage and some anguish she chose a lesser evil in order to achieve a higher good; she sent the soldiers away. Her decision was like Rahab's misleading of the king of Jericho (Joshua 2) and Elisha's deception of the foreign soldiers (2 Kings 6).

Sometimes a minister must decide if revealing the whole truth would do more harm than good. A wife asks her pastor, who is counseling her husband, if her spouse is having an affair. Is the minister guilty of breaking the eighth commandment if he conceals what he knows?

Though it may appear to be the best you can do in a certain situation, never forget that a lesser evil is an evil and not a good. A repentant spirit is in order. The Christian minister should always regret the necessity of such a choice and should work toward the day when such conflicts are eliminated or at least minimized. Lewis Smedes reminds us that in the "crooked ways of the world," we can deceive ourselves into believing that our loving lies are gallant when they may be only a way to save us from trouble.

> Telling one loving lie does not turn a person of integrity into a liar any more than one wrong note turns a concert violinist into a barn dance fiddler. But if you get used to getting away with a wrong note, you may get careless with yourself, and become just another fiddler when you could have been an artist.[60]

Being a good minister is a matter of learning how to *do good*. Doing good is a matter of values, deciding what moral goods are worth preserving and what rules, principles, and ideals apply to each moral question. Theological perspectives are basic; what we believe about God as creator, redeemer, and governor influences our ability to make good moral choices. For the minister, there are moral duties that must be followed, relevant norms that must be heeded, and social consequences that must be considered.

Yet making good moral choices is more than being a good person (character) and doing the right thing (conduct). There is also a third component called moral vision or integrity, which is the most unique one of the three, for this approach to decision making creates a new way to perceive ourselves and others.[61] This moral vision not only completes the trilogy of major components in ethical decision making but also unifies both character and conduct into a wholeness of life that is best described by the moral ideal of integrity.

Living Good—The Ethics of Integrity

In his hotel room the night before he delivered the Yale lectures, the Reverend Beecher wiped blood from his cleanly shaven face. He had cut himself, for in the mirror he had faced a contradiction between the person he saw and the message he preached. His life lacked integrity as he prepared to deliver the first lectures on preaching at New Haven.

In vivid contrast is the testimony of another person who later delivered a Yale lecture on preaching. George Wharton Pepper, one of the few laypersons to deliver such a lecture, spoke for the laity when he said, "It is impossible to exaggerate the weight that the man in the pew attaches to the integrity of the preacher."[62]

No professional is expected to model integrity as much as a church minister. "Misconduct is inexcusable among professionals, but glaringly so among preachers."[63] After challenging the notion that ministers are superhuman and not subject to normal human faults and foibles, Lebacqz nevertheless states:

> The minister is expected to embody trustworthiness in such an integral way (i.e., to have such integrity) that even the slightest failure becomes a sign of lack of integrity. This does not mean the minister is permitted no faults. It means that the minister is permitted no faults *that have to do with trustworthiness.*[64]

The term *integrity* best describes the ethical wholeness of life demanded of the Christian minister. The morally mature minister experiences concommitant growth in three vital areas: character, conduct, and moral vision. These three elements interface to produce a morally complete person. Each is necessary, and none is complete without the other two.

A virtuous person who lacks the ability to discern values usually fails to touch the world around him or her. Restricting the ethical life to the task of discerning right and wrong values often causes people to lose touch with the world above them. The absence of responsible "being" and "doing" in a minister prevents the development of moral vision, the world within. As Birch and Rasmussen concur:

> [M]oral vision establishes the reference point for the other elements in the moral life. It sets the terms for that which will be included and excluded. It confers status upon that which is of greater importance, lesser, and, indeed, of no importance at all. Formation of moral character, together with decision making and action, are pervaded by the reigning moral vision.[65]

As three concentric circles form a new shape at the center where the trio overlaps, so in the minister's moral life a dynamic center is formed that integrates character, conduct, and moral vision into one complete life of integrity.

The Meaning of Integrity

The term *integrity* appears sixteen times in Scripture. The Hebrew word for it is *tōm* or *tummah* and means "whole," "sound," "unimpaired," "perfection." It is used to describe biblical characters such as David (Ps. 7:8), Solomon (1 Kings 9:4), and Job (2:9). None of these men was morally perfect, but they each modeled a life of wholeness and maturity.

In the New Testament, Paul reminds Timothy that a pastoral overseer must be blameless (1 Tim. 3:2). In personal character, family relationships, and spiritual commitments, the one called to shepherd God's flock must be above reproach (1 Tim. 3:1–7). The apostle counsels the young preacher Titus, "In your teaching show integrity" (Titus 2:7).

Jesus is the supreme example of integrity. Even his enemies admitted, "Teacher, we know you are a man of integrity. You aren't swayed by men, . . . but you teach the way of God in accordance with the truth" (Mark 12:14).

Modern dictionary definitions of *integrity* define it as "soundness, adherence to a code of values, the quality or state of being complete or undivided." Charles Swindoll adds, "When one has integrity there is an absence of hypocrisy. He or she is personally reliable, financially accountable, and privately clean . . . innocent of impure motives."[66]

Integrity includes both who one is and what one does. It involves the way one thinks as well as acts. It is

> ethical soundness, intellectual veracity, and moral excellence. It keeps us from fearing the white light of close examination and from resisting the scrutiny of accountability. It is honesty at all cost . . . rocklike character that won't crack when standing alone or crumble when pressure mounts.[67]

The Creation of Integrity

How does a minister develop character, conduct, and moral vision into one organic whole called integrity? Theology and ethics have recently emphasized the role of narrative, or story, in the Bible and in the Christian life. Narrative ethics asserts that we create ourselves and write our own stories according to moral convictions we receive from the communities to which we belong. As noted earlier, our characters are shaped by our communities and their stories. Duke professor Stanley Hauerwas contends that this claim about the significance of narrative and community for theological understanding is not

> just to make a point about the form of biblical sources, but involves claims about the nature of God, the self, and the nature of the world. We are "storied people" because the God that sustains us is a "storied God," whom we come to know only by having our character formed appropriate to God's character.[68]

As believers identify with God's story and make it their own story, they become a part of the Christian community, which nurtures and reinforces in them the virtues and values of the kingdom of God. When they make this story their own, they receive moral guidance and hear the moral demands of the gospel. Sometimes called the ethic of discipleship, narrative ethics focuses on the life and teachings of Jesus as a call to radical obedience. "Rather than reducing Jesus' teachings to principles or values, costly witness is called for. It is to live in the liberty that the new age has dawned in Christ."[69]

In short, the approaches called narrative, community, and discipleship ethics all point to the importance of integrating character and conduct in decision making. The virtues and values revealed in Scripture are not isolated from the biblical story, which is the story of the people of God, who share a new vision.

The ultimate test of any story is the sort of person it shapes. Ministers of Jesus Christ and proclaimers of "the story" are compelled to ask, "Does my story fit God's story?"

At the beginning of the twentieth century, Charles Sheldon wrote the devotional classic *In His Steps,* which posed the ethical question, "What would Jesus do?"[70] Though idealistic in its application, the novel was accurate in its basic theme. The example of Jesus is our guiding story.

How do we follow the example of Jesus? Is it possible in this modern world for a minister to live the way Jesus lived and to love the way Jesus loved? Acceptance as a disciple involves learning to imitate a master. It is not a matter of merely doing our duty. It means living Jesus' story. "The problem lies not in knowing *what* we must do, but *how* we are to do it. And the how is learned only by watching and following."[71]

Whether you call it discipleship or moral vision or integrity, the challenge is the same: We are to "walk as Jesus did" (1 John 2:6). T. B. Maston's last book, *To Walk as He Walked,* was based on this his favorite Scripture passage. The renowned ethicist called for Christians to reexamine the historic Jesus and the life he lived. "The major recurring question for us is, How much do we walk as He walked?"[72] What gives a minister integrity is the way the events of his or her life embody the gospel story, the life and teachings of Jesus the Messiah.

For example, the stories told by Christ, such as the parable of the good Samaritan, teach us how to perceive people. Lebacqz reminds us that we often miss the point Jesus makes here. The question introducing the story, "Who is my neighbor?" was addressed to Jews. The parable tells the injured Jew lying on the roadside, your neighbor is your enemy! The Samaritan you hate and the race your friends despise is the compassionate one who stopped and gave you aid. "The meaning of the story goes far beyond simple rules about helping others. . . . It has to do with vision."[73]

The Practical Question

At this point you may be saying, "All of this sounds well and good, but specifically, how does a minister put this into practice?" First, let us agree that every person called to the ministry wants to be a person of integrity—wants to achieve that wholeness of life and soundness of character that result in good moral choices.

Second, let us reaffirm the inadequacy of singular approaches. Any list of moral rules fails at several points, even if the rules are from the Bible or from orthodox church teachings. Likewise, great ethical principles such as love and justice, though important values, do not by themselves give complete guidance. Listening for an inner voice alone is also inadequate, for it is too subjective. Even looking for the lesser evil or the greater good does not resolve all moral conflicts.

What then can a church's moral leader do? Different styles of moral reasoning fit various moral questions. In a book written to help professionals, Darrell Reeck concludes:

> [A]stute people in actual practice use a mix of types of ethics. In day-to-day situations they may operate with reference to a set of principles that are perhaps even only somewhat dimly perceived. When they face unique, nonrepetitive decisions, they may bring calculations of consequences into operation. If really pushed to the wall in a situation in which they cannot compromise, they may act according to principle without any regard to consequences. As people mature in decision making they achieve an artful ability to make appropriate ethical responses by drawing selectively from their repertoire of ethical knowledge.[74]

"Artful ability" seems to allude to the quality called moral vision.

Perhaps the most important characteristic not mentioned until now is consistency. For the minister to be inconsistent in moral thinking and actions is not only irrational but also raises serious questions about personal integrity. The vice Jesus condemned with his harshest words and most scathing denunciation was hypocrisy (Matthew 23).

> Hypocrisy can mean a failure to practice what one preaches; it can also entail an attitude of rigorous moral scrupulosity in one area co-existing with an attitude of libertarian indifference in a comparable area. Hypocrisy may consist in a failure to carry through the implications of one's moral stances consistently.[75]

For example, if a minister denounces explicit sexual scenes on television, does he also condemn excessive violence? Are a minister's views about war and peace compatible with those regarding euthanasia and abortion? Would he or she be honest if it were possible to get away with not being so?

Our contention has been that of all the methods used to make good moral decisions, three are basic: character, conduct, and moral vision. The character of a Christian minister is foundational; being precedes doing. Developing the right virtues are absolutely essential to effective ministry.

The ability to discern and apply social values are also crucial. A well-grounded minister recognizes which duties are obligatory and which goals serve as guidelines for achieving the will of God.

Finally, through personal identification with Jesus Christ and full participation in the gospel story, an ethical leader gains a moral vision that synthesizes and harmonizes being, doing, and living into a life of moral integrity—living the truth.

Fyodor Dostoevsky eloquently described the effects of living a lie in his novel *The Brothers Karamazov:*

> Above all don't lie to yourself. The man who lies to himself and listens to his own lie comes to such a pass that he cannot distinguish the truth within him, or around him, and so loses all respect for himself and for others. And having no respect he ceases to love, and in order to occupy and distract himself without love he gives way to passions and coarse pleasures, and sinks to bestiality in its vices, all from continual lying to other men and to himself.[76]

We return to the initial question of this chapter: Are a minister's moral choices endowed or acquired? By now, the answer should be clear. Ethical integrity is not genetically inbred at conception or miraculously infused at baptism or ordination. The prophet of God must grow in faith and morals as do all believers. Learning how to make good moral choices is a lifelong process called Christian discipleship.

Thus far we have attempted two tasks. First, we have explored the meaning of the minister's vocation, suggesting that the traditional professional role of the clergy has significant ethical implications. Second, we have sought to establish a method for making good moral choices by properly combining character, conduct, and moral vision to form a life of ethical integrity.

Now it is time to move into the more practical aspects of ministerial ethics by addressing what it means to be an ethical minister in relation to one's personal life (chap. 3), congregational life (chap. 4), life with colleagues (chap. 5), and life in community (chap. 6).

Suggested Reading

Birch, Bruce C., and Larry L. Rasmussen. *Bible and Ethics in the Christian Life.* Rev. ed. Minneapolis: Augsburg, 1989.

Hauerwas, Stanley. *A Community of Character.* Notre Dame, Ind.: University of Notre Dame Press, 1981.

Higgenson, Richard. *Dilemmas: A Christian Approach to Moral Decision Making.* Louisville: Westminster John Knox, 1988.

Smedes, Lewis B. *A Pretty Good Person.* San Francisco: Harper & Row, 1990.

Trull, Joe E. *Walking in the Way: An Introduction to Christian Ethics.* Nashville: Broadman & Holman, 1997.

3

The Minister's Personal Life

Incidental or Intentional?

Political writer and analyst Theodore White concluded his study of former president Richard Nixon and the Watergate scandal with these words:

> The true crime of Richard Nixon was simple: he destroyed the myth that binds America together. And for this he was driven from power.
>
> The myth he broke was critical—that somewhere in American life there is at least one man who stands for law, the President. That faith surmounts all daily cynicism, all evidence of suspicion of wrong-doing by lesser leaders, all corruptions, all vulgarities, all the ugly compromises of daily striving and ambition. That faith holds that all men are equal before the law and protected by it; and that no matter how the faith may be betrayed elsewhere, at one particular point—the Presidency—justice will be done beyond prejudice, beyond rancor, beyond the possibility of a fix.[1]

Consider also the corporate scene. In the early part of the twenty-first century, the corporate world was shocked by the revelation of accounting irregularities at Enron and MCI/World Com. The chief executive officers of both these businesses were professing Christians and active churchmen. A pastor in Houston, Texas (the city in which Enron was headquartered), wrote a book entitled *The Tao of Enron*. In it he pointed out that integrity was listed as one of Enron's four core beliefs. The pastor observed, "A select group of Enron executives embraced a philosophy so far from traditional ethics that they ended up adopting a lifestyle completely contrary to their company's stated beliefs on integrity."[2]

Both the nation and the corporate world need the assurance that their leaders act with integrity. Yet this is even truer for Christians. Christians and churches need to be assured that their ministers have integrity. A minister's ministry is built on the trust that people have in his or her spiritual and ethical wholeness. If integrity is missing, the ministry is in danger.

Integrity appears in a minister's personal life and conduct. The incident of Jesus and the Samaritan woman at the well recorded in John 4 gives instructive insight into ministerial integrity. The disciples had gone into Sychar to buy lunch. At noon Jesus was seated at the well when the unnamed Samaritan woman came for water. Jesus engaged her in conversation. "Just then his disciples returned and were surprised to find him talking with a woman. But no one asked, 'What do you want?' or 'Why are you talking with her?'" (John 4:27). The disciples had such trust in Jesus, such confidence in his personal integrity, that no one questioned his relationship with the woman.

Integrity in a minister's personal life is intentional. Integrity does not just happen because of an individual's commitment to ministry. A minister must work at being a person of integrity in his or her personal life.

What are the major problem areas in the minister's personal life? R. H. Whittington, longtime religion professor at Louisiana College, repeatedly warned his students, "Boys, pay your bills and keep your zippers up." He identified sex and finances as major areas of potential problems. Richard Foster cited a triple ethical threat to Christian discipleship: money, sex, and power. Foster wrote, "The issues of money, sex, and power catapult us into the arena of moral choice."[3] In a *Time* magazine article, Billy Graham said that Satan attacks God's servants in the three areas of sex, money, and pride.[4] With these problem areas in view, this chapter addresses a minister's conduct in relation to self, family, finances, and sex. Chapter 4 considers the problem of power.

In Relation to Self

Self-esteem

Ministers are people before they are ministers. A positive self-concept and appropriate self-esteem are essential for a healthy, effective ministry. Walter Wiest and Elwyn Smith remind us that "persons called to the clergy profession live always in tension between two realities: their humanity—who they are and what they are, their best and their worst, their gifts and their limits—and the special demands of their calling."[5] That tension can work on a minister's self-esteem if not handled properly. Two areas particularly demand attention: ego and role identity.

An inflated ego is a problem for many ministers because they command attention from others and have authority over others. The ability to serve humbly and to live gently and kindly is difficult for those who struggle with massive egos. Such people are often unwilling to share credit or attention with fellow church members or staff, have an assertiveness that leaves little room for the initiative of others, and insist on their own views.

Some ministers, however, suffer from underassertiveness. Their ego is so small that humility becomes a vice. These people have difficulty leading a congregation and confronting persons with either the demands of the gospel or the specifications of a job.

The problem of role identity plagues those who cannot find personal identity outside their ministry. They define their lives entirely in terms of their ministerial vocation. These individuals face difficulty when anything jeopardizes their ministry or when they face retirement.

Ministers with a healthy self-esteem recognize that they have worth, value, and dignity apart from the ministry to which God has called them. Their identity rests in who they are as persons more than in what they do as ministers.

Health

In addition to a healthy self-esteem, ministers must also pay attention to physical health. Working to the point of exhaustion, without days off or vacations, seems like commendable dedication, but it actually may be a foolish expenditure of strength. A loss of health means a loss of ministry. If dedicated ministers pace themselves, care for their bodies, and guard their health, they can expand their ministries rather than cut them short by an early death or failing health.

Catherine Marshall memorialized her husband, Peter Marshall, in *A Man Called Peter.* Immediately after recovering from a heart attack, he plunged back into his duties as pastor of the New York Avenue Presbyterian Church in Washington, D.C., and as chaplain of the U.S. Senate. Shortly thereafter he suffered another heart attack and died at a relatively young age. How much longer could his ministry have lasted and how many more lives could he have touched had he properly regarded his health?

Kenneth Cooper, the physician who pioneered aerobics, emphasized total well-being through aerobic exercise, a positive eating plan, and emotional equilibrium. He asserted that total well-being can provide the physical and emotional base for finding and savoring . . . goals. For example, it will undoubtedly enrich a career or a deep spiritual commitment, especially as you get more involved in these endeavors and as the time and energy demands they place on you grow greater.[6]

Cooper emphasized the importance of health for both achieving and enjoying the goals one has in life. The same principle applies to ministry. A healthy person can minister better and enjoy it more over a lifetime. This is a matter of Christian stewardship. Stewardship involves how one uses money, but it also involves how a person uses the body God has entrusted to him or her.

Nutrition, rest, exercise, and recreation combine to enrich one's health. These may seem secondary to high-energy, high-achieving, hard-driving persons. However, when it comes to extending and enriching ministry, good health habits are important components of a minister's life. A day off each week and a vacation each year contribute to the overall health of a minister. Recreation or a hobby that provides enjoyment and diverts the mind from ministering tasks is important for a balanced life.

Lifestyle

The lifestyle of a minister is another important element in his or her total witness. A lifestyle should confirm rather than contradict the gospel he or she proclaims.

Near the close of the last century, in the span of several months, the lifestyles of several well-known American ministers revealed serious differences between what they practiced and what they preached. One televangelist announced that God would take his life unless his listeners responded with a large contribution before a deadline. Another lost his television network after revelations of an extravagant, opulent lifestyle combined with sexual immorality. Ironically, one well-known televangelist who made another televangelist's moral failures public was himself disciplined by his denomination and deprived of his ministerial credentials as a result of his own moral failure. The lifestyles of these ministers simply did not square with their proclamations.

Preaching restraint and personal discipline while practicing conspicuous consumerism is not consistent. Asking for sacrificial giving and personal commitment from church people while refusing to give sacrificially or to alter personal plans to meet another's needs is not a convincing testimony of Christlikeness.

The minister's parking area of a denominational hospital in a major Texas city often contained a white Cadillac with a red leather interior. That luxury car sported a personalized license plate with the Greek word *doulos,* meaning "servant" or "slave." In a metropolitan area with many pressing human needs, *doulos* was not an appropriate insignia for a white Cadillac with a red leather interior.

Spiritual Growth

The cleric is a ministering person as well as a pilgrim of faith. Continual spiritual growth is as important for a minister as it is for a parishioner. The apostle Paul advised, "Run in such a way as to get the prize. . . . I beat my body and make it my slave so that after I have preached to others, I myself will not be disqualified for the prize" (1 Cor. 9:24, 27).

"Familiarity breeds contempt," states the proverb. Few ministers treat the Bible or spiritual disciplines with contempt, but some ministers may treat both the Bible and spiritual disciplines with such familiarity that they lose some of their mystery and wonder.

When David consolidated his kingship and established the capital at Jerusalem, he moved the ark of the covenant to Jerusalem. The narrative in 2 Samuel 6:6–7 records, "When they came to the threshing floor of Nacon, Uzzah reached out and took hold of the ark of God, because the oxen stumbled. The LORD's anger burned against Uzzah because of his irreverent act; therefore God struck him down and he died there beside the ark of God." One obvious element in Uzzah's death was that he showed too much familiarity with the holy.

In handling spiritual things regularly, ministers can easily become too familiar with the holy. The spiritual disciplines and exercises they teach others may become perfunctory to them. A serious ethical issue arises when ministers require of others what they do not practice themselves or what they practice so routinely that the act loses all meaning.

Education does not end with seminary. Learning about the Bible, God, and the relationship between God and humankind is a lifelong activity. As life unfolds and one encounters new life experiences, one's understanding of God and of spiritual matters should grow. Spiritual matters always have a challenge to them and an element of mystery about them. No matter how often a minister performs a wedding or baptism, conducts a funeral, preaches a sermon, or offers a prayer, the event must never become a repetitious act with no heart in it.

God commanded Moses to say to the people of Israel, "Be holy because I, the LORD your God, am holy" (Lev. 19:2). Jesus commanded his disciples to "be perfect, therefore, as your heavenly Father is perfect" (Matt. 5:48). The word translated "perfect" can mean "whole" or "complete" or "perfect for its purpose." Whatever meaning is assigned to the word, the basis of comparison is God, made known in Jesus Christ. The apostle Peter admonished us to "grow in the grace and knowledge of our Lord and Savior Jesus Christ" (2 Peter 3:18). To follow the directive of Moses, the command of Christ, and the admonition of Peter, a minister must continue to be a true disciple of Jesus Christ, a student of the Word of God, and a practitioner of the disciplines of the Christian life.

For the preacher, the Bible should never become simply the source of sermons and the texts for teaching. Seminary professor Charles Bugg asked, "What about approaching the Bible in a formational way instead of just information to be explored? By this I mean, what about allowing the Bible to speak to my own life and to continue to form and reform me."[7] A cleric should read the Bible devotionally. Other material such as classic Christian devotionals, sermons by pulpit masters, or contemporary devotional materials should also be used. The growing minister needs to read theological, biblical, historical, and ethical materials as well as more general works.

The common spiritual disciplines that ministers recommend to others must become their practice if their lives are to ring true. One does not have to look for esoteric methods or hidden keys to spiritual growth. For ministers as for other Christians, spiritual growth comes from the regular practice of prayer, Bible study, worship, and Christian service.

The secret of an effective ministry is the continual growth of the minister. As long as one is growing spiritually and relating personally to the people one serves, effective ministry can continue.

In Relation to Family

The Minister's Family Life

For many years a billboard on Louisiana Highway 1 just north of the city of Natchitoches contained a message from the Church of Jesus Christ of Latter-Day Saints, the Mormons. The message proclaimed, "No other success compensates for failure in the home." This quotation should be prominently displayed on every minister's desk. The family is a very important ingredient in a pastor's life. Why then does it often rank second, or even lower, in a pastor's list of priorities?

In Protestant churches, the general assumption is that the minister will be a married person with a family. That assumption is reinforced by the ministerial qualifications for both pastors and deacons given in the pastoral epistles (1 Tim. 3:1–11; Titus 1:6–9). Some church groups even require that clergy be married and have children before they are eligible for ministerial leadership positions.

For many years, divorce was unthinkable for ministers. Troubled marriages continued in quiet desperation or armed truce. The incidence of divorce among clergy is higher today, but it is still not well accepted. Dean Merrill observed in *Clergy Couples in Crisis:*

Some denominations still automatically defrock a divorcing pastor; others require an unpaid sabbatical of varying lengths. In still others, leadership may be willing to aid, counsel, and eventually guide the divorced minister to another parish, but local congregations remain wary. If a church does vote to accept such a pastor, the official act is only part of the battle; the trust and respect of individuals must still be won, often over a long time and at great cost.[8]

The failure of a minister's marriage is considered a tragedy, in many cases a fatal tragedy, as far as continuation in the ministry is concerned.

But divorce is not the only issue in regard to a minister's family. The quality of the marital relationship between a minister and spouse must also be considered. For his doctoral dissertation, a Mississippi Southern Baptist pastor conducted research on marital satisfaction among pastors' wives. He discovered four factors that caused a lack of satisfaction in their marriages: the disruption of time together, the state of anxiety brought on by church expectations, loneliness, and fewer days of dual devotions.[9] The primary relationship in a clergy family is the relationship between the minister and spouse. That husband-wife bond must be stable and strong before the family can be stable and strong.

Part of the challenge for ministers and their spouses is that their marriages are considered a model for church families. Healthy marriages can model to others how a couple can remain in love, stay married, and function as a Christian couple even when dealing with stress, long work hours, inadequate income, and the demands of children.

A minister's marriage can present problems, however, when the model is negative rather than positive. As David and Vera Mace observe:

> A Christian minister's task is to proclaim the message of divine love and to help those who respond to it to grow in love for one another. A married minister can therefore be reasonably expected to provide in his own marriage relationship an image and example of how other people, through their united love for God, can grow in the quality of their love for each other. When a minister's marriage does not demonstrate the warmth and tenderness of human love at its best, an observer could justifiably say, "If his religion doesn't work in this closest of all human relationships, how can we be sure that it is really true?"[10]

Ministers' children also often find themselves in the spotlight. Ministers' children are no different from other children. They face the same stresses and temptations as others, and they experience the same disappointments and failures as others. There is no proof that ministers have more problem children than non-ministers, but the problems ministers do have with their children may be more apparent because of the high visibility of ministers' families. High achievers such as Orville and Wilbur Wright, Martin Luther King Jr., Harriet Beecher Stowe, Walter Mondale, George McGovern, Condoleeza Rice, Albert Schweitzer, and Paul Tillich were all ministers' children.[11] J. Clark Hensley suggested, "Look at *Who's Who* and you will discover more sons and daughters of clergymen than any other profession."[12]

Time spent together is the key ingredient for a happy home life. Unfortunately, time spent together is a most difficult feat for a ministerial family.

A chapel speaker once said that if a minister were away from home every evening, it would not make any difference to his children whether he was at church or a bar. He was not home with them. Perhaps this is an overstatement, but it makes a valid point. Time spent with family is necessary for a strong and fulfilling home life. Every preacher has probably sermonized about affluent parents who gave their children everything they wanted but themselves. That same principle applies to the minister's family.

How can time be reserved for the family? By scheduling it and protecting it. Such times are just as important as other appointments a minister may have. Many ministers set aside specific times each week or each month to spend with their children. Some ministers block out an evening weekly or monthly for a date with their spouse. In a study of clergy couples conducted by David and Vera Mace, 68 percent of the wives surveyed listed a lack of time alone together as the greatest difficulty in adjusting to being married to ministers.[13]

A popular religious writer tells how he set aside time for his family. Each year he would take a new appointment calendar and write down each family member's birthday, his wedding anniversary, and family vacation time. Later in the year if someone would call about a project or a meeting on one of those dates, he would reply by saying that he already had a commitment. After he started that practice, he was invited to participate in a big meeting on his child's birthday, and he said no. The caller asked why he could not come since it was a big convention and his witness might reach many people. The writer was a little embarrassed to say that it was his daughter's birthday and that he was the only daddy his daughter had. The man was quiet on the other end of the line for a few seconds, then he replied, "I wish I could do that." The writer concluded, "I may not make as many speeches, attend as many meetings, or write as many books for Christ. But I hope I will at least have lived for Him in my own home."[14] Pastors need to spend quality time with their children and their mates. Effective time management techniques and specific agreements with the congregation can help pastors achieve that worthy goal.

Yet another factor in a successful family life is commitment. There should never be any question about the personal commitment each partner has made to the other.

Because of the nature of ministry, ministers often deal with people of the opposite sex. This calls for a high degree of trust on the part of the spouse. A minister must be a person of absolute integrity and one whom a spouse can trust because of his or her commitment.

Commitment is also a way of building family solidarity. Children who see by their parents' actions and attitudes that they love and trust one another grow up with a model of commitment in Christian marriage. However marital love is defined, exclusive commitment to one another must be at the center of it.

Commitment to one another is both undergirded and strengthened by commitment to Christ. In the Maces' study, 63 percent of the husbands and 65 percent of the wives cited "shared Christian commitment and spiritual resources" as the leading advantage of clergy marriage.[15]

The Single Minister

Ideally, no difference should be seen between a single minister and a married minister with regard to serving a church. However, we do not live with the ideal but with the actual. In many cases, churches hesitate to call a single minister. People may question why a pastor is single. Married persons may be suspicious of an unmarried minister spending time with their spouse. Parents may be hesitant to trust their children with single clergy.

More people today are waiting longer to marry or are consciously choosing singleness. A single minister may be widowed or divorced. Jesus never married, and it is doubtful whether Paul was married during his time of missionary activity. A person is no less a person or no less a minister because he or she is single, whether by choice or by circumstance. The single minister is still a part of a family, his or her family of origin, and all are a part of the family of God.

Should a single minister date a church member? A minister who chooses to date a church member should exercise great care. Other church members could become concerned about the exclusive attention given to that member. Rumors and innuendoes about their relationship could circulate through the church. Should the relationship fail, the breakup may affect not only the individual but also that person's family and friends, and the minister's ministry at the church could be jeopardized.

The question takes another turn depending on whether the minister is widowed, divorced, or a young single minister just out of seminary. The minister in question may also have children to consider. Whatever the circumstance of his or her singleness, the single minister should always show discretion in dating a church member. In most cases, it is not a good idea.

A church should not expect a single minister to spend more time in ministry just because he or she does not have a spouse and a family. A church should call a person to ministry on the basis of that person's dedication to Christ and the ability to perform the tasks required. Neither should a church attempt to pay an individual less money for the same or similar ministry just because he or she does not have a family to support.

The same principles of ethical behavior and personal integrity apply to the single minister as to the married minister. In some cases, the single minister will have to be even more certain that he or she has lived ethically and above suspicion for the ministry to be effective.

In Relation to Finances

Managing Money

"Boys, pay your bills," a professor warned in earlier days. The warning was well deserved, for many ministers have not developed the ability to manage money. So notorious have clergy often been in regard to financial mismanagement that in some circles people are warned against lending money to the professions that begin with P: plumbers, painters, prostitutes, and preachers.

Even though clergy salaries have risen, the executive director of the Minister's Financial Services Association in Lubbock, Texas, made an important observation. When a minister's salary is compared with the median income of people across the nation with graduate education, many ministers "could possibly be significantly underpaid."[16] According to a Church Compensation Report compiled by *Christianity Today,* Christian clergy salaries rose an average of only 7.4 percent during the four-year period included in the survey, which was less than half the inflation rate for that same four-year span. Even when total compensation, which rose 12.6 percent in the same period, was considered, pastors' salaries still lagged behind inflation, which was 16 percent for that period of time.[17]

Among the ministers in the *Christianity Today* survey, only 1 percent felt they were overpaid. Sixty-six percent of the senior pastors and 59 percent of the solo pastors surveyed felt they were "fairly paid." That means that 34 percent of the senior pastors and 41 percent of the solo pastors felt they were underpaid.[18]

Christianity Today International conducted follow-up studies in 1996 and 1999. Although seven out of ten pastors in these studies felt they were paid fairly, 30 percent felt underpaid. Of that 30 percent, 6 percent considered themselves severely underpaid. These results were consistent with the 1991 study. This study found that in the 1990s, total pastoral compensation (base salary plus housing/utilities allowance) stayed ahead of cost-of-living increases by approximately 1 percent a year. The Consumer Price Index increased by 21.9 percent from 1991 to 1999, while the total compensation for senior pastors increased an average of 31.2 percent, and that of solo pastors rose 27.8 percent.[19]

Many churches offer their clergy a pay package in which they designate from the church budget a lump sum for pastoral compensation. The minister is then given the opportunity of dividing the total compensation into his personal pay, housing and utility allowances, automobile and other ministry related expenses, and retirement benefits. The danger in this approach is that many clergy, especially younger ones with younger families, may opt for the immediate money needed for expenses and neglect to put aside money for retirement or other future needs. A better approach is for the church to divide the compensation into personal income, ministry related expenses that are reimbursed to the minister, and expenses for retirement and insurance.

A former Duke University professor who became the director of analytical research for a denominational pension fund asserted that male clergy fear falling out of a middle-class lifestyle and not being able to meet the middle-class expectations for their children's education and their retirement. He opined that clergy cannot assume the gradual income growth that most Americans with graduate degrees take for granted. Indicating that the clergy's place within the professional middle class is becoming increasingly tenuous, he pointed out that mean clergy income remained relatively flat over a twenty-year period. During a decade toward the end of the twentieth century, the average mean salary for a married clergyman with a graduate degree was 11 percent higher than the previous decade. For all married males with graduate degrees, salary levels rose by 25 percent. For married male doctors, income rose 37 percent, and married male lawyers saw their income rise 30 percent during the same period. With these figures in mind, the analyst stated, "Although ministers like to think of themselves as members of the professional middle class, they are hanging on to that status by their fingernails."[20]

Another study by Duke University looked at clergy salaries from the basis of a competitive, market-driven salary structure. The report illustrated how the free-market forces that drive secular salaries are also at work in church salary structures. To fill clergy positions, churches often have to increase the salaries they are offering. Ministers can also demand higher salaries because other ministers are making more money. The study also examined the impact of clergy compensation on calling and commitment. Low clergy salaries make it difficult for pastors to be true to their calling, causing many talented ministers to enter other professions or other forms of ministry. Inadequate compensation is also inadvertently changing ministry from a calling to a career. To accumulate savings, provide for their families, and pay off educational debt, many clergy feel compelled to move up a career ladder to larger congregations. Some are forced to take on second jobs or to rely on an income-earning spouse, both of which limit the type of churches and ministries a pastor can serve.[21]

Given the fact that the minister's salary is below average and that his or her family has the same needs as similar families in the community, many ministers have performed nothing short of the financially miraculous in adequately feeding, clothing, and educating their families. Enough examples exist, however, of ministers who have owed money to many merchants in town, who have been late paying their bills, or who have expected discounts, gifts, or special favors that the belief that ministers cannot manage money persists.

People are very sensitive about money. Church leaders do not appreciate being embarrassed by their minister's financial irresponsibility. One large church in a metropolitan southwestern city actually garnished one of its minister's paychecks for a year in order to rescue him from indebtedness.

The discipline to plan a budget, the ability to live within that budget, and the art of balancing a checkbook are all essential skills for Christian ministers. Handling finances responsibly may even be seen as a spiritual discipline. The failure to handle finances properly has diminished the witness of too many church overseers.

John Wesley's rule of life was to save all he could and to give all he could. When he was at Oxford, Wesley had an income of 30 pounds a year. He lived on 28 pounds and gave away 2 pounds. As Wesley's income increased to 60 pounds, 90 pounds, and 120 pounds annually, he still lived on 28 pounds and gave the balance away.[22] The founder of Methodism managed his money well.

A minister should certainly practice the basic principles of Christian money management, beginning with Christian stewardship. For many clergy, the tithe (Mal. 3:10) is considered a biblical standard and a minimum starting point for Christian stewardship. A minister should also practice the responsible handling of debt. Taking their cue from Romans 13:8, some think that a Christian should have little or no debt. A disciplined savings plan, conservative spending, and the avoidance of conspicuous consumerism are all important factors in Christian money management.

Richard Foster referred to the "dark side of money" and the "light side of money." The "dark side of money" relates to the way money can be a threat to a relationship with God. The "light side of money" refers to the way in which money can be used to enhance a relationship with God and bless humankind.[23]

The misuse of credit looms as an expression of the dark side of money. Many ministerial families have drowned in an ocean of debt. Well-meaning, good-intentioned people have often prompted ministers into more credit than they can handle on their ministerial salaries. Businesses may think they are helping by extending easy credit. It may be their way of showing appreciation for a minister. But before the church leader realizes what has happened, the total amount of money owed has become more than he or she can handle. Some payments are skipped, other payments are delayed, and the minister falls farther behind in repayment. The word will then often circulate around the community that the preacher does not pay his bills. The pastor's credit rating will show him to be a bad credit risk. If he is called to a new ministerial responsibility, the cleric leaves the community while still having debits on his accounts. The report circulates through the community that "Pastor Jones left owing everybody in town." The result is not positive either for the ministry in general or for that minister in particular.

In some communities, ministers are given professional discounts by health professionals and businesses. The practice probably began as an attempt to help ministers, whose salaries were often low. The health professional may have recognized the minister as a fellow professional in a caring vocation and responded by giving a professional discount. Such discounts may have been considered a form of donation to the church.

A minister's insistence on a discount, however, or an inquiry about a discount before making a purchase only adds to the perception that ministers are money-grubbers. Some people think ministers always have their hand out for a special favor. Some ministers have perfected the art of begging or of making subtle suggestions to the extent that people feel an obligation to do them special favors.

If a person knows that an individual is a minister and voluntarily offers a discount, then the minister may feel free to accept it as a gift and to respond accordingly. That is different from placing the clergy sign next to the gas tank of the car or of making an issue out of being a minister when introductions are made.

A bank slogan proclaimed, "Where money matters but people count." In a minister's relationship with money, people should always count and money should always be handled responsibly and with care.

Practicing What You Preach

The teaching of Christian stewardship is practiced in most churches. For many of these congregations, tithing is both taught and promoted as the biblical standard. As a basic practice, the minister should consistently practice what he or she preaches concerning Christian stewardship. Landrum Leavell II, former president of the New Orleans Baptist Theological Seminary, in a commencement address urged students to adhere to their monetary vow of tithing. To the graduates he said, "God has called you to be a leader and if you don't have enough faith to trust God with your material possessions and be a storehouse tither, you don't have enough integrity to make it in the ministry."[24]

By definition, a steward is one who manages the affairs of another. Christian stewardship speaks to a Christian's, in this case a minister's, management of what God has entrusted to him or her. Christian stewardship is the total response of an individual to the grace of God. While stewardship is often narrowly defined only in terms of money, it involves more than money; it involves the self. All that a minister is, as well as all that a minister owns, is a trust from God. How that trust is managed is Christian stewardship. When it comes to money, the practice of Christian stewardship by the parson is essential. A minister's message on stewardship will hardly ring true if he or she has not practiced it as well as taught it.

In Relation to Sex

At the time this book was first written, a spectacular trial was under way in New Orleans, Louisiana. One well-known Christian evangelist was suing another nationally known televangelist for $90 million for defamation of character. In the lawsuit, Marvin Gorman accused Jimmy Swaggart of conspiring to destroy his television ministry through false accusations of immorality, while Swaggart himself was dallying with prostitutes. Gorman admitted a single "immoral act" with a woman. On his television show, Swaggart made a tearful confession that he had sinned. While he did not specify his sin, the confession came after Gorman provided church officials with photographs of Swaggart outside a motel with a prostitute.[25]

In more recent days, the religious world has been rocked by the revelation that numerous Roman Catholic priests are guilty of sexual abuse and by the cover-up of those incidents. Some estimate that the lawsuit costs to the Roman Catholic Church in the United States may reach as much as half a billion dollars.

Obviously, the personal and professional lives of these ministers, as well as those of the victims and their families, were deeply affected by sexual misconduct. Clergy sexual abuse has become such a major problem in ministerial ethics that this issue is addressed in greater detail in a new chapter (chap. 7) in this revised and expanded edition. A brief overview is given here in relation to the minister's personal life.

Incidences of Sexual Misconduct

Most Christian ministers are people of integrity who behave ethically with regard to sexual matters. Yet one three-year study of religious and secular counselors conducted by the Wisconsin Coalition on Sexual Misconduct found that 11 percent of the perpetrators were ministers and that 89 percent of the victims were women.[26]

Leadership, a journal for church leaders, published a survey of three hundred pastors. Twelve percent of the ministers polled admitted to having had sexual intercourse with someone other than their spouse since they had been in ministry. Thirty-three percent of those polled acknowledged that they had engaged in "sexually inappropriate" behavior with someone other than their spouse (without any definition of that behavior). Another 18 percent confessed to other forms of sexual contact with someone other than their spouse.[27]

One of the early studies, conducted in 1984, included questions about sexuality that revealed startling statistics about ministers. Among four major denominational groups, 37.15 percent of the respondents acknowledged that they had engaged in "inappropriate sexual behavior for a minister." In addition, 12 percent admitted to having had sexual intercourse with a member of their congregation.[28] More recently, the research of G. Lloyd Rediger led him to assert that 10 percent of clergy are guilty of sexual malfeasance. Another 15 percent are approaching the line of misconduct.[29] In many instances, clergy sexual offenders have had multiple offenses. In one case reported by *Newsweek,* while attempting to seduce one woman, a minister boasted of having slept with thirty other women.[30]

Causes of Sexual Misconduct

Any number of factors can cause a minister to practice sexual indiscretion. Some male ministers are sexual predators who prey on women in the church. Many of these would be considered sex addicts who have a deep-seated emotional illness as well as a moral problem. On the other hand, it is precisely because clergy are "generally compassionate, people-oriented professionals that some may yield to inappropriate intimacy."[31]

Peter Rutter, a San Francisco psychiatrist, emphasized the vulnerability of any professional to sexual misconduct.

> What I have come to call sex in the forbidden zone—sexual behavior between a man and a woman under his care or mentorship in a professional relationship—can occur any time a woman entrusts important aspects of her physical, spiritual, psychological, or material welfare to a man who has power over her.[32]

One *Newsweek* article provided a profile of the male minister who strays sexually. According to this profile, he is usually middle-aged, disillusioned with his calling, neglecting his own marriage, and a lone ranger who is isolated from his clerical colleagues. His failure commences when he meets a woman who needs him.[33]

Glen Gabbard, a psychiatrist who is the director of Menninger Hospital in Topeka, Kansas, identified a common characteristic of ministers that can lead to sexual infidelity. Ministers who go into ministry with a longing to be loved, to be idealized, or to be godlike may become disappointed by a congregation's response to him. He wants to be idealized, but the congregation sees his human frailties. When a young woman comes to him for counseling, the minister may see in this woman the fulfillment of his original wish to be loved as God is loved.[34]

Some people are intentionally seductive and may attempt to lure their minister into sexual activities. Those who view the pastor as a person of power may see this sense of power or intimacy with a power figure as attractive. For some emotionally insecure persons, sexually seducing a minister gives a sense of pseudo-satisfaction by making them feel they have established a more intimate relationship with God through intimate contact with a minister. George Parsons of the Alban Institute in Washington, D.C., observed, "This notion, in effect, is that they can seduce God. It is an irrational dynamic, but it's there."[35]

Another cause of sexual misconduct is that many ministers who counsel people do not understand the concept of transference or how to deal with it. Transference has been defined as "the process in which people project their own (often unmet) needs onto an idealized figure. Such transference can be 'positive' (affection, warmth, and so on) or 'negative' (anger, rejections, and so on)." Transference often involves dependency, romantic feelings, feelings of hostility, and ambivalence about authority.[36] These feelings occur because of the role of the minister, not because of the minister's personal attractiveness or qualities. Countertransference can also occur. In this case, the minister projects his or her unmet needs on to someone else. While marital dissatisfaction does not always explain ministerial sexual impropriety, it does make a minister more susceptible.[37] Most counselors are trained to understand transference and countertransference. Unfortunately, ministers generally do not receive training in these areas; thus, they are more vulnerable to them.

In his book on ministerial infidelity, Tim LaHaye identifies three "forces that can lead to sexual sin":

1. the power of sexual attraction
2. the power of seductive women
3. the power of emotional bonding

In addition, he points out some attitudes that can lead to a moral fall:

- pride
- resistance to accountability
- anger
- the press for success
- the drive to fulfill goals
- work, work, work

LaHaye believes these are "the values that corrode a pastor's moral life."[38]

In the *Leadership* magazine survey referred to earlier, the most common cause cited for sexual impropriety was physical and emotional attraction (78 percent). This leading cause of sexual misconduct was followed by marital dissatisfaction (41 percent).[39]

Researchers in the *Newsweek* article cited earlier also pointed to a possible cause: Many ministers are underpaid and overstressed workaholics who put in sixty to eighty hours of work per week. Peter Carnes, a pioneer researcher in sexual addiction, added that ministers are always on display and always on call, which makes them susceptible to a double life.[40] These stresses can cause a minister to let down his guard and thus become more vulnerable to sexual temptations.

In the *Leadership* survey, the pastors who admitted to having had sexual intercourse or sexual contact with a person other than their spouse were asked who the other person was. Their responses were:

- a counselee (17 percent)
- a ministerial staff member (5 percent)
- other church staff member (8 percent)
- a church member in a teaching/leadership role (9 percent)
- someone else in the congregation (30 percent)
- someone outside the congregation (31 percent)[41]

In most cases, ministers who are vulnerable to sexual misconduct act out this behavior with those closest to them—church staff or members of the congregation.

Consequences of Sexual Misconduct

In a parable about discipleship, Jesus urged people to count the cost before signing on as his followers (Luke 14:25–33). Before a minister engages in an act of sexual indiscretion, he or she should count the cost. No matter what the extenuating circumstances, a choice has to be made, and a poor choice has serious consequences. A minister who conceals sexual misconduct is rarely able to continue that duplicitous behavior indefinitely. In most cases, the truth comes out.

Robyn Warner (a pseudonym) pointed out the costs of irresponsible sexual behavior in terms of personal loss. Warner experienced the loss of

- self-esteem
- position
- respect in the community
- his children
- financial security
- his partner[42]

In view of these consequences, it is at great personal risk that a minister yields to sexual temptation. The losses detailed above do not include the damage to lives, the church, ministry at large, and the larger work of Christ. It really does not matter what denomination a fallen minister belongs to. All ministers are hurt when one minister fails. The loss of faith in ministers and ministry affects all clergy.

The study of ministerial sexuality entitled *Sex in the Parish* by Karen Lebacqz and Ronald Barton grew out of the work of the Professional Ethics Group of the Center for Ethics and Social Policy at the Graduate Theological Union in Berkeley, California. The book reveals three reasons why sexual intimacy with parishioners is wrong:

1. previous commitments, specifically marriage covenants
2. professional obligations, including a sense of identity and a responsibility to guide people in their spiritual journey
3. past experiences of either their own or other people's pain arising from sexual involvement between pastor and parishioner[43]

These factors demonstrate moral failure on the part of those who hold up standards of moral conduct for others.

Sexual indiscretions have cost some ministers their ministry. More than one minister has confessed an affair to the church, counting on the congregation's forgiveness, and been terminated rather than forgiven. Church people expect exemplary behavior from their ministers.

Marie Fortune, founder of the Center for the Prevention of Sexual and Domestic Violence in Seattle, Washington, wrote a book about a fictional minister named Peter Donovan who was guilty of sexual exploitation of several women in his church. In the book, Fortune indicated the frustrations felt by the exploited women. Their first frustration resulted from the reluctance of people to believe their stories. The next frustration involved the extremely slow response of denominational officials to their charges. With keen insight, Fortune proposed that a significant aspect of the problem is the reality that the church functions as a family. The family image, with God as Father and fellow believers as siblings, suggests a positive relationship of trust, intimacy, caring, commitment, and respect, which are the bases of human family life. Just as the role of the parent can be misused, so can the role of the minister. Fortune then stated, "When the irresponsible pastor does engage in sexual activity with parishioners, the result is incest in the church family; the parallels to incestuous abuse are disturbing."[44]

Others have joined Fortune in likening the sexual abuse of church members to incest in the family. Some of the same traits occur in the church as in incestuous families, such as:

- social isolation
- blurred boundaries
- the paradoxical feelings of inadequacy and perfectionism

- the "no talk" rule, which distorts communication
- unequal power[45]

Respondents in Lebacqz and Barton's study likened the violation of trust by one in a ministerial role to the violation of trust that occurs with incest. One woman pastor expressed it by saying, "To be their savior and then to cross sexual boundaries is devastating to people." To that statement the authors added, "Because clergy represent God, Christ, and the church, to be violated by a member of the cloth is to feel violated by God, Christ, and the church."[46]

Prevention of Sexual Misconduct

From any viewpoint, the number of clergy guilty of sexual misconduct is alarming. What can ministers do to protect themselves from the very real danger of violating sexual boundaries?

In her writings, Fortune has suggested that prevention should begin during the preparation for ministry. Those preparing for ministry need information about and clarification of ethical standards for ministry. They need to understand the nature and meaning of ethical behavior in sexual relationships. Fortune asserts that a ministerial code of ethics would help to clarify ethical sexual behavior for ministers.[47]

In that regard, Richard Blackmon and Archibald Hart proposed that a code of ethics be established to help regulate ministry relationships. Unlike mental health professionals, ministers are only loosely bound by a commonly understood moral code that is subject to differing interpretations. Clearly articulated boundaries for ministry relationships would help to prevent problems from arising in regard to a minister's relationships with others.[48] The subject of a code of ethics for ministers is addressed in chapter 8.

Ministers should be aware of their professional boundaries and always seek to maintain those boundaries. Lebacqz and Barton write, "Many pastors argue that, even if the *boundaries* for sexual intimacy are the same for pastor and layperson, the *responsibility* for maintaining those boundaries falls to the professional person. It is he or she who must establish and keep those boundaries."[49] With this in mind, Fortune dispelled the idea of "consenting adults" in pastor-parishioner sexual relationships. She insists that the responsibility always lies with the minister for keeping the relationship within moral bounds. "The dynamics of a pastor-parishioner or counselor-client relationship create a context such that any behavior moving beyond those bounds 'takes place in the absence of meaningful consent'—that is, without mutuality, equality, shared power, and a non-punitive outcome."[50]

Some commonsense principles can aid ministers in avoiding compromising situations. In an interview in *Time* magazine, Billy Graham identified sex as an area in which ministers are vulnerable.

> I learned . . . that I would be tempted in those areas. So I never rode in a car with a woman alone. I never have eaten a meal with my secretary alone or ridden in a car with her alone. If we sit in here and I dictate something to her, the door is open. And just little things like that, that people would think are so silly, but it was ingrained in me in those early years.[51]

Graham cited several principles that a minister can follow:

- Never be totally alone with a person of the opposite sex (in counseling, another person should always be in an adjacent office).
- Be careful about being in questionable environments (take a deacon or another church member with you).
- Be cautious about friendships that could be considered inappropriate.
- Be aware of the risk of emotional bonding.
- Avoid placing yourself in a position in which moral compromise could happen.

As the apostle Paul said, "Abstain from all appearance of evil" (1 Thess. 5:22 KJV).

G. Lloyd Rediger developed the acronym PREVENT to outline a seven-step plan for preventing clergy sexual misconduct:

- Preparation: Prepare for appropriate behavior before encountering an intimate and vulnerable situation. Anticipate potential problems.
- Regularity: Develop a consistent pattern of appropriate responses for nurturing and caring. Draw on training, consultation with clergy and professionals, and God's guidance.
- Evaluation: Establish appropriate ways to be accountable to congregational leaders. An annual review of professional behavior is also valuable.
- Value: Remember to value and take seriously the need for intimacy, for consistent emotional closeness with other human beings and with God.
- Excellence: Keep in touch with the joy of ministry.
- Network: Associate regularly with peers.
- Terror: Be mindful of the traumatic consequences of clergy moral malfeasance.[52]

Recognizing a minister's sexual vulnerability is vital to prevention. Each one of us should recognize that as human beings we are vulnerable. Because of this, restraint and responsible sexuality are necessary. Two of the best ways to ensure responsible sexual behavior are for a minister to build a strong marriage and have a healthy attitude toward sexuality. Another resource is ministerial accountability. Ministers are accountable to God, the church, the community, and their family. Ministers can also make themselves responsible to a support group, a church committee, or a mentor.

Ministerial Restoration

When considering the moral failure of ministers, the question of restoration must be addressed. Some denominations have specific procedures for the discipline and restoration of erring ministers. Independent churches and denominations that emphasize the autonomy of the local church do not have methods of dealing with the issue at the denominational level.

One of the key problems associated with clergy sexual abuse in the Roman Catholic Church was that the church covered up the offenses. The bishops often reassigned the offending priests to another parish with the hope that they would not repeat the offense. But that secretive method of restoration did not work; in fact, it usually opened the door to more misconduct by the offending priests.

In preparing for his book *If Ministers Fall, Can They Be Restored?* Tim LaHaye sent a questionnaire concerning restoration to fourteen well-known conservative evangelical leaders. All agreed that fallen ministers would need to repent of their sin and then work diligently to save their marriages. These leaders believed that any future service would depend on reconciliation of the clergy with his or her family. All the questioned leaders believed that forgiveness of the fallen cleric was possible and that God could use the restored minister in some place of service. They did not agree on whether the person could return to a pastoral ministry. All thought that the minister would have to prove himself or herself worthy of trust before assuming any public ministry, and they recommended a delay of as many as five years before returning to ministry.[53]

After advocating a restoration committee in the church in which a minister has transgressed, LaHaye proposed an eight-step restoration process, which included:

1. genuine repentance
2. helping to rebuild the minister's spiritual life
3. helping to rebuild the minister's marriage
4. helping the minister to find work
5. the establishment of a waiting period

6. a restoration service
7. the consideration of the "open door" (the door that might open for ministry, possibly a ministry other than the pastorate)
8. the establishment of ongoing voluntary accountability[54]

Following an article dealing with a high-visibility pastor who resigned from the church he served because of sexual indiscretion, *Leadership* published the results of a forum between four ministerial leaders concerning recovery and restoration. They believed that sins that violated trust and invalidated the minister's ongoing ability to provide spiritual leadership, particularly sexual sins, required some sort of restoration process. The forum recommended a restoration committee that included laypersons under the oversight of a church. Each of them agreed that a restored minister could be returned to some type of ministry, though not normally in the same church previously served.[55]

Consideration should be given as to whether a minister's sexual indiscretion is a one-time occurrence or a recurring pattern of life. Most survivors of clergy sexual abuse question whether a guilty minister should ever return to pastoral work. Certainly a "predator" (see chap. 7) should never be entrusted with ministerial responsibilities.[56]

People recommending a minister to a church should be honest about the minister's sexual misconduct. Too many times a minister who has been guilty of sexual sin is recommended to a church with the idea that if he or she moves on to another place of service the problem will disappear. When a church is considering a person for a ministerial position who has been guilty of sexual indiscretions, the church should be aware of the failure. If that church chooses to call the individual even with that knowledge, then it has made the decision with full understanding and has not been duped.

At least one state convention of churches affiliated with the Southern Baptist Convention maintains a confidential list of known perpetrators in order to protect churches and future victims. A minister's name is placed in a file when he or she confesses to abuse or sexual misconduct, has a legal conviction, or there is substantial evidence that abuse took place. The information about a particular individual can be released only to specific officers of a church. The information is accompanied by the following disclaimer:

> In keeping with the mission and a spirit of public service, the Convention endeavors to maintain records of allegations of sexual abuse or sexual improprieties by members of the clergy. We do not have the resources to make independent investigation of these allegations nor can we vouch for the accuracy of the information reported to us. Churches are advised to investigate the background of potential employees or members of the clergy independent of the Convention and not to rely exclusively on any information provided by the Convention.[57]

The Christian Life Commission of this Texas Baptist group has also developed a Covenant of Clergy Sexual Ethics, which calls on ministers to "commit to God and the congregations they serve to be faithful to the biblical sexual ethic of fidelity in marriage and celibacy in singleness."[58]

Interestingly enough, the Levitical code specifies certain stipulations regarding the sins of priests, including what sacrifice was to be made and how it was to be offered (Lev. 4:3–12). While an Old Testament priest certainly differs from a New Testament minister, the implication is that through repentance, restoration, and recommitment, a contemporary church leader can resume a ministry for God when such acts are done openly and honestly.

Marie Fortune differentiates between clergy sexual immorality that occurs outside a congregation and sexual involvement that abuses the role and authority of a pastor or Christian counselor. She notes that while Jimmy Swaggart's involvement with a prostitute showed "a problem with his own sexuality" and created a dilemma for the church, he "evidently did not betray his pastoral relationship" with any congregational members. In contrast, "Jim Bakker used his position and power to coerce and manipulate" a woman within his own ministry into sexual involvement. She concluded, "There's an ethical distinction here most people don't make."[59] Both cases, however, indicate improper sexual activities that require accountability.

Ministers' personal lives are distinct from their professional lives. Yet they are also curiously interwoven. Stanley Grenz observes that "the ministry is the one profession which can countenance no disparity between private morality and public performance."[60]

In some personal areas, however, ministers should be especially careful. Historically, ministers have been uniquely vulnerable in four categories: self, family, finances, and sex. In his farewell address to the leaders of the Ephesian church, Paul said, "Keep watch over yourselves and all the flock of which the Holy Spirit has made you overseers" (Acts 20:28). Most ministers have been faithful to keep watch over the flock. They must be as faithful to keep watch over themselves.

Early in Christian history, John Chrysostom (A.D. 347–407) counseled:

That minister's shortcomings simply cannot be concealed. Even the most trivial soon get known. . . . However trifling their offenses, these little things seem great to others, since everyone measures sin, not by the size of the offense, but by the standing of the sinner.[61]

An examination of the minister's personal life has revealed that integrity must be intentional rather than incidental. Integrity in ministry does not just happen.

From the minister's personal life we now turn to the minister's congregation to determine what is required of a good minister in relation to congregational issues.

Suggested Reading

Fortune, Marie M. *Is Nothing Sacred? When Sex Invades the Pastoral Relationship.* San Francisco: Harper & Row, 1989.

Foster, Richard. *Money, Sex, and Power: The Challenge of the Disciplined Life.* San Francisco: Harper & Row, 1985.

Heard, Gerry C. *Case Studies in the Ministry.* East Rockaway, N.Y.: Cummings & Hathaway Publishers, 1996. (These case studies deal with the minister's moral character and personal life and the minister's relationship with the congregation, colleagues, and community.)

Mace, David, and Vera. *What's Happening to Clergy Marriages?* Nashville: Abingdon, 1980.

Merrill, Dean. *Clergy Couples in Crisis.* Carol Stream, Ill.: Leadership; Waco: Word, 1985.

4

The Minister's Congregation

Friend or Foe?

One of us was visiting a theological seminary when he chanced upon a friend who was a longtime professor of theology at that school. After an exchange of greetings and inquiries about family, the professor brought up the problem of forced termination. "Is the basic problem theology?" he asked.

"No," was the reply to the scholar who had spent most of his adult life teaching theology. "Churches have an amazing tolerance for bad theology. The basic problem is relational."

Relationships between a minister and the members of a congregation are essential. Does a minister view the congregation as friend or foe? Do the members look upon the minister as a friend who will care for them, laugh with them, cry with them, and share life with them, or as a foe whom they ought to resist and whose teachings, motives, and methods they ought to question?

The way a minister and members view one another depends on the relationships they have with one another. To a large degree, those relationships depend on the ministry skills the minister displays with them. Some of these skills are personal—the personal integrity of the minister. Others are professional—the ministering ability of the minister.

Relationships are more important in ministry than in any other profession. The morals of the carpenter who framed your house probably did not concern you greatly. You probably do not worry much about whether you like your dentist personally as long as he or she is competent in dentistry. When you look for a surgeon, your primary concern is more than likely the person's professional qualifications and competence, not the surgeon's personality. In these areas, professional competence is of more importance than personal relationships.

That is not true in the ministry. No matter how competent church leaders may be in regard to biblical exposition, grasping church growth principles, and the intricacies of organization, they cannot adequately minister without good relationships with church people. Relationships determine whether a cleric and the congregation view each other as friend or foe. Many issues in churches are decided based on whether members love and trust their ministers, not on the issues themselves.

Good relationships between ministers and congregations must be developed. How are they developed? They are developed in the normal course of ministry. As pastors bury the dead, visit the sick, comfort families, marry people, and generally share in living with people, they build lasting relationships.

Knowing one another personally and sharing the experiences of life aid in building good ministerial relationships between ministers and members. Through compassionate care and genuine concern, a minister lets people know that they are meaningful and important. And all of this rests on the personal integrity of the minister.

How should a minister relate to a congregation? This chapter examines this crucial question from the standpoints of ministerial leadership, ministerial duties, transitions in ministry, and success in ministry. Being a good minister is closely related to the way a minister relates to a congregation, ideally as friend and not as foe.

Ministerial Leadership—Authority and Power

Models for Ministry

All ministers have a model for ministerial leadership. That model may come from a previous pastor or a respected professor or it may be a composite based on people they have known and characteristics they have observed. Such models can be described by the following labels.

Some ministers model their ministry after a chief executive officer. Their model is the corporate executive, and they aspire to be a spiritual CEO. *Active* is the operative word for this style of ministerial leadership. This leader makes things happen, no matter what it takes. Rather than actively doing ministry, however, this minister often directs ministry. William May described the spiritual CEO model for ministry when he wrote:

This model apparently offers the most powerful conception of leadership: the CEO leads the organization largely (but not exclusively) by command and obedience. . . . [A]uthority moved from the top down without the formal or substantive need to persuade. This mode of leadership obtains largely in the modern world in authoritarian governments and in the modern corporation, where the effort to persuade may exist but does not constitute the sine qua non of the enterprise.[1]

May believes this model does not work in the church for reasons both extrinsic and intrinsic to church life. The extrinsic reason is based on the democratic setting in America. In both political life and voluntary organizations, leadership depends on the consent of the governed. The intrinsic reason is that Christian churches believe in the lordship of Christ; Christ the Lord "rules the inward motions of the human spirit." May also observed that "salvation takes hold of the whole person, the deliberative processes included. . . . The notion of the CEO . . . foreshortens the deliberative process and therefore diminishes the reach of the salvation to which the faith testifies."[2] One Baptist asserts that "pastors who see themselves as chief executive officers and operate their churches like large corporations seem to have forgotten they were called by God to be servants."[3]

The primary descriptive term for the political dictator model for ministry is *authoritative.* These ministers are authority figures who make their desires known to the congregation, often couching these desires in terms of the will of God or the direction that God has revealed to them and expects them to carry out.

A well-known pastor of a church in a major city often said that people had accused him and the deacons of running the church. "There is not a word of truth in it," he would reply with tongue in cheek. "The deacons have nothing to do with it!"

Authority is earned and not assumed. Simply because a person occupies the position of pastor does not automatically give that person the authority to order others around or to assume that he or she is the only person in the church to whom God makes his will known. Dictatorship may be the most efficient form of government, but it leaves out the consent of the governed. May identified this model as "the leader of the republic."[4]

The office of the president in its U.S. political setting combines several ingredients, one of which we may wholly reject as germane to the ministry—the president as commander-in-chief. The pastor has no troops to command and very minimal power of command over subordinates on the executive side to his or her responsibilities.[5]

He then noted that the "more important substantive powers of the presidency lie in the powers of persuasion." These powers of persuasion, according to May, take the forms of exemplary persuasion and deliberate persuasion.[6] Effective ministers do not order; they persuade.

A third model followed by some ministers is the hired-hand model for ministry. The operative word for this ministry model is *passive*. Hired-hand ministers simply do what they are told and go where they are directed. They exert little leadership and give no direction for the ministry. The hired-hand pastor is subservient to the board, the congregation, or either an individual or group of individuals who exert power in the church. The negative effects of this type of ministry on both the church and the minister are apparent.

A better model for ministry is the servant model, which was given by Jesus Christ, who embodied this type of ministry: "The Son of Man did not come to be served, but to serve, and to give his life as a ransom for many" (Matt. 20:28). Jesus further exemplified this model when he tied a towel around his waist and washed the feet of his disciples, none of whom was willing to take the servant role (John 13:1–17). In describing Jesus, Paul wrote that he took "the very nature of a servant, being made in human likeness" (Phil. 2:7). Concerning Jesus' servant model, Leonard Griffith observed, "He appeared on the stage of history in the role of a servant, the man for others, who asked nothing for himself—no home, no money, no leisure, no privacy. He had everything to give and he gave it freely."[7]

Responsive is the word that best describes the servant model of ministry. The minister who acts as a servant responds to the needs of the people, the directives of God, and the guidance of the Holy Spirit. Based on the parable of the unworthy servant in Luke 17:7–10, a Bible expositor explained that a servant is someone who works in somebody else's house, who ministers to somebody else's needs, who works at somebody else's convenience, and who does not expect to be thanked.[8]

Of the many models for ministry that modern ministers may choose, the servant model carries with it the commendation of the Lord as well as the Master's example. Franklin Segler points out that "in the teaching of his disciples Jesus emphasized serving as the fundamental quality of ministry. He pointed to himself as the *model* and the *example*."[9]

One minister preached a sermon to a gathering of ministers based on Jesus' act of washing the feet of his disciples. In that sermon, the minister said that when we each appear before the Lord in the end, he will not ask, "What is your title?" but, "Where is your towel?" Ministers should serve God and his people as servants, being responsive to his leadership in their lives and his guidance in their ministries.

Authority in Ministry

The authority of the minister is directly related to the model of ministry followed by a pastor. In recent years, the issue of ministerial authority, particularly pastoral authority, has become prominent.

The authority of the pastor is often asserted by citing the King James Version translation of Hebrews 13:17: "Obey them that have the rule over you, and submit yourselves: for they watch for your souls, as they that must give account, that they may do it with joy, and not with grief: for that is unprofitable for you."

Commenting on this verse, Herschel Hobbs observed:

> The Greek phrase is "the ones leading [or guiding] you." This suggests a shepherd [pastor] leading his flock.
>
> "Obey" translates a verb which has many usages. Arndt and Gingrich Lexicon (Greek Dictionary) cites the meaning in Hebrews 13:17 as "obey" or "follow." In light of "the ones leading you" it seems that "follow" is the preferred meaning. It is like the sheep following the Shepherd. "Submit" renders a verb meaning to yield, give way, submit to one's authority (Arndt and Gingrich). In terms of leadership, the first two seem preferable. If the shepherd leads one way and the sheep wants to go another way, the sheep should yield or give way to the shepherd's way.
>
> In terms of the pastor-church relationship, the sense is to follow the leader in carrying out the Lord's work.[10]

Hobbs concluded that the pastor's authority is earned, not conferred, and it is found in leading the people of God, not in ruling over them. Hobbs also stated that "nowhere in the New Testament is the pastor presented as a *ruler*."[11] Segler adds, "Undoubtedly the phrase '*ministerial authority*' is an *oxymoron*, the combination of two ideas or terms that are incongruous or contradictory." He would prefer paradoxical terms such as minister-leader and servant-leader.[12]

Jesus had authority. According to the Gospel of Matthew, at the conclusion of the Sermon on the Mount, "the crowds were amazed at his [Jesus'] teaching, because he taught as one who had authority, and not as their teachers of the law" (7:28–29). Charles Bugg commented on this reaction by stating, "The authority of Jesus did not come from sticking his finger between the eyes of people and saying, 'You must listen.' Rather, Jesus had a freshness in his message that caused people to say, 'This man has a word from God.'"[13]

Felix Montgomery provides insight into a definition of authority in ministry.

> [T]he New Testament suggests a divine purpose and direction for ministry. Authority is important for the reason that it claims the right to do the ministry for which one has been called. Ministers hold a right, a legitimacy to fulfill the task the Holy Spirit sets before them. The church grants a part of ministerial authority by affirming the call and by providing a place of service. . . .
>
> Ministry's purpose and direction come from God, yet take place in terms of human interaction. We include both dimensions by defining ministerial authority as "the power or right the minister possesses and the church grants for the purpose of fulfilling God's call."[14]

The minister serves God in a human organization, the church. Samuel Southard recognized that a minister serving in a church must be authoritative in regard to:

- the maintenance of traditional values
- being sensitive to personal feelings and community relationships to move the church organization toward specific goals
- influencing the lives of persons so that they and the world in which they live may be changed toward God[15]

The authority of a minister appears in prophetic and evangelistic forms when he seeks to change people and movements. It appears in pastoral emphases when he is called on to reflect feelings or understand group relationships. His authority as a priest or a reminder of values comes through his preaching and sacramental ministry. Organizational authority is manifested in his power to move the church toward a specific program of action.[16]

The authority for these responsibilities comes from:

- the derived authority the minister has received from church and community tradition
- a legal responsibility to function as a representative of an established institution and to uphold the norms of that institution
- the charismatic hold a saintly or heroic individual has on hearers
- the technical knowledge a person offers without coercion to those who need that person's help[17]

Taken together, these traditional designations give the minister authority.

Obviously, some authority goes with any leadership role, including ministerial roles in churches. One writer observed, "The fact of the matter is that the people expect their minister to exercise leadership both in and out of the pulpit. He is not called to 'lord it over them,' but the pastor is called to send a clear signal about what he thinks is important in the life and work of the church."[18] The minister's authority should be used and not abused, for "the real danger of authority is authoritarianism."[19] The minister's authority should be used to build up the church, to strengthen and teach people, and to fulfill the ministry to which God has called the minister.

Effectiveness in ministry depends greatly on a clear understanding of authority by ministers and churches. Real authority in ministry comes from affirmation of duties and rights (sacred office), personality and capability (human person), preparation and approval (human office), and personal encounter with God for mission or call (sacred person). Every minister needs to work out of these four dimensions to effect substantial results in serving.[20]

With that in mind, Montgomery asked the question, "How much authority is enough?" He answered his own question by saying, "Enough to be respected, accepted, believed, trusted, and followed."[21]

The Use of Power

The issue of power is closely related to a minister's authority. As a professional and an authority figure, a minister has power over other persons. Karen Lebacqz observed that professionals have both power—the ability to influence behavior—and authority—legitimated and institutionalized power.[22] Roman Catholic ethicist Richard Gula wrote that "in the pastoral relationship, the use of power is the key moral issue. We inevitably have power over those seeking pastoral service because we have something they need."[23] Ministers represent not only themselves and society but also God. A minister, by his or her very presence, exerts a measure of power.

Power has been defined as "a measure of a person's potential to get others to do what he or she wants them to do, as well as to avoid being forced by others to do what he or she does not want to do."[24] According to such a definition, ministers certainly have power. From an ethical perspective, the use of that power is a key factor in ministry. Wayne Oates believes that the "integrity of a Christian leader is measured by his or her sense and use of power in relation to others."[25]

The major problem with power is what it does to relationships. Richard Foster observed that "power hits us in our relationships. Power profoundly impacts our interpersonal relationships, our social relationships, and our relationship with God."[26] When ministers use the power they possess in a destructive manner or to gain power over others, it destroys relationships and hurts people.

Ministers always live with the realization that they risk misusing the power they have. Marie Fortune was on target when she wrote:

> A healthy professional, pastoral relationship realizes the fact of pastoral power, acknowledging both the gift that it brings and the implication that the pastor is at risk to misuse that power. The laity are vulnerable to harm should that occur. The risk of misusing the power is a risk for all pastors. This risk is a function of the role itself, not just the character of the pastor.[27]

Power is influenced by the way people view themselves. When ministers view themselves as people of power who have the power to do what they want and get what they want, even if it is directed toward church goals or spiritual ends, they misuse power.

When we are convinced that what we are doing is identical with the kingdom of God, anyone who opposes us must be wrong. When we are convinced that we always use our power to good ends, we believe we can never do wrong. But when this mentality possesses us, we are taking the power of God and using it to our ends.[28]

Simon Magus attempted to buy the power of the Holy Spirit in order to use it for his own purposes. Simon Peter rebuked him for doing so (Acts 8:9–25). The attempt to use the power that one has as a minister for personal gain or for the display of personal strength must still be rebuked.

Power, however, can be constructive. Foster described the creative use of power when he pointed out, "The power that creates gives life and joy and peace. . . . The power that creates restores relationships and gives the gift of wholeness to all."[29] Creative power is the power to restore relationships. It is the power a pastor uses to bring unity to a divided fellowship, to heal the hurts between two friends, to help people work together rather than pull against one another. It is the power of moral persuasion rather than coercion. Martin Luther King Jr. used his power to help bring civil rights to all Americans. A pastor may use his power to lead a church to direct involvement in a mission activity.

A minister has power as a person, a professional, and a pastor. That power can be used wisely or unwisely, destructively or constructively. "The task of the pastor is to use the authority image that he carries as a professional and to use it properly. . . . It is his by virtue of his profession, and he is therefore responsible for its use."[30]

Leadership

In a study of world leaders, former president Richard Nixon noted, "Great leadership is a unique form of art, requiring both force and vision to an extraordinary degree." He went on to say:

Leadership is more than technique, though techniques are necessary. In a sense, management is prose; leadership is poetry. The leader necessarily deals to a large extent in symbols, in images, and in the sort of galvanizing idea that becomes a force of history. People are persuaded by reason, but moved by emotion; he must both persuade them and move them. The manager thinks of today and tomorrow. The leader must think of the day after tomorrow.[31]

Those same characteristics are necessary for ministerial leadership, for a minister functions as a leader in a church and among people. A minister convinces rather than coerces, persuades rather than pressures.

John Maxwell asserted, "Leadership is leadership, no matter where you go or what you do. Times change. Technology marches forward. Cultures vary from place to place. But the true principles of leadership are constant. . . . Leadership principles stand the test of time. They are irrefutable."[32]

Defining leadership as an action-oriented, interpersonal influencing process, Robert Dale stated that leadership is roughly equal parts of vision and initiative. "Vision defines the task and provides the content for the leadership setting. Initiative allows followers to be approached and designs the interpersonal processes for the group or organization." He also observed that effective congregational leaders tend to be "visionary and people-approachers, dreamers and doers."[33]

One of the forms that leadership takes is leadership by example. Writing to Timothy, a younger minister, Paul advised, "Don't let anyone look down on you because you are young, but set an example for the believers in speech, in life, in love, in faith and in purity" (1 Tim. 4:12). In the model chosen for ministry, the leader sets an example for other believers. As the Boy Scout leadership manual states, never ask anyone to do anything that you are unwilling to do yourself.

Two Baylor University management professors (who were also directors of the Baylor Center for Church Management) wrote that a balanced church leader must combine both active and passive leadership traits. Ministers who lead must be capable of making things happen through planning, budgeting, and programming; they must also have the patience to wait for things to happen as the result of prayer and congregational action. This type of leader also expands the leadership base to include people in the church. "The search for balanced leadership really involves creating a leadership team or body within which active and passive orientations complement one another."[34]

Dale strengthened that idea: "When leaders in ministry use one style of leadership exclusively, they discover that they are ineffective in circumstances that do not mesh well with their rigid approach."[35] Good leaders are both balanced and flexible. Different leadership styles are needed in different situations. The good ministerial leader is flexible enough to use the proper style of leadership in a given situation.

The way a minister leads helps to determine whether the minister and the congregation view each other as friend or foe. The task is so great and the interpersonal relationships so essential that a minister must work hard to develop good leadership skills.

Ministerial Duties—Roles and Responsibilities

Relationships between a minister and members of a congregation are formed as the minister performs his or her duties. Consider some key ministerial duties with regard to the ethical obligations involved.

Preaching

Most ministers consider preaching their primary responsibility. And well it is. More people are touched through preaching than through any other ministerial activity. Many ministers identify themselves as "the preacher" and explain their commitment to vocational Christian ministry as "a call to preach."

How ethical are ministers in their preaching?

> "Ministerially speaking" is a phrase synonymous with gross exaggeration. The secular person, and many Christians, use "preachy" and "preaching" as pejoratives. . . . Should the congregation not be able to listen to persons who wear the mantle of spokespersons for God without weighing each bit of evidence?[36]

The most effective preaching is done within the context of a pastoral relationship and with pastoral concerns for the people. Preaching is then not just a spiritual exercise but a real attempt to apply the Word of God to the lives of people with whom the preacher is intimately involved. Harry Emerson Fosdick's prayer as he got up to preach was always, "O God, someone here needs what I am going to say. Help me to reach him!"[37]

One pastor answered the question, "What does it mean to do pastoral care through preaching?" by saying, "It means taking the Bible and a basic understanding about a human problem and ministering to the folks in the pew. . . . Using preaching as a means of doing pastoral care means always preaching in love and not using the pulpit as your Sunday whipping post. It means proclaiming God's Word with a caring heart."[38]

Pastoral preaching is done in the context of worship. Ministers should see their sermons as an integral part of the worship service and not just as a time for them to perform. The prayer and the praise in the order of worship are not just preliminaries to the sermon. They all fit together as a planned expression of the worship of God. Each sermon should be thoughtfully planned, prayerfully prepared, and effectively delivered. Preaching is that moment when God's truth is delivered through a human personality. If a minister merely wings a sermon, depending on the inspiration of the moment or the effectiveness of delivery, he or she debases the preaching moment.

In a doctoral dissertation on clergy ethics, James Allen Reasons argues that ethical preaching is more than preaching on ethical issues; it is also preaching in an ethical way.[39] Two issues in particular are involved in ethical preaching: the use of Scripture and plagiarism.

> Although ethical responsibility to Scripture is not debated in many circles, it is still a vital issue in ministerial ethics because of its abuse. At some point in his ministry, the preacher must establish personal guidelines to ensure faithful interpretation of the text.[40]

Through allegory, symbolism, or the spiritualization of a passage, skillful preachers can make Scripture texts mean whatever they want them to mean with little concern for context or the intended meaning of a passage. A professor of homiletics and Christian ministry cited a well-known preacher in his denomination who changed the words of the Scripture passage he was reading in order for them to better fit his sermon.[41] J. Clark Hensley offers some hermeneutical principles that were first formulated by D. P. Brooks. The minister should determine

- the exact meaning of the text
- the literary form the writer used
- the context
- the historical and cultural setting
- the meaning in the light of Christ
- what the passage means now[42]

Eisegesis, reading into the text one's own meaning, is to be avoided.

Many preachers are also guilty of plagiarizing. In regard to this clergy sin, Nolan Harmon notes, "Taking someone else's message and giving it as one's own is known as *plagiarism*. It is condemned by all ministers and defined differently by all. However, the honest minister will know when he or she takes what is in reality the work of another."[43]

How common is plagiarism? Late in the last century, three well-known, high-profile pastors of prominent churches in the Southwest were accused of plagiarism in their printed or taped materials. An official of the publishing house that had produced both the original material and the plagiarized work defended it by saying, "There's a whole oral tradition that exists that would be very complicated to trace down. . . . It's just drawing on that oral tradition that circulates."[44]

A staff member of a fellowship group of a large denomination preached a sermon at a national women's meeting. The sermon, it turned out, was practically identical in title, Scripture text, and content to a previously published sermon in a book on women's issues. The offending preacher blamed the plagiarism on her paid research assistant, who had provided her with the material.[45]

At a large urban church at Christmastime, the pastor's sermon for the morning was entitled "Christmas Ho-Hum or Christmas Golly-Gee." That unique title, together with the content of the message, which included two stories attributed to John Killinger, raised suspicion that the sermon was not original. It turns out that the message came from a book of Christmas sermons by Killinger. The pastor, however, had passed off the sermon as his own creation. Obviously, plagiarism in preaching is all too common.

All preachers have been influenced by other people. In some cases, it would be difficult to trace the origin of a statement or a concept. Getting an idea from another person, researching the concept, and developing it, making it one's own, is not dishonest. Simply lifting material and preaching it as one's own, however, ventures into the area of plagiarism. The ready availability of sermons on the internet has made the temptation to plagiarize even greater. Too many preachers have followed the dictum of one well-known minister, now deceased, who often declared, "When better sermons are published, I will preach them!"

Two other areas in which dishonesty is often practiced in preaching are confessional preaching and sermon illustrations. In confessional preaching, one may embellish a story and confess more than was actually experienced. Several years ago, a preacher in the Northwest claimed that he had worked for Murder, Inc. for fifteen years and had killed twenty-eight people as a Mafia hit man. He claimed he had been counseled by Charles Colson and Billy Graham and had found God on death row while reading a Bible in a prison cell. The truth, however, was that he had violated parole after killing his wife and leaving his girlfriend for dead after choking and stabbing her. He was a murderer, but not in the way he had claimed. Upon learning of his whereabouts, authorities from the state in which he had violated his parole arrested him.[46] That is carrying ministerial embellishment a bit far!

Dishonesty may also occur in regard to sermon illustrations. A minister should never picture himself or his family members as smarter, better, or more spiritual than they are. Neither should a minister claim for himself experiences that were actually someone else's.

An executive of a national denominational agency spoke at a chapel service one morning and concluded his message with a moving account of an experience he had had in India. A mother had dropped a sore-encrusted baby into his lap through the open window of an automobile and said, "It's your baby now!" He applied it to our world mission task. The next Sunday a seminary student heard a fellow seminary student preach. In that sermon, he told of his military experience in North Africa and of a mother dropping a sore-encrusted baby into his lap while he was in a Jeep. She had said, "It's your baby now!" He applied it to our world mission task.

Could both preachers have had the same experience in different parts of the world? Possibly, but not probably. The student preacher's credibility was reduced for those who heard both messages.

In examining ethics in preaching, Raymond Bailey mentions five other matters called "specious sermonic fallacies and persuasive devices" that are ethical concerns in preaching. They are:

1. poor preparation and faulty exegesis
2. glittering generalities
3. loaded language and name calling

4. emotional manipulation
5. misrepresentation and partial truth[47]

Proclaimers of God's truth must always remember their own humanity:

> The authority leader is under constant temptation to self-aggrandizement and the use of power in the pulpit. He thinks of himself as God's "prophet," "spokesman," "ambassador"! He can easily be deceived into thinking his own word is the authority, that he is infallible. His use of pious and even ecstatic language, in order to gain power by means of emotional persuasion, may belie or undercut the word of God he is supposed to proclaim and exemplify.[48]

Teaching

Two ethics teachers, Walter Wiest and Elwyn Smith, remind preachers of the need for truthfulness in both proclamation and teaching:

> Truth—which includes both truthfulness and being true—is the key both to ministry and the ethics of ministry. Ministers of the gospel have something to be true to. We have a message to proclaim that is given to us, we do not make it up ourselves, and we are to witness to that truth faithfully and with integrity. This is a moral commitment.[49]

The teaching ministry of the church has always been considered an essential element of church life. Jesus came preaching, teaching, and healing. The contemporary church continues to preach the Word of God, to teach the truths of God, and to heal the brokenness of persons. A Yale ethics professor expressed the importance of the teaching function by saying, "The pastor shares an ethical obligation with other teachers: the quest for and sharing of truth and knowledge. Many an ordination ritual includes the joint assignment, to be 'pastor and teacher.'"[50]

In a Christian context, teaching is more a matter of education than indoctrination. Passing on the religious heritage of the faith community is essential, yet truth cannot be guarded so closely that only one approach or interpretation is presented. Freedom to think, to research, and to ask questions without fear of reprisal must be maintained. A minister cannot protect people from confrontation with other approaches to life or learning. The goal of teaching spiritual truths is to help people become mature Christians. This does not mean that all Christians must look alike and think alike.

> Those who build a creed on a selected teaching of the Bible or on a narrow segment of Christian theology become defensive about testing the belief by the wider expanse of truth. This often results in an attempt to suppress teachings which threaten the fixed doctrine. Such authoritarian views of education may result in the molding of creedal clones as ministers for our churches.[51]

The credibility and the integrity of ministers are demonstrated by the way they teach. The Word of God must be handled responsibly and respectfully. Those being taught must be treated with dignity. Neither the dignity nor the personhood of an individual should be trampled in the attempt to teach that individual.

Administration

The practical matter of the administration of a church is a part of a minister's duties. Many ministers consider this the most disagreeable part of their work, partly because administration is usually the most time-consuming aspect of their work.

How persons are viewed and treated is one ethical issue relating to church administration. People should always be viewed as having intrinsic worth and value. They should never be exploited or manipulated. Neither should they be considered intrusions on a minister's time. One minister, whose work was mainly administrative, would get perturbed when people would interrupt his work, until he realized that the interruptions were his work.

Trust is also a key ingredient. The trust that a minister and a congregation have in each other affects the way they work together. Neither the minister nor the church members should be defensive toward one another. Instead, they should be positive and supportive.

Trust begins with openness to and acceptance of a person and results when one person has respect for another as a person. The motives of a person are also involved in trust. One should never judge another's motives as less than pure. Trust extends to the belief that a person is capable of functioning in a position. Training, teaching, and instructing may be necessary to help a person become fully functional in a position. That responsibility is a part of both the teaching ministry of the church and the administrative function of the minister.

People respond better to programs when they have some ownership in them. Many churches use the committee system to great advantage. One strong component of the committee system is that it involves church members in decisions. People like to have a part in the decisions that affect their lives.

A minister should also use good organizational practices in the work of administration. A church that is properly organized and functioning can follow the leadership of its ministerial leaders. A church's organizations should have well-defined purposes and goals. Volunteer leaders should understand these purposes and goals and be trained to implement them. A minister should offer help, guidance, and encouragement.

The proper handling of finances is a key ethical factor in the administration of a church. Christian stewardship is more than a scheme to raise money for a church. It is the response in love of a Christian to God's grace.

The teaching and promotion of Christian stewardship are administrative as well as pastoral functions. Christian stewardship and the annual church budget are closely connected. Ministers can become involved in stewardship promotion in the church in several ways. They may emphasize money as the major basis of the church. They may see stewardship promotion as a necessity, as a means through which ministries are accomplished. Or they may view stewardship as a ministry of growth among members and an avenue through which to share commitment.[52]

How Christian stewardship is presented is one ethical concern. Gaylord Noyce advises, "Integrity, therefore, must be our byword; congruence of ends and means. Fund raising should be straightforward and not devious, open rather than secretive."[53] He outlines some of the ways to guard integrity in fund-raising for Christian causes:

- by applying ethics in promotion
- by avoiding the exploitation of vulnerable people
- by applying the highest in promotional material
- by avoiding "undue influence"
- by using the right method[54]

How money is used is another concern of ministerial ethics. In recent years, the nation has been shocked by the misuse of funds given by faithful followers to highly visible Christian leaders. An Associated Press release reported that one evangelist who asked people to give money to help the poor and needy spent more than 60 percent of the funds received on overhead, including his salary, housing, expensive sports cars, watches, and other personal items. Little of the money actually reached the poor.[55] The money given to churches should always be scrupulously audited. The people responsible for finances must be sure that the money is spent on the tasks for which it was given.

Pastors who control a pastor's discretionary fund should be particularly careful in using it. Such a fund is usually intended for benevolent purposes, the entertainment of prospects for church membership, or visiting people, but it is open to abuse. Too many ministers have not been discreet in using a discretionary fund and have had trouble telling the difference between their money and the church's money. Access to church funds and church accounts is also an issue. Such access should be carefully guarded with checks and balances so that the integrity of the pastor is beyond question.

Openness in financial matters creates trust in a church and in the integrity of a minister. A congregation should know where its money goes and have the assurance that it is being spent on the purposes for which it was given. Full financial reports should be made available to a church on a regular basis.

Counseling

Wayne Oates points out that ministers, whatever their training, do not enjoy the privilege of deciding whether to counsel people or not. "His choice," he said, "is not between counseling and not counseling, but between counseling in a disciplined and skilled way and counseling in an undisciplined and unskilled way."[56] Inevitably, people will bring their problems to their pastor, seeking personal guidance and care.

One immediate ethical concern regarding counseling is whether a minister is prepared for it. For many counseling situations, no particular training is necessary. A pastor can answer a question, listen to a concern, be a friend, provide reassurance, or give encouragement. Much pastoral counseling is what Oates calls "the brief pastoral dialogue."[57]

Other counseling is on the level of what Oates calls "pastoral counseling and psychotherapy."[58] This type of counseling calls for appointments and multiple sessions. Ministers who do not have specialized training or clinical experience and are uncomfortable with long-term counseling should refer people needing help to specialists. Generally speaking, pastoral counseling should be confined to the area of relationships.

Counseling people of the opposite sex is also an ethical concern. "There is no more frequent and painful a ministry-wrecking blunder than sexual involvement growing out of cross-gender pastoral care. A minister 'falls in love' with a parishioner, and an affair or divorce ensues. What also ensues is a crisis for the congregation."[59] In the *Leadership* magazine survey concerning ministers' sexual indiscretions cited in chapter 3, 17 percent of the pastors who had intercourse or other forms of sexual contact with someone other than their spouse had the experience with a counselee.[60]

Noyce suggests some "rules of thumb to serve as reflexes in the pastor and pastoral counselor." These rules of thumb designed to protect ministers are:

- When a cross-gender church member issues repeated appeals for pastoral help and time that are unusually repetitive and persistent, look at the probability of romantic transference.
- Discretion should be exaggerated in pastoral care rather than relaxed.
- While maintaining visual and acoustic privacy, cross-gender counseling should be done in the proximity of other staff or church people.[61]

Confidentiality

Confidentiality concerns determining the boundaries protecting shared information and guarding those boundaries. At times, it is difficult to know what information should be kept confidential. Some guidelines to help in that decision concern

- what is said
- why it is said

- the way it is said
- the context in which it is said[62]

Richard Gula states that keeping a confidence is one of the firmest rules of professional ethics. Not only ministers but also physicians, attorneys, and counselors have ethical standards to guide them in keeping a confidence.[63]

Clergy confidentiality in regard to counseling and the confessional has a long tradition in Christian churches. Noyce observes, "That pastoral conversation be confidential and not subject to forced disclosure is as important for the clergy as for psychiatrists and psychotherapists, and it is rooted for us in a much longer tradition."[64]

From a legal standpoint, two issues are involved in clergy confidentiality. The first issue is testimonial privilege, whether a minister can be compelled to testify in a judicial proceeding about matters told to him or her in confidence. The second issue involves the rights of privacy, whether the person who reveals confidential matters to a minister has a legal right to expect that these matters will not be revealed to others.[65]

With regard to the issue of testimonial privilege, generally the courts have held that the information given to a minister in counseling or in confession is privileged. A minister is protected from being forced to reveal such conversations in court. Child abuse cases are exceptions. About this Lynn Buzzard and Dan Hall reported, "Few privileges are absolute, the clergy-penitent privilege is no exception. Today, in some states members of the clergy are required by state child abuse 'reporting' statutes to report known or suspected cases of child abuse, even if confidentially disclosed to them."[66] Even in states in which ministers are not mandated reporters for child abuse, a minister must consider carefully his or her response to the knowledge of a suspected case of child abuse. Other legal responsibilities of the minister are discussed in chapter 6.

Not all pastoral communication is confidential. According to Gula, three virtues should guide a minister in the ethical commitment to confidentiality. They are fidelity or trustworthiness, justice, and prudence. "Since the decision to disclose a confidence is not easy to make, prudence is needed in order to exercise discretion in determining those situations in which the vulnerable are at serious risk and when the receiving of information is or is not an invasion of privacy."[67]

Since ministers know so much about so many people, confidentiality also concerns power. People entrust much personal information to ministers. The person with the most power also has the most responsibility. Ministers need to respect the dignity of individuals by maintaining confidentiality.

A minister should never take sermon illustrations from counseling experiences. Doing so violates the confidence of the person involved. Furthermore, when parishioners hear the experiences of others used in sermons, they will not trust a minister to keep their confidences. Pastors should guard against casual conversations, even with their spouses, lest they leak something told to them in confidence. They should also carefully consider whether it is appropriate to discuss certain matters with deacons, elders, or a church board. Confidential information must be kept inviolate, except in those cases in which a minister is required to report information.

Visitation

Personal visitation or pastoral calling has long been considered a primary responsibility of a minister. In today's busy society, personal visitation has become difficult. Yet personal contact with church members is still very important. In many church communities, personal visits by the pastor are expected.

Visitation can be broken down into several categories. Pastoral visits can be used to enlist new members. Other calls are evangelistic in nature. Visiting the sick is a necessary element of pastoral care. Some pastoral visits may be primarily social. Those who are homebound or institutionalized also need visits from ministers.

In hospital visitation, a minister is a part of the healing team. Even so, a minister must not take liberties with his or her privileges. A minister should never interfere with the treatment being given to a patient or enter areas of a hospital where special permission is required, such as the intensive care unit or the surgical recovery room. Hospital visits ordinarily should be brief, about five to ten minutes. Ministers should remember that they are neither God nor the physician. Answers to some questions are beyond their knowledge. Loud talk, too much levity, and boisterous behavior of any kind can be self-defeating. In most cases, prayer is appropriate, but it is often better to ask before offering a prayer.

Evangelistic visitation is for the purpose of presenting the claims of Jesus Christ. An individual's decision to accept Jesus Christ as his or her personal Savior should never be forced or coerced. The dignity of the individual should not be violated. Such a visit should be made in the spirit of prayer and with the power and presence of the Holy Spirit.

A minister must consider the ethical obligations to a member of another church. "Sheep stealing" is universally disdained. Many ministers do not visit a member of another church unless that person takes the initiative by requesting a visit. In all home visits, ministers should remember that they are invited guests. They should not be rude or ungracious. They should always leave a way to come back to a home with the gospel of Christ.

When visiting members of the opposite sex, in either their homes or hospital rooms, the same care should be taken as with counseling. Appointments for visitation are helpful so that other family members can arrange to be present.

Or ministers can take another person along. If no one but the opposite-gender person is home, the visit can be done at the front door without entering the house. In a hospital room, the door should be left open.

Weddings and Funerals

Weddings and funerals are two other basic ministerial duties that involve ethical responsibilities. Strong relationships between a minister and members of a congregation are formed through these two common human experiences.

A wedding is one of the significant moments of a person's life. From ancient times, marriage has been considered a religious rite. Ministers were at one time the sole judges of who might be married, for there was no state license for marriage. When the state gained control of legitimizing marriage, that obligation was removed from the church. Nevertheless, ministers still have an important spiritual responsibility for marriages.

A church wedding is actually a private event done in a public place. A wedding is performed in the context of the church, the place for worship and witness, to give a spiritual emphasis to the marriage. Yet a Christian union requires more than merely holding a wedding ceremony in a church sanctuary.

A church should begin to prepare people for marriage long before the wedding service occurs. Through Christian family emphases, special studies on human sexuality, sermons on the Christian home, and appropriate literature, a church prepares Christians for marriage.

Most ministers insist on at least one, and often more, sessions of premarital counseling before performing a wedding ceremony. In those sessions, topics such as gender roles in the home, work and vocation, finances and money management, relationships with parents-in-law, religious differences, and children are discussed.[68]

An ethical dilemma for many ministers concerns whose marriage ceremonies they will perform. Some consider themselves "Marrying Sams" who will perform the ceremony for anyone who comes along with a license and the fee. Others perform the ceremony only for members of the church they serve. The choice becomes even more difficult when considering whether to perform a marriage ceremony for a person who has been divorced. Ministers usually take one of four approaches in these cases. Some, of course, make no distinction and perform the ceremony for anyone with a valid license. Another approach is a blanket refusal. They do not perform a ceremony for anyone who has been divorced. Others perform the ceremony only if the divorced person was the "innocent" party in the divorce. This approach is difficult to uphold, as there is usually no truly innocent partner in a divorce. The fourth approach is to consider each case on its own merits. This approach has difficulties also, but it does seem to follow the example of Christ in accepting people where they are and helping them back into wholeness with God and one another. Some denominations have guidelines for their ministers to follow in these cases.

One pastor had strict standards about divorce and remarriage. He absolutely refused to perform the marriage ceremony of anyone who had been divorced, whatever the reason. One day he was approached by the child of an active church family with the request to perform his wedding. The young man, it turned out, had been married briefly as a teenager and then divorced. Now he was a university student. The minister explained his normal practice but did not give a definite answer at that time. Several days later, he called the young man to tell him that he felt compelled to stick by his position; he would not perform the ceremony. Then he said to the student, "If there is any other way that I can help you, please let me know." The icy answer was, "Don't worry. There won't ever be any other way." That evening the pastor preached from Jonah 4:1–11, the story of the prophet sitting under the gourd vine and complaining about the vine wilting while the people of Nineveh were living in spiritual darkness. God reminded Jonah of that disparity. The point of the passage was the contrast between gourds and human souls. Was Jonah's concern for principle more important than God's concern for people? In that sermon, the preacher was convicted. He had made his marriage principle more important than the people involved. Following the service, he rushed into his office, called the young man, and agreed to perform the wedding ceremony. The couple is still married, and the man is a leader in his church. The minister often wonders what would have happened to this family had he stuck by his original position.

Whether a person has been divorced is not the only special condition a minister must consider. What about couples who have been living together, a bride who is pregnant, interfaith marriages, and interracial marriages? Each minister has to make decisions based on his or her understanding of the nature of the gospel, the nature of pastoral care, and the responsibility of the church for ministry.

A minister's responsibility does not end with, "I now pronounce you husband and wife." A follow-up visit to the home of the newly married couple is helpful. Certainly the minister will be available for further counsel and help as they are needed. The marriage begins when the wedding is over; a pastor's ministry also continues after the wedding is over.

Performing a funeral is another basic duty of a minister and often one of the most difficult. Yet the ministry provided during the time of bereavement is also particularly meaningful. A pastor represents God, under whose watch and care all events, even death, take place. A minister represents the people who in sympathy, concern, and support seek to ease the sense of loss and the intense hurt of the hour. He or she also represents an ecclesiastical organization and profession in conducting a public service.[69]

A funeral service has several functions. Through the service the family

- faces the reality of death
- expresses its grief in a socially acceptable manner
- gives witness to the Christian faith by celebrating the life of the deceased and the promises of God
- participates in a rite of closure[70]

Each of these serves a distinct function. Ministers must guide a family through these functions and help members find wholeness and healing rather than manipulating them or exploiting their feelings.

Other ethical questions ministers face at funerals are the following:

- Will the minister be truthful about the person or bestow instant sainthood on him or her at death?
- Should a minister accept fees for funerals?
- If fees are accepted, should they be discussed before the service?
- What is the distinction between a fee and a love gift?
- Will the minister conduct a funeral service for a non-Christian?
- Should the service be held in the place of worship or in a funeral home chapel?
- What about the involvement of fraternal organizations in the burial?

Each of these issues must be individually faced and answered.

A pastor should get in touch with the family as soon as possible after being informed of a person's death. A personal visit is best when possible. To perform this ministry, a cleric should have knowledge about death, grief, and grief ministry. As far as possible, a minister should participate in planning the funeral service. Questions need to be answered: Where will the service be held? Who will conduct the service? What will be included in the service? Some basic guidelines for a service include:

- Make it positive.
- Make it Christian.
- Make it helpful, strengthening.
- Make it brief.

Through the entire service, the strengthening, encouraging, helping presence of God through the Holy Spirit should be emphasized.

A minister's responsibility does not end after the flowers have faded. Ministers can help those who have lost loved ones by helping them do the necessary grief work, sharing helpful literature with them, and conducting follow-up visits.

Ministerial Transitions—Beginning and Closure

Ministry, by nature, involves mobility. New positions open, new challenges arise, and new approaches offer ministers the opportunity to change churches or ministerial responsibilities. Some denominations appoint ministers to a church. Many evangelical churches seek out and call their own ministers. Some religious groups operate with a combination of the two systems. Whichever process is used, most ministers feel that through a confluence of the leadership of the Holy Spirit, the desire of a church, and their own willingness, a call is issued and they begin a ministry of service.

The Committee

In most cases, a prospective minister deals with a committee. The committee may be a pastor search committee, a pastoral advisory committee, a personnel committee, or a specialized committee commissioned to recommend a minister for a particular position. In the case of search committees, they are normally composed of laypersons who have volunteered their services and donated their time to the church for this task.

A search committee composes a list of potential pastors through the recommendations of others. This introduces the first ethical consideration. How honest should a recommendation be? A letter of recommendation commending an individual for a position in ministry should be truthful. Two Pittsburgh Theological Seminary professors state:

> It is expected that in a letter of recommendation one will say as much as possible that is positive and as few negative things as honesty allows. What is crucial is that the truth should be told where it really counts, as kindly as possible. Thus the failure to mention a negative factor that is crucial in the job consideration falls outside the range of the ethical.[71]

Many times those who give information about a minister will not be completely candid. Perhaps they think they are helping a friend. They may feel that the people will discover "the whole truth" after the person is in the position. Maybe they are fearful that the complete truth will prohibit the minister from landing the position. Many churches have been hurt because the person providing a reference was not completely truthful.

In a similar vein, a minister is expected to be honest in regard to his or her resume. Few fabricate degrees or falsify positions of service, though that has been known to happen. More often resumes leave misleading impressions, such as when a minister lists a school on a resume, giving the impression that he or she graduated from that institution, when in fact he or she attended there only a short time.

Should divorced ministers reveal on their resumes that they are divorced? Not necessarily. That fact will often cause a committee to discard the resume immediately without considering the details or other relevant factors. Such pastors should, however, tell the committee about the marital failure very early in the process, even in the first meeting.

A minister and a committee must deal with each other on the basis of honesty. A committee should be honest about the church and community. A minister should be honest about personal experiences and abilities. Still, both the minister and the church should do their homework about each other. Just as location, location, location are the three most important factors in real estate, so investigation, investigation, investigation are the three most important factors for a search committee. A committee cannot know too much about a prospective minister, and a prospective minister cannot know too much about a church.

Lyle Schaller suggests a series of questions a prospective minister can ask. One group contains *what* questions:

- What is the reason you are a member of this church?
- What does the church do best?
- What would you change?
- What are the church's major goals?
- What was the period of greatest strength of the church?

Another group of questions contains *why* questions. These have to do with the statistics of the church and the trends in the church. These include questions such as, Why did the church membership figure change, either positively or negatively, over a period of years? Why did the church reduce or increase staff? Why did the church relocate? Why did the church budget increase or decrease? Looking at these figures, why is there a difference? Did something dramatic happen either in the church or in the community? Next come the *what's the type* questions, which deal with the type of church, community, and people involved. The final group of questions contains *what are your expectations* questions. These also deal with the priorities of the church.[72]

The Conditions

Both a committee and a minister should be clear about the conditions of the call. Agreement should be reached concerning expectations, which would go a long way toward avoiding a forced termination. Financial arrangements should also be discussed. What is the base compensation? Does that include housing and utility allowances? If a church-owned home is provided, who pays the utilities? What about retirement benefits and insurance? Is the entire family or just the minister covered by medical insurance? Is there a car allowance or a reimbursement program? What about expenses for conventions, conferences, and continuing education? Will the church provide a book allowance?

The conditions that relate to work schedules, days off, vacations, holidays, time for revivals, leading or attending conferences or workshops, and participation in denominational meetings should also be discussed. Who will pay for the pulpit supply when the position must be filled during the minister's absence?

The final set of conditions concerns the transition. When will the minister come before the church for presentation and election? When will the minister resign from his or her current position? When will the new responsibilities begin?

While these questions may seem mundane, they must be answered for both the church and the minister to act ethically. By settling them before issuing a call and making a move, churches and ministers can eliminate many possibilities for misunderstanding and trouble. In churches with congregational government, these agreements should be presented to the church by the committee and adopted by the church. The agreements will then be a part of the church's records. The prospective minister should receive a written copy of the minutes spelling out the agreements.

The Call

The committee has made its decision, and the call has been issued. The prospective minister then faces the decision as to whether to accept that call.

A number of factors go into the decision. Ministers should consider their abilities. Are they well equipped for the position? If it is a minister of education position, for instance, that calls for a person who is interested in detail work, then candidates who are given to directing broad, sweeping programs, leaving the details to others, obviously would not be a good match. Ministers should also consider their ministry goals. Will this position help them fulfill what they see as God's will for their life? Self-fulfillment in ministry must also be considered.

The Closure

By accepting a call to a new place, a minister must bring his or her present ministry to a close. Although the excitement of new possibilities may seem attractive, the actual move may be traumatic. The future promises new friends, new vistas, new approaches, and new experiences, but the present means leaving behind old places, old friends, familiar scenes, and the known. The unknown can be scary.

The church shepherd must first resign the present position. In many cases, church bylaws specify the amount of advance notice required. Two weeks is usually the minimum. Enough time should be given to enable an orderly exit but not so much that the work is crippled or the people begin to wonder when the "ex-pastor" is ever going to leave. A month is probably the maximum, unless unique circumstances exist.

Courtesy demands that some advance notice be given to selective persons. A pastor may want to discuss his or her plans with a trusted advisor, the leader of the deacons or church board, or the entire board before announcing them to the church. A staff minister should let the immediate supervisor know.

An exit interview is helpful. Whether done formally or informally, an exit interview allows ministers to reflect on and evaluate their ministry and allows churches to evaluate their programs.

As the departure approaches, the minister begins to disengage from the people, the place, and the position. The last days should be spent in an effort to make an orderly exit and to clear the way for ongoing ministry. As Ron Sisk observed, a departing pastor should leave prescriptions sparingly. "No one's more irrelevant to a church's decision-making process than a pastor who's just announced his or her resignation. Trying to determine what the church should do next is always a mistake. For the pastor's friends it is important that they know that the pastor trusts them to do well; for the others it is important that they know the pastor is not trying to exert leadership from afar."[73] The next chapter examines the relationship between a departed minister and the former congregation, as well as relationships with the predecessor and the successor.

The Challenge

When ministers accept new challenges in the Lord's work, they do not come to new positions with all the answers and a ready-made program. A new shepherd discovers a different community and must adapt to a new ministry.

Any new ministry is begun with a certain amount of anxiety. A minister will have to get acquainted with new policies, new procedures, and established customs. "We never did it that way before" may be the first seven words a new minister hears.

A minister will have to establish a new support system. In multi-staff churches, each minister will have to carve out a niche among the other clergy. In single-staff churches, the minister will have to discover who the power brokers are in the church and learn how to relate to them.

New beginnings are difficult. From an ethical perspective, new pastors can show integrity in the way they move into a position and among the people.

They can prove their honesty by providing a ministry consistent with what they offered and the church accepted. Major changes in the church should not be made during the first few months. Instead, the minister and the congregation should establish and nurture relationships that will carry them through the years to come.

Ministerial Success

The Measure of Success

How does one measure success in ministry? As professionals and as Americans, ministers are success oriented, but knowing how to measure that success properly is more difficult. Richard Bondi wrote, "[S]uccess or failure forces us to examine the standards by which we measure either one. We may well fear to discover that our standards have more to do with the story of the world than the story of the Church."[74]

Three methods of measuring success are often used. The first of these measures of success is the bottom-line approach, which is the approach used by businesses. The bottom-line definition of success goes strictly by the numbers. Are statistics better this year than last year? Is the count up? Measurement may be geared to the three Bs: buildings, budgets, and baptisms. Or measurement may focus on the three Ss: membership size, amount of salary, and number of staff.[75]

The second way to measure success is by personal satisfaction. How satisfied is the minister with the ministry? Has the ministry been fulfilling? Has the minister given his or her best to God and the people?

William Willimon cited a survey conducted by sociologist of religion Robert Wilson of clergy of the Episcopal Church and clergy of the Church of God (Anderson, Indiana) inquiring into their happiness and satisfaction with ministry. The Episcopal ministers had greater financial compensation for their work, lived in larger, better-equipped parsonages, and had more generous pension programs than the ministers in the Church of God. But the Episcopal pastors were less happy and content in their ministries. When compared to the Church of God ministers, many of them showed low morale and deep unhappiness. Wilson believed part of the problem lay in differences between how each group conceived of its ministry. The Episcopalians saw themselves as professionals—well educated and trained, though poorly employed and compensated. The Church of God ministers saw themselves as called, willed by God to work in the church of God, people sent on a mission. Wilson said, "You can't pay people to do the things that ministers routinely must do. They need to think God has called them, or ministry is miserable."[76]

The third measure of success is a spiritual approach that evaluates commitment and faithfulness. Consider Isaiah's response to the vision of God in the temple when he was called and commissioned.

> Then I said, "For how long, O Lord?" And he answered: "Until the cities lie ruined and without inhabitant, until the houses are left deserted and the fields ruined and ravaged, until the LORD has sent everyone far away and the land is utterly forsaken. And though a tenth remains in the land, it will again be laid waste. But as the terebinth and oak leave stumps when they are cut down, so the holy seed will be the stump in the land."
>
> Isaiah 6:11–13

The standard of success was not measured in results but in faithfulness to God.

In an article in *Context,* Martin Marty referred to another publication in which a pastor and his wife were discussing success in ministry. They remembered the seminary commencement speaker who had concluded his message with a text of his own: "You have heard that it was said, 'God does not call you to be successful but to be faithful.' But I say to you that in God's eyes faithfulness is success. Down here success is the sign of faithfulness, but up there the only sign of success is faithfulness." The pastor's wife had cross-stitched and framed a piece for her husband with these words: "Up there the only sign of success is faithfulness."[77] Good ministers need to remember that.

A pastor and wife, Kent and Barbara Hughes, wrote a book that grew out of their achievement of a sense of success after feeling despondency when a new church they served did not grow. They included this testimony: "We found success in a small church that was not growing. We found success in the midst of what the world would call failure." From their study of Scripture, they came to the conclusion that "we are not called to success, as the world fancies it, but to *faithfulness.* We realized that the results are for God and eternity to reveal."[78] They shared what they called "the basic plan for biblical success" by which they were liberated from the success syndrome. To the best of their ability they were striving:

- to be faithful (obedient to God's Word and hardworking)
- to serve God and others
- to love God
- to believe God is (to believe what we believe)
- to pray
- to pursue holiness
- to develop a positive attitude[79]

Robert Raines wrote, "Success is a moving target." He explained, "Our goals change by reason of age, circumstance, growth and experience."[80] These four factors are certainly involved in any ethical assessment of success. With growth and maturity, the standards for success usually change.

That must be what Richard Bondi had in mind when he observed, "[I]t is when we forget the story that called us into ministry in the first place that we place a misguided importance on our own success or failure, or the expectations placed on us by people in a particular time and place."[81]

In a *Christian Century* article, William Willimon cited thirty "characteristics of effective pastors." Then he stated that Exodus 3 makes only one characteristic essential: the call and authorization of God. Willimon then referenced a 1970 study by Harold Quinley of activist pastors that set out to discover what made pastors strong, courageous, and bold in leading congregations to confront the social evils of the day. Quinley concluded that a strong sense of external authorization, a sense that "I am here because I have been authorized and sent here by God and the church," was the main source of pastoral courage.[82] And what a source that is!

The Goal for Christians

A denominational executive once wrote about measuring a pastor's success. He concluded that a pastor's main goal should be to disciple the church into Christlikeness. He defined functional Christlikeness in terms of three activities that characterized Jesus' life: "He prayed, He bore faithful witness of His Father's love, and He shepherded His Father's sheep."[83] In addition, Jesus challenged the social injustices of his day by his very life.

Jesus himself called us to be Godlike and mature disciples when he said, "Be perfect, therefore, as your heavenly Father is perfect" (Matt. 5:48). A standard of success can never be based on people or our own accomplishments. The standard of measurement is Christ Jesus, and success is determined by obedient faithfulness to him and progress toward Christlikeness. Christlikeness is the goal for the minister, as it is for all Christians. As both minister and congregation progress toward that goal, they can be friends instead of foes.

Being a good minister means being an ethical minister who serves a congregation with effectiveness and integrity. The relationships developed determine whether the minister and the congregation view one another as friend or foe.

Suggested Reading

Bondi, Richard. *Leading God's People: Ethics for the Practice of Ministry.* Nashville: Abingdon, 1989.

Brister, C. W. *Pastoral Care in the Church*. 3d ed. San Francisco: Harper, 1992.

Carroll, Jackson W. *As One with Authority*. Louisville: Westminster John Knox, 1991.

Dale, Robert D. *Ministers as Leaders*. Nashville: Broadman, 1984.

Gula, Richard M. *Ethics in Pastoral Ministry*. New York: Paulist Press, 1996.

Harbin, J. William. *When a Search Committee Comes . . . or Doesn't*. Nashville: Broadman, 1985.

Sanders, Randolph K. *Christian Counseling Ethics: A Handbook for Therapists, Pastors, and Counselors*. Downer's Grove, Ill.: InterVarsity, 1997.

5

The Minister's Colleagues

Cooperation or Competition?

John Donne, a minister and a poet, once wrote, "No man is an island entire of itself; every man is a piece of the continent, a part of the main."[1] While Donne was actually referring to the fact that each person's death diminishes each one of us, his statement also enunciates a principle for ministry: No one performs ministry entirely alone. Each one ministers in collegiality with others. How do ministers view those with whom they minister? Do they see them as colleagues with whom they cooperate to achieve a spiritual goal, or do they see them as competitors and try to outdo them? Consider the following scenarios.

John Jones has just been called as pastor of Mt. Pisgah Church. He has particular expectations of what he will accomplish during his ministry in that church. He will lead the church to new heights in church growth; he will lead in building a fellowship hall, which some of the people on the pastor search committee assured him the church wants; he will develop a stewardship program that will involve all the church members and will set new giving records for the church. John Jones, however, has not reckoned on Uncle Jack. Uncle Jack is a longtime member of the church. He is a deacon and chairman of the finance committee and has functioned for years as a permission-giver in the church. No matter whose name is on the church sign as pastor, Uncle Jack is actually the one who gives permission for church programs to be adopted. He does not mind church growth; he just does not want all those new people in the church. Rather than build a new fellowship hall, he would prefer to increase the cash reserves of the church by swelling the certificates of deposit owned by Mt. Pisgah Church. As far as giving to the church goes, he determined years ago the amount of money he would give each year, and it has never varied. Considering the expectations with which John Jones is coming to the pastorate of Mt. Pisgah Church, will he have competition in this church?

Mary Jacobs is a staff addition to First Church as minister to single adults. That responsibility had previously been covered by Joe Smith, who continues to minister to youth and university students. Since he is a single adult, he feels as though he has been cut off from his own group by the addition of Mary to the staff. In conversations with other single adults, he often sharply questions Mary's approaches to ministry. In staff meetings, he plays the devil's advocate regarding any issue involving Mary. When he and the pastor talk together, Joe inquires about Mary's loyalty to the pastor. When he meets with the church business administrator, he asks how Mary handles the financial accounts for which she is responsible. On the staff of First Church, is Joe Smith a cooperating colleague or a competitor of Mary Jacobs?

At the denomination's monthly pastors' conference, Rev. Fred Friendly always lets it be known that his church has gained many new members during the past month. Rev. Sam Cureton, a fellow pastor, often observes Rev. Friendly and his braggadocio, his manner with the parishioners of other churches, and his desire to be known as the most aggressive advocate of outreach in the area. Rev. Cureton has also observed a steady stream of members moving from neighboring churches to the church served by Rev. Friendly. Most of the other pastors are convinced that Fred Friendly is a renowned "sheep stealer." Is Fred Friendly cooperating or competing with the other pastors in his area?

Jesse DeWitt insists on injecting his denominational distinctives into every discussion of the General Minister's Association of Casual County. At times, he questions the degree of Christian faith and even the salvation of the pastors in other denominations. The church served by Rev. DeWitt never participates in community services, such as the community Thanksgiving service or community hymn sings. Would the other churches in the community consider him a cooperating colleague or a competitor?

Every minister serves with other ministers and relates to them either cooperatively or in competition. They work together either willingly or grudgingly, either with one another or against one another.

Ministers are accountable to God for their personal lives and ministries. They are also accountable to other ministers. What one minister does can impact the ministry of many others, even though they may not serve in the same denomination. Ministerial accountability to one another, to the ministerial profession, and to God is vital to the work of the kingdom of God. Being a good minister involves relating to colleagues in cooperation rather than in competition.

Church Leaders

The Foundational Relationship of Trust

Church work is different from any other kind of work. In a church, members are not only clients or customers but also colleagues. The clergy minister to church members, but they also work with them. In a single-staff church, in which the pastor is the only staff person, many church officers actually function as members of a church staff would function. These church leaders are colleagues with the minister. In churches of all sizes, members form the committees, teach Sunday school, and perform the work of the church. In these ways, church members are colleagues as well as clients.

Obviously, good relationships among ministers and church leaders are crucial, and trust is essential for these relationships to survive. The changes that must be made in a church can be made because the people trust the pastor to lead them properly. They trust the leader to be sensitive to the Holy Spirit's leadership, to be concerned about their spiritual welfare rather than his or her ministerial reputation, and to be a person of integrity.

The Book of Ruth contains the beautiful story of Ruth the Moabitess, who followed her mother-in-law, Naomi, home to Israel. As she pledged her love to Naomi, Ruth said that Naomi's people would be her people, Naomi's home would be her home, and Naomi's God would be her God (Ruth 1:16). Ruth believed in Naomi's God because she first believed in Naomi. People believe in a minister's program, project, or preaching because they first believe in him.

When Trust Is Broken

LeaderCare of LifeWay Christian Resources of the Southern Baptist Convention, formerly the Church Administration Department of the Sunday School Board of the Southern Baptist Convention, defines forced termination as "the severing of the formal relationship between the minister and the church either by coercion or by vote."[2]

Forced termination is every minister's nightmare. A group from the church, a committee of deacons, or members of the board may say, "Pastor, we feel that your effectiveness in this church has come to an end. We think you ought to resign." Or the nightmare may take place at a church meeting, with some members supporting the minister and others calling for dismissal. In churches with a congregational form of church government, the incident may occur by someone standing up at a business meeting and saying, "I move that we declare the pulpit vacant."

In 1984, the research department of the Southern Baptist Convention Sunday School Board made its first study of forced termination. In Southern Baptist churches, eighty-eight ministers were being fired each month across the nation. The two primary causes cited were disunity of the congregation and the interpersonal skills of the pastor. The pastors claimed that they were terminated by a small powerful minority who controlled the decision-making process of the church. The churches insisted that the pastor could not get along with church members, especially church leaders.

Four years later, another study showed an alarming increase in the number of forced terminations. Within four years, the number of forced terminations among Southern Baptist ministers had increased from an average of 88 a month to 116 a month. A different set of causes emerged. The leading cause was a lack of communication between the minister and church leaders. The second leading cause was immorality.[3]

Since 1997, the Church-Minister Relations Directors of the state conventions of the Southern Baptist Convention have been tracking forced terminations. Perhaps because of this added attention, the number of forced terminations of Southern Baptist ministers actually decreased in 1997. But unfortunately, about 45 percent of those who were involuntarily terminated did not return to church-related positions.[4]

Norris Smith, a consultant with LifeWay Christian Resources in 1997 and an authority on the subject of forced termination, observed, "Research . . . seems to declare that forced termination is no respecter of place. No area seemed to be more susceptible to terminations than any other."[5]

These studies reveal the importance of good relationships between ministers and church leaders. Everyone suffers when a forced termination occurs. The fellowship of the church is fractured. Individuals in the church experience a wide range of emotions. The church assumes a defensive posture rather than an aggressive pursuit of its mission. The reputation of the church is sullied in the community. The minister's feeling of self-worth is deeply affected. The minister's spouse is shaken by insecurity, and the minister's children are badly hurt. "[Forced termination] leaves the minister's family and the congregation devastated. Everyone loses something. No one really wins."[6]

Baptists are not the only ones who are subject to forced termination. It can happen in any church with a congregational government. Many denominations have procedures that must be followed when a minister is terminated. All ministers, however, face the possibility of the breakdown of relationships and the sundering of the bond between the minister and the church.

A number of ethical issues are related to the forced termination of ministers. They include:

- the minister's personal integrity
- the acceptance of the worth of the individual as reflected in the way ministers are treated by churches when involuntarily terminated
- the responsibility to develop pastoral skills and competence in ministry

One minister who experienced forced termination indicated that ethics, the sense of right and wrong and the exercise thereof, plays a primary role in forced terminations. He presented biblical guidelines and principles that relate to the topic:

- showing the reverence for the minister and the church demanded by the Bible
- practicing loving forthrightness and communication in relationships
- understanding the issues before undertaking any course of action
- practicing *agapē*
- resisting using the secular legal system to settle disputes in the church[7]

Avoiding Forced Termination

A good minister is not concerned simply with avoiding forced termination. That is a negative approach to life and ministry. A positive approach is to develop competent and effective ministry skills so that forced termination never becomes an issue.

Ministerial competence involves developing the pastoral skills necessary to minister effectively. In the previous discussion of professionalism, a professional was defined as one having particular skills for specific responsibilities. Ministerial competence is developed through the educational process, continuing education, reading, and on-the-job training. Many of the necessary ministerial skills cannot be taught; they are acquired by doing. Learning to preach, for instance, is done by preaching. One can learn the methods of preaching, but one can never really learn to preach until one actually preaches. Developing pastoral skills is a lifelong process. No one ever arrives at total perfection in every area. Ministers are ethically obligated to continue to develop their skills as long as they minister to others in God's name.

Ministerial competence also involves developing personal skills. The need for good interpersonal skills is evident from the studies previously cited. Speed Leas of the Alban Institute, a recognized authority on church conflicts and conflict management, conducted a study that showed that ministers' lack of interpersonal skills caused 46 percent of involuntary terminations.[8] In ministry, a great deal rides on interpersonal relationships.

Knowing and agreeing on expectations also help clergy to avoid forced termination. Edward Bratcher, stressing the involvement of both clergy and laity, states, "Both must have a sense of direction for the church and its ministry. Both must be prepared to set goals, to seek to achieve them, and to be open to negotiation when differences arise."[9] The Southern Baptist Theological Seminary and the Lily Foundation conducted a study titled "Quality in Southern Baptist Pastoral Ministry," which revealed that those who lead the churches and those in the pew emphasize different aspects of quality. "This research would point to the need for greater sensitivity to the expectations of laity, if ministers are to function with greater effectiveness in the future."[10] What is true in Southern Baptist ministry is true in the ministry of other evangelical churches as well.

Both ministers and church leaders should be open and honest with one another. If a lack of communication is a major cause of forced termination, the practice of clear, open, and honest communication is a major factor in avoiding forced termination.

In churches, communication occurs on two levels: the formal level and the informal level. The formal level of communication involves those ways in which someone intentionally and consciously attempts to communicate matters to people in the church. These include such things as public announcements, posters, signs, church papers, bulletins, and advertisements. The informal means of communication involve telephone conversations, hall discussions, coffee break chats, discussions between friends, and conversations that occur among the little groups that gather on the parking lot. Which level of communication is more effective? Probably the informal. Many formal messages are stopped before they ever get out. And if there is a broken trust, formal means of communication may be suspect in some members' minds. Clear communication is essential. One characteristic of churches in conflict is that information is hoarded and decisions are made by a few.[11]

Becoming a healthy minister also helps one avoid forced termination. Healthy wholeness as a person and a parson is a goal for all ministers. Brooks Faulkner states, "Being a healthy minister will prevent forced termination. The reason is simple: Not all churches are healthy, and some churches that have the potential of being healthy have unhealthy and/or unsteady influences." Faulkner indicates that being a healthy minister is essential for self-preservation, effectiveness, personal growth, and dealing with the possibility of forced termination. Both physical and spiritual health are necessary.[12] From Titus 3:1–5, Faulkner derives characteristics of a healthy minister. Healthy ministers:

- respect authority
- are ready for every good deed

- malign no one
- are not contentious
- are gentle
- are kind[13]

Based on several lines of research, Faulkner, a church administration authority, summarizes good health in a minister by asserting that healthy ministers:

- grow
- have a place for retreat
- have a sense of humor
- can live with not knowing
- are not preoccupied with suspicion and resentment
- have learned the art of forgiveness[14]

Bratcher contends that "ministers are not miracle-workers—they cannot walk on water, but they can learn to swim."[15]

Church Staff

Much of ministry is performed in multi-staff churches. Some churches have a ministerial staff comprised of a number of ministers who function in specialized ministries. Even single-staff churches have volunteer church staff. William Tuck states, "Attitude toward and treatment of one's fellow staff workers are indicators of one's theology. The practice of ministry is intrinsically involved in one's understanding of theological truth. Relationships . . . with fellow staff members become theological action."[16] Relationships with fellow staff members also become ethical actions.

An incident from the Hebrews' exodus experience, related in Exodus 18:13–23, provides a biblical model for church staff. After the Hebrews crossed the Red Sea and were camped near Mount Sinai, Jethro, Moses' father-in-law, came to visit Moses. Observing how Moses was both leader and judge of the people and noting the personal toll this took on him, Jethro made a suggestion. Jethro counseled Moses to choose people who could serve as judges over groups numbering one thousand, one hundred, fifty, and ten. These people would decide the minor disputes. Moses would teach the people and make decisions concerning major matters that were referred to him. This biblical event has much to teach us about staff relationships and serving the Lord together.

Called

The people who served with Moses were called from among the congregation. All ministers, whatever their function in ministry, have been called by God from among the congregation.

Both Romans 12 and 1 Corinthians 12 indicate that Christians are gifted in different ways. All gifts are from the Holy Spirit, and all gifts are to be used for building up the church. Responsibilities may vary and functions may differ, but each minister on a church staff is a real minister, and each ministry is a valid ministry. "What these other ministers do is just as surely ministry as that which a pastor might do. Ministry is ministry because of what is done rather than by whom it is done."[17]

Generally speaking, staff members are called by the church and not by the senior minister. Charles Tidwell suggests, "Let all of a church's ministers be called by church action, not just employed by an individual or a committee acting independently and alone. If the church requires evidence of a call of God to qualify one of its ministers, then it seems wise to have the church endorse the minister's call by church action."[18]

The practice of "cleaning out" a staff when a senior minister moves to another church or retires fails to recognize that each person on a church staff was at some time presented to the church as the person whom God had called to that position. The call of God to the senior minister to move or to retire does not rescind the call of God to other staff ministers. Allowing a senior minister to choose his or her own staff may result in more efficiency and closer initial relationships among staff members, but it does not give sufficient recognition to the call of all staff ministers. It also creates a sense of "my staff" on the part of the senior minister rather than "our staff ministers" on the part of the church.

Collegiality

Collegiality is a second concept gleaned from Moses' experience. Ministers serve God together. They serve as colleagues in the Lord's service. One pastor commented, "Each minister understands that his or her ministry is significant as a part of the team, but, due to the variety in talents, experience, and training, responsibility may not always be totally equal."[19] This pastor also said that the senior minister is the key to creating a climate of cooperation, trust, support, communication, love, and mutual understanding.

The idea of a ministering team comes from the concept of collegiality. A pastor who used the team ministry approach in one church for nearly two decades found the scriptural basis for that approach in 1 Corinthians 3:9: "We are partners working together for God" (GNB). Two matters in this verse demonstrate a team ministry. First, all the members of the church work for God in ministry. The second matter leads directly from that concept. "We are partners working *together.*" This pastor observed, "If one feels jealous when a colleague experiences success or achieves recognition, the problem is not likely with the colleague. The solution is not in the suppression of the colleague's individuality, but in one's becoming more secure in one's own ministries under God."[20]

Understanding staff ministry as collegiality fits with Jesus' teachings about servanthood. Collegiality in ministry follows a team model rather than a hierarchial model for organization. It also follows a servant model for expression. Jesus challenged the leadership of his day when he taught his followers that the mark of effective leadership was not lording it over others but serving others (Mark 10:42–45). His servants rule only by serving. Another pastor stated:

> The ministers on a church staff can provide the congregation with a model of servant ministry through their relationships with each other and by their performances of their responsibilities. . . . If church members see staff workers who are constantly putting each other down, circumventing each other for a place of greater recognition in the church, and unable to relate well with their fellow ministers, they will have great difficulty in understanding what it means to be servants in Christ's name. . . . The servant image provides a model which is patterned after our Lord's own ministry. When the staff is committed to this kind of ministry, they can serve as a catalyst for the whole congregation.[21]

Characteristics

The characteristics expected of a church staff member come from the Exodus passage referred to earlier (Exod. 18:13–23). The description of the kind of people chosen to aid Moses in his ministry reveals the basic characteristics of those who serve.

The first characteristic is capability. The person who serves in any ministering task must be capable of doing the job. Capability comes through

- God-given spiritual gifts
- the natural gifts the person possesses
- the acquired skills the individual gains through education and experience

People are not called to church staff positions just because they are nice but because they have the capability of performing a specific task.

The second characteristic is commitment. Christian commitment is expected of each staff member, not just the pastor or senior minister. Such people are committed to Christ, to the church, and to the kingdom of God.

Competence is a third characteristic. The Exodus account called for "trustworthy" leaders. Trustworthy people are worthy of trust. They are competent to fulfill the task to which God and the church have called them. Competence is an ethical imperative for each person ministering with a church staff.

The fourth characteristic mentioned to Moses was character. Jethro described persons with character as those "who hate a bribe." A retired professor of Christian ethics noted that in the Lyman Beecher Lectures at Yale, character is most frequently described as the essential characteristic of a minister. This may be true, he continued, because people are more impressed by a preacher's life than by sermons. They hear the person more than the sermon. "Ministers of good character incarnate into their lives the spirit of Christ."[22]

These four characteristics apply to all persons who minister in the name of the Lord Jesus Christ. Whatever an individual's function on a church staff, he or she should possess these positive characteristics.

Consequences

Do ethical staff relationships make a difference in a church? Look back again to the account in the Book of Exodus. Such relationships have two consequences.

One consequence relates to the staff members. Jethro told Moses, "You will be able to stand the strain" (Exod. 18:23). Ethical and fulfilling relationships on a church staff enable the staff to work more effectively. Creating a climate in which each staff person can do his or her best work is the responsibility of the staff leader, usually the pastor or senior minister. He or she does this by removing some of the stress from the ministry and challenging the staff to the highest standards of work.

A study conducted by a denominational research department reported that most staff members feel accepted, affirmed, and appreciated by one another. "Staff members feel personally accepted (94.7%), loved and cared for (93.2%) by other staff members all or most of the time. They also feel their opinions are important to other staff members all or most of the time (90.3%)."[23] This kind of ethical relationship among staff members enables them to "stand the strain" as they minister together.

The second consequence of ethical staff relationships relates to the church. Jethro expressed it to Moses by saying, "All these people will go home satisfied" (v. 23). Ethical relationships help staff members perform the ministry, meet the needs of the people, exemplify the servant model of ministry, and satisfy the congregation.

A pastor turned professor shared some "rules of the road" related to ethical staff relationships.

- Respect one another as persons and ministers.
- Give one another the gift of attention.

- Recognize that every staff has problems and see these as opportunities for growth and not division.
- Handle conflict fairly.
- Spend some time away from the pressures of the church and get to know one another as persons.
- Remember that the staff models relationships for the rest of the church.[24]

Following these guidelines enables members of a church staff to serve God together as colleagues rather than as competitors. In turn, the church benefits, and the ministry is exalted rather than debased. The main concern is getting the work of the church done without worrying about who gets the credit. Working as a team with a spirit of collegiality accomplishes that goal.

Other Ministers

Ministers all have predecessors and successors and serve in areas with ministers of their own as well as other denominations. In these relationships, too, ministers must cooperate rather than compete.

The Predecessor

Often, departed ministers, like deceased husbands, assume sainthood. The incoming pastor hears nothing but good reports of the excellent work of the former pastor. After a while, he or she may wonder if the predecessor ever did anything wrong.

One of us followed pastors with long tenures in two successive pastorates. After hearing nothing but glowing reports about all the preceding minister had accomplished, a civic club meeting brought humorous relief. One of the members told a story about the former pastor running out of gas on a bridge in the middle of town. While others at the table laughed at the minister's embarrassing situation, the response of the newer, younger minister to the story was, "I'm just glad to know that he ever ran out of gas." Memories are selective. A former minister may have experienced failure, disappointment, and discouragement, but they are often not fresh in members' minds.

Generally speaking, an incoming minister does not need to fear those who speak well of the predecessor. Those who loved, appreciated, respected, and supported the former minister will likely do the same with the new minister. The church member of whom the minister should be wary is the one who speaks ill of the previous minister. Those who criticize, find fault with, and express disappointment in the former minister will probably react to the new minister in the same way over time.

Ministers all build on the foundation that others have laid. All are recipients of the ministry of their predecessors. In 1894, Bishop Charles Galloway of the Methodist Episcopal Church spoke to a conference at Boston University on ministerial ethics. Galloway said:

> Much of our work is to reap where others have sown. Their sowing should have equal honor with our reaping. A circuit, station, or district may be served full term without the earnest pastor's noting much fruit of his labor. Another comes whose mission is to gather golden sheaves and whose joy it is to sing a harvest song. Though possibly much honored, credited with being a more successful workman, he really enjoys the fruit of another's planting. . . . He that planteth and that watereth are one.[25]

Ministers should honor and respect those who preceded them. People never exalt themselves by debasing others. Ministers do not look good or act ethically when they criticize or question the character of those who preceded them.

Ministers should invite former ministers back for special occasions in the church. For example, if a building is completed that a former minister helped to plan, perhaps the former minister could deliver the dedicatory message. If a minister never recognizes the contributions of former ministers or involves them in the life or affairs of the church, it only reveals his or her insecurities.

Ministers can also keep predecessors informed of events in the life of the church. One of us was the pastor of a church when several teenage girls were struck by a car when crossing a street on a university campus where they were attending a conference. One girl was reported brain dead, but six years later when this girl walked across the stage to a standing ovation to receive her high school diploma, her former pastor greatly appreciated a telephone call telling of the girl's graduation and hearing a description of the joyous event.

The Successor

Nolan Harmon's comment in a book on ministerial ethics and etiquette first published in 1928 still rings true:

> Above all, when a man leaves a charge, let him leave it. No minister should be constantly back to gossip with the brethren or hear comments on the work of his successor. Great harm has been done in this way by some ministers. The outgoing pastor should get all his supplies, trunks, boxes, barrels, the piano, the bread box, the garden hose and Willie's shotgun—everything loaded at one time, should give a good-by, making it as tearful as desired, but having started the moving van, don't look back! . . . "Get out and stay out" is the injunction here.[26]

Obviously, a departing minister will leave behind friends. Interest in them and concern for them will continue. However, the work of that church is now in the hands of another. The sucessor should be given the freedom to conduct ministry without the interference of the predecessor.

The current minister needs to get to know the people, to form close relationships with them, and to become a part of their lives. The best way to do this is through sharing the major milestones of life with them. If the former minister continues to perform weddings and funerals, he or she cheats the current minister out of developing those relationships.

Leadership journal formed a panel of Christian leaders to discuss eight ethical choices among ministers. The question was introduced with these words: "Courtesy of one's predecessor and successor in a pastorate extends beyond matters of backbiting and malpractice." Then this question was asked: "When can a pastor return to a prior pastorate to preach or to perform weddings, funerals, or baptisms/dedications?" Three members of the panel answered "never." Six thought it permissible upon invitation or permission by the successor. Two panel members felt good about returning at any time, saying that they were not engaged in some kind of competition. One minister explained, "If the present pastor has difficulty with my returning, then it's his problem. He doesn't have to 'establish himself'; the Lord establishes a pastor."[27]

A Yale Divinity School professor of pastoral theology passed on a list of negative influences on a congregation compiled by the Alban Institute:

- Contacts between a former minister and church members cause whatever negative emotions were present at the pastor's departure to continue to surface. (These emotions may be regret, guilt, anger, frustration, or relief.)
- Continued contacts deny members the opportunity to work through those emotions of grief directly and constructively, and the contacts encourage their futile grappling with ghosts.
- Contact discourages members' working through their feelings within the community ("I'd better not tell my deacon that I called the old pastor.") and encourages a rivalry among members ("The pastor called *me!*").
- Private contacts with individuals deprive the community of the opportunity to share grief and loneliness, to build the strength that comes from shared suffering, to discover resurrection hope that emerges from shared struggles.
- Contacts with former ministers focus member energy outside the congregation at a time when that energy may be needed most within the community.
- Private communications encourage holding on to the past and fighting former battles, but this time with invisible contenders; they decrease a

person's ability to struggle with present realities and diminish hope in the future.

- Contacts confuse persons as to where and how to direct their commitment to new leadership; they make that difficult task even more difficult for members.
- Each contact places the resident pastor in the awkward position of interloper. Interim specialists are trained to deal with negativism so that the installed pastor can begin positive building at the earliest opportunity.
- By surfacing implicit comparisons between new and old, contacts between the former minister and church members undermine the choice of a new pastor and inhibit a wholehearted commitment to the new relationship.
- Contacts keep the new pastor on the defensive and subvert that pastor's morale and effectiveness. The new pastor can never successfully compete with the old pastor's ghost as long as that ghost is actively present.[28]

Retired Ministers

A minister also deals with retired ministers. Sometimes these ministers continue to live in the community in which they served. "One can think of painful situations in which the retiring minister's own sense of human worth and identity hinges heavily on the pastoral status. If that minister stays on in a neighborhood near enough to be accessible to or active in the last congregation, the pressures flood in, coming from parishioners and the retired pastor alike."[29]

Some retired ministers find it difficult to separate themselves from their ministry. They need to secure their self-worth in their own selfhood rather than in their ministry so they are able to function as a person when no longer able to function as a minister.

Active ministers should remember that retired ministers no longer have a church to love and to return love. The current minister needs to be sensitive to the needs and feelings of the retired minister. A sensitive, caring relationship can bring satisfaction to both.[30]

Retired ministers who continue to attend the church they once served should be recognized, appreciated, and allowed to be full and contributing members of the church. Some churches bestow a title such as "pastor emeritus" on these ministers, perhaps providing a small stipend and office space. Retired ministers can assist in funerals and weddings on occasion (but this should be done with great care for the same reasons outlined under "The Successor") or fill in behind the pulpit when the new minister is away. New pastors who encourage these activities show that they are not threatened by the presence of retired ministers. The counsel that older, experienced ministers give to younger, inexperienced ministers is helpful. In times of congregational crisis, their insight and active help is invaluable. Above all, no effort should be made to discredit the retired minister or to wean the congregation away from the retiree.

> If they have much love for him, be assured that they have enough to go around and their hearts can be stretched to love you, too. Just thank God that he taught them to love their pastor or enabled them by being loving to thus love you, their present pastor. An unloving attitude by the new pastor toward the retired pastor can hinder the congregation from loving the new one.[31]

All ministers deal with other ministers in a variety of relationships. Ministry is better served and the Christian faith is advanced when ministers view themselves as colleagues rather than as competitors.

Other Churches

A minister's colleagues also include ministers in churches of other denominations. Unfortunately, these relationships are not always exemplary.

In earlier times, denominational distinctives were emphasized more than at the present. Denominational loyalty is now shrinking. When people seek a church home, they often look for a church that meets their personal and family needs rather than a church of their denominational family. Because of particular emphases in church life—charismatic experiences, for instance, or a celebrative style of worship—churches of different denominations may have more in common than churches of the same denomination. Many churches have no denominational ties. Since churches no longer hold Saturday afternoon debates on the courthouse square defending their positions and deriding others' views, what is the relationship between ministers of differing denominations? Gaylord Noyce affirmed, "We are called on to encourage and affirm, not denigrate, the work of other pastors."[32]

Proselytism, or sheep stealing, is no more acceptable between denominations as between churches of the same denomination. A general practice is to let a person or family of another denomination make the first move toward joining another church. Ministers who are contacted by people who want to switch denominations should answer questions about their churches honestly. They should point out differences but should not use the occasion to be derisive about other people's beliefs.

When a person decides to join a different denomination, the pastor or the church should inform the previous church of the person's decision. Letters of dismissal or certificates of transfer are often exchanged between churches of the same denomination but not between churches of different denominations.

A simple note informing the church of the individual's decision is courteous and allows the church to adjust its records.

Ministers within a community should know one another personally. They will more than likely work together on projects of community interest and bump into one another in hospitals. The better they know one another personally, the better they can serve together. Relationships are often achieved through a ministers' association in the community. Another avenue is an interdenominational study group, support group, or fellowship group in which ministers of various denominations share their commonalities and their community interest.

A pastor who is already established in a community should visit an incoming pastor of a neighboring church regardless of the denomination. If a reception or welcoming party is held to introduce a minister to the community, other ministers should attend. Ministers can also respond to the needs of other ministers when they are hospitalized or face personal tragedies.

Many denominational groups or independent churches have opted not to become a part of organized national or international ecumenical movements. Yet on the local scene, churches of these denominations often work well with other churches to relieve human hurts and to advance the cause of Christ. Shelters for the homeless, food for the hungry, clothes for the needy, and aid for transients are often provided in a community through the efforts of churches of several denominations working together.

The contemporary minister always lives with the tension between being a priest and a prophet. When the prophetic prevails, the minister often needs the support of other prophets to make an impact on the community. At times, the community must be called to account for its actions and reminded of Christian values. Ernest Campbell, former pastor of Riverside Church in New York City, states:

> I have held to the view that a preacher, to be prophetic, must live out of phase with his times. Our prototypes in Israel and Judah seemed impossible to please. When the nation was consumed with delight over its accomplishments the prophets predicted disaster and called for repentance. Conversely, when the spirit of the nation was low (as in the Babylonian Captivity) the prophets came through with words of hope and the promise of a better day.
>
> The time has come for ministers in this country to counter the despair that has gripped the nation. To live out of phase in these days is to point to a better way. As in recent years we warned about American pride and pointed out the injustices that mock our public rhetoric, so now the hour has come to lift this people up.
>
> It is when we are weak that we can be strong. It is when the false gods fail that the God of grace and glory has a chance. It is when the old balances of power shift and leave us vulnerable that the power of the Spirit can give us the vision of a world at peace. It is when we have spent and spent for that which

cannot satisfy that the bread of life, proclaimed in love, can nourish a weary people back to health.

To believe in God is to believe that in every situation, personal and collective, there is an alternative to despair. We may be dead, but God isn't. Our sins may have done us in, but there is a grace greater than our sin.[33]

To live "out of phase with his times" is a part of the prophetic presence of the preacher. Richard Bondi said that there "is no substitute for the personal presence." He went on to claim, "The leader must remain on the edge in order to lead. . . . But the leader must also have an active presence with the community in order to claim solidarity with it."[34] Remaining on the edge and living out of phase with the times while living in solidarity with the community are challenges for the minister. As a moral leader, the minister must speak prophetically, but he or she must also work redemptively as a priest. Ministers who work with other ministers on moral issues help Christians address the contemporary world with a more unified front.

Wholesome, healthy relationships with ministers of other denominations are desirable. Life is enriched and ministry is expanded when a minister knows, respects, and appreciates ministers of other faith groups. While not compromising denominational distinctives or approving of all the methods of others, ministers can affirm, appreciate, and count others as allies on many issues. Harmon concluded, "When a person is found to be genuine, whatever the methods, others neither fear nor are jealous; they rejoice to have another worker for Christ in their community."[35]

Other Professionals

A Professional among Professionals

Chapter 1 revealed that a minister functions as a professional among professionals. Many ministers have a certain ambivalence about the concept of ministry as a profession. One writer found this ambivalence centered in the minister's search for a vocational role.

The concept of the professional is not that of a person who acts out an image for the public twenty-four hours a day. A minister can retain his integrity and proper self-identity at the same time that he carries his role with professional concern for the good of those to whom he ministers. There is no reason for him to feel guilty for carrying himself with professional competence.[36]

Ministers should be professionals without becoming mere professionals. They should always be competent in practicing their ministry, exemplary in their personal conduct, capable of meeting the demands placed on them, and responsive to calls for ministry. *Professional* should never mean a cold, calculating, uncaring person.

"Each of the classic professions—medicine, law, and the church—carries an implicit profession of faith. The very word 'profession' has significance because it implies a profession of faith in some person or concept."[37] The medical person has faith in the healing arts, the lawyer has faith in the system of law, and the minister has faith in God and in the visible church.[38] Or as Karen Lebacqz put it, "A professional is called not simply to *do* something but to *be* something. A professional 'professes.'"[39] Professionalism involves both being and doing, what a person is and what that person does. Ministers profess faith in God through Jesus Christ, whom they serve through the church. If ministers act in a manner that is unbecoming to a minister, they are said to have behaved unprofessionally.

The concept of ministry as a profession is both freedom producing and anxiety producing. By being involved in a vocation that calls for loyalty to a visible body of believers, the minister has a specific, defined task. Knowing what the job is and what is expected in terms of competence, capability, and character can be freedom producing. There are times, however, when a person's understanding of God's will conflicts with the good of the institution, the church. In those cases, ministry as a profession is anxiety producing.[40]

Because a minister is a professional, he or she must know how to relate to other professionals in the church and the community. A minister should show respect for other professionals, each of whom has also prepared for work, professed faith in a field, and acted professionally. These professionals are to be respected and honored for who they are and what they do.

Ministers relate to doctors, lawyers, and other professionals by not encroaching on their fields. Concerned ministers spend a lot of time in hospitals, but that does not qualify them to pass judgment on the treatment being given. While pastors counsel people, they are not psychiatrists. Legal matters are too complicated and technical for ministers to hand out legal advice freely. Each person acts out of his or her experience. The physician, lawyer, and minister—members of the "learned professions"—should know where the work of one stops and the other begins.

A Part of the Community Team

A minister works with other professionals in a community to meet the needs of people. Not every need a minister faces is a spiritual need. Some needs can be better met by other trained persons. A minister may not be able to give a job to a person desperately seeking employment, but he can introduce that individual to someone in the community who can provide the employment needed.

Wayne Oates suggests that a pastor's first responsibility to a new community is to become friends with other pastors of all denominations. After that, ministers should become acquainted with the medical community, physicians of both general practice and specialties. The third group they should get to know includes social workers, heads of institutions, and school teachers. They should also become acquainted with parent-teacher organizations and child care agencies. "These," Oates observed, "are all members of a 'community team' of healing helpfulness to people. As a general rule, they, like the minister, are passionately devoted to what they are doing."[41]

Ministers often help people best by referring them to people who can help them with a particular problem. In this way, ministers are functioning and valuable members of a community team that is dedicated to meeting human needs and helping people. Walter Wiest and Elwyn Smith are of the opinion that "pastors cannot perform their pastoral duties at maximum effectiveness if they have not worked out some way to communicate with doctors, attorneys, law enforcement personnel, and many others."[42]

A Member of the Healing Team

A specific community team composed of professionals attempting to meet human need is the healing team. Most ministers spend a great deal of time in hospitals ministering to people who are sick or dying. When ministers visit a hospital room, they bring hope and help to others and guide them in spiritual development. This spiritual ministry is an integral part of the healing process.

Howard Clinebell, a recognized authority in pastoral care and counseling, commented on this truth.

> During the time I served as a hospital chaplain, I often felt frustrated by some hospital personnel who perceived my role as exclusively that of bringing religious resources, anxiety-reduction, and comfort to patients—especially when medical treatment had done all it could and failed. Although I regarded those traditional functions as valuable, I sensed that a minister's role with the sick also had another significant dimension—to help enable healing. Experience in recent years has increased my appreciation of the great importance of this second aspect of the minister's role with the sick. The skillful use of listening, caring, and counseling methods with those who are ill can help them become more open to the God-given healing resources within their bodies, minds, spirits, and relationships. When those counseling skills have a vertical dimension and use religious resources appropriately, they can be particularly helpful in enabling

people to open themselves to experience the healing energies of the ever-present love of God—the ultimate source of all healing.[43]

Clinebell states that the words "health, heal, hale, whole and holy are all derived from the same or closely related Old English root words,"[44] which underscores the connection between religion and healing. A minister is a part of the healing team and helps the people of the church and community find and experience wholeness.

For ministers to relate properly to their professional colleagues, they must be emotionally mature. Yet what does it take to be emotionally mature? A longtime professor of Christian ethics indicated that a minister must have

- the capacity for healthy self-acceptance
- the capacity to maintain durable relationships
- the ability to work with people who hold different value orientations
- the capacity to delay present gratification for future and more permanent satisfactions
- the ability to cope with indecision or mental paralysis
- the ability to achieve a large measure of objectivity
- the ability to get along with other people, to tolerate their views and values without becoming dogmatic and defensive about one's own
- a sense of humor
- love
- the capacity to care[45]

Each of these marks of maturity helps a person to be a good and effective minister. The next chapter shows how these principles apply to a minister's community.

Suggested Reading

Bratcher, Edward B. *The Walk-on-Water Syndrome.* Waco: Word, 1984.

Brister, C. W. *Caring for the Caregivers.* Nashville: Broadman, 1985.

Chandler, Charles. *Minister's Support Group: Alternative to Burnout.* Nashville: Broadman, 1987.

Faulkner, Brooks. *Forced Termination.* Nashville: Broadman, 1986.

Griffith, Leonard. *We Have This Ministry.* Waco: Word, 1973.

Lebacqz, Karen. *Professional Ethics: Power and Paradox.* Nashville: Abingdon, 1985.

6

The Minister's Community

Threat or Opportunity?

Walker Percy's *Thanatos Syndrome* is an apocalyptic tale set in Feliciana, Louisiana, during the late twentieth century. The plot develops when a psychiatrist discovers that well-intentioned but misguided medical researchers have slipped a Sodium 24 ion into the water supply. The drug has made a measurable impact on deviant behavior in Feliciana. By inhibiting certain activities of the brain, the drug has caused a significant decline in crime, the spread of AIDS, wife and child abuse, teenage suicide, and other social maladies. Unfortunately, the drug has side effects: dramatic emotional, linguistic, and sexual changes. The Felicianans may be better behaved, but the price is high—the loss of human traits.

Father Simon Smith, the priest who plays a prominent role in the novel, perches like a postmodern Simeon Stylites (the fifth-century pillar saint who spent his lifetime "above" the world) in a fire tower on the outskirts of town. Father Smith fled to the tower in despair over the success of the Qualitarian Movement, which proposed quick and painless death for those suffering in hospitals. Once a hospice director, this priest has given up on conventional attempts to stop this mercy killing, hoping his absurd act might raise questions. When a psychiatrist does question the priest, the jeremiad response is reminiscent of the prophets of the Old Testament.

You are a member of the first generation of doctors in the history of medicine to turn their backs on the oath of Hippocrates and kill millions of old useless people, unborn children, born malformed children for the good of mankind—and to do so without a single murmur from one of you. Not a single letter of protest in the august *New England Journal of Medicine*. And do you know what you're going to end up doing? You a graduate of Harvard and a reader of *The New York Times* and a member of the Ford Foundation's Program for the Third World? . . . You're going to end up killing Jews.[1]

Percy's critique of an unquestioning trust in technology and science also offers insight about pastoral ethics and what James Wind calls "our ministerial moment."[2] As with Jeremiah or Jonah, there are times when the modern minister is called into the community to engage in hand-to-hand combat.

Yet the public role of a minister is not just that of a prophet but also that of a pastor. The shepherd of God is concerned about community needs and ministry opportunities, as well as public morality. Along with congregation building and pastoral caring, a minister has a public ministry that is larger than the claims of a particular church. This dilemma raises the question: Is the community a threat or an opportunity for the modern minister?

The role of a minister in society is mandated by both biblical tradition and professional responsibility. How to interact with the world has been the basis of much theological debate and the occasion for many historical movements. Perhaps no one has better portrayed the struggle of Christians to relate to the world than H. Richard Niebuhr in his classic work *Christ and Culture*.[3]

Though written in a day when American culture was much more monolithic, the book poses a question that remains relevant. In the midst of society (family, state, church), how does a Christian choose between loyalty to Christ and faithfulness to other loyalties in society?

Niebuhr outlined five relationships between culture and the church that have occurred throughout history. The first two are what he called "radical answers."

Christ against culture is the response of sectarian groups that condemn culture and separate themselves from it. Partly due to persecution from an immoral and pagan Roman society, early Christians such as Tertullian took this stance. Later groups such as ascetics, monastics, and modern Amish communities illustrate this same rejection of culture.

The second radical answer is called Christ of culture. Early Christian Gnostics and modern cultural Protestants selectively identified certain aspects of culture as Christian. For them, the culture interpreted Christ; the best insights of civilization (science, philosophy) harmonized with revelation.

The temptation still exists for Christian leaders today to relate to the community in one of these two ways. A pastor may give up on the world and withdraw from society, assuming it is sold out to Satan and sin and is beyond redemption. Many conservative Christians in the past century sought to separate themselves from evil by renouncing "worldliness," usually defined as certain immoral activities.

A more common attitude among twenty-first-century evangelicals is the way of identification with culture. Many would see in the Religious Right and the trend toward civil religion a repetition of that age-old strategy of "Christianizing" some part of culture. Another form of identification is the attempt of many churches to reach younger generations by adopting their music, mania, and mind-set. In an attempt to be relevant, however, the church can so accommodate itself to society that its distinct message is lost.

Niebuhr rightly rejected both of these extreme positions for several basic theological reasons. One thinks only nature is good, while the other looks to culture for salvation. Both separate God the creator from God the governor of the world. The "against" position focuses only on Christ, the "of" group only on culture. The Yale theologian prefers a better alternative: the "Church of the Center," which works to change society by properly relating Christ to culture.

Three positions represent this preferred approach of the church in regard to the world. Christ above culture affirms both the world and faith but gives superior value to Christ over culture. Christians such as Thomas Aquinas believed the natural world revealed much truth about God and life, forming a base to which supernatural revelation could be added.

Christ and culture in paradox is a dualistic approach to life in community. Martin Luther taught that a person lives in two kingdoms: The state has the final word on secular matters; the church has authority over spiritual concerns. The Christian lives in paradoxical tension between the two worlds, which do not always agree but must always be obeyed.

The preferred approach offered by Niebuhr is Christ the transformer of culture. This "conversionist" approach seeks to transform the world into conformity to the will of God. It works from the conviction that the claims of Christ extend to all of life and society. Christian thinkers such as Augustine and John Calvin, as well as modern leaders of the Great Awakenings (1726–1810), the social gospel movement, and mainline Protestantism, represent this position.

What do these historical examples teach contemporary clergy about their life in community? They obviously warn Christian leaders to be wary of negative withdrawals from the world and a utopian identification of the gospel with culture. To seize Niebuhr's theme, the Christian minister must affirm absolute loyalty to Jesus Christ while accommodating his or her loyalties to culture.

Christian involvement in a community must always be realistic: Every culture is corrupted by sin. At the same time, the gospel of Jesus Christ is powerful: Societies can be transformed. These two realities create a healthy tension between Christian ideals and appropriate social action.[4]

One fact remains: The church is in the world, and the world is also in the church. A community, therefore, can be for a minister both a threat and an opportunity. At times, a pastor leads the congregation to minister in the community as friend to friend. At other times, when social evils raise their dragonic heads, the prophet must go forth like a medieval knight to battle the forces that ravage human life. To be God's minister in the world is ethically demanding, for it requires of the clergy a dual role of pastor and prophet.

Basis for Ethical Involvement

What biblical basis do ministers have for ethical involvement in the community? One of the first revelations of Scripture is that God is creator of all that is: "God saw all that he had made, and it was very good" (Gen. 1:31). This good creation, both the world of nature and the world of culture, is governed by a sovereign Lord to whom humanity is responsible (Genesis 2; Matt. 25:31–46). But God's created order did not remain untainted for long. Sin and evil quickly entered the picture, corrupting the earth and all persons on it (Genesis 3). The ultimate revelation of Scripture, however, is not about ruin but redemption. God the creator and governor of the world is also God the redeemer. The story of the Bible, from the Red Sea to Golgotha, is about the one and only Redeemer who works and is working to transform the kingdoms of this earth into the kingdom of God (Revelation 21). This is why ministers must view society as an opportunity for ministry. God has not abandoned the world; neither should the church or its leaders.

The Old Testament prophets proclaimed the need for social justice and community righteousness (Amos 5:21–24). Isaiah condemned the religious festivals and meaningless offerings of Judah because their religion was ethically deficient; it did not work in the marketplace. "Stop doing wrong, learn to do right! Seek justice, encourage the oppressed. Defend the cause of the fatherless, plead the case of the widow" (Isa. 1:16–17).

Perhaps Micah summarizes best the call of the Old Testament messengers for social righteousness: "He has told you, O mortal, what is good; and what does the LORD require of you but to do justice, and to love kindness, and to walk humbly with your God?" (Micah 6:8 NRSV).

The New Testament continued this concern for social justice expressed in the old covenant. The Gospels reveal this prophetic emphasis in the life and teachings of Jesus, who often confirmed his intent not to "abolish the Law or the Prophets . . . but to fulfill them" (Matt. 5:17). Christ explained in the Sermon on the Mount that Christians are citizens of a new kingdom and live by a new law—the law of righteousness (Matt. 5:20). As the "salt of the earth" and the "light of the world," disciples of Jesus are mandated to have a positive influence on a darkened and decaying society (Matt. 5:13–16). Both in character (Matt. 5:3–11) and in conduct (Matt. 5:21–7:28), the followers of Jesus are called to live in the world according to ethical ideals that are based on the moral character of God: "Be perfect, therefore, as your heavenly Father is perfect" (Matt. 5:48).

As God's new covenant community, the Christian church is not to be an end in itself; disciples of Jesus are the body of Christ in the world. The Christian community is to be involved in doing what Jesus did, for the Lord said, "As the Father has sent me, I am sending you" (John 20:21). The position of the "called out ones," like that of Israel, is one of service, not of privilege.

In two respects, the church differs from Israel. For the Hebrews, church and state were the same; the religious and political communities were identical. Not so with Christianity, for the Roman emperor was never the Davidic king. Second, Christians must never expect a political ruler to enforce their faith or morals. The church must never become a political power broker.

> Whatever may be said for the Constantinian establishment of Christianity and for the cultural achievements of the medieval church in the West, the state-established church cannot be the norm of Christian ethics.[5]

Does this separation of church and state mean that ministers should not get involved in economic or political issues? What did Jesus teach about the role of the state? Although Christ lived under an imperial dictatorship, he accepted the authority of the state and recognized its legitimate functions (Matt. 17:24–25; Mark 12:17). Christ's classic statement about God and government came in response to the Pharisees' question about Roman taxes. Holding a Roman coin between his fingers, Jesus replied, "Give to Caesar what is Caesar's, and to God what is God's" (Matt. 22:21). Jesus rejected the Zealot way of violent revolution, not because God's kingdom is socially irrelevant but because the methods of the Zealots were not God's way.

In teaching about an ethical kingdom, Jesus continually challenged the social order of his time.[6] Jesus was crucified not for being a nice fellow but because he threatened the social and political powers of the first century, both Jewish and Roman. Jesus was radical in many of his actions: He identified with the poor, the oppressed, and the outcasts of his society. He outraged many by associating with women in public, treating them as equals. His concern for the weak was a challenge to Rome's unjust treatment of the "worthless" and Israel's many social distinctions.

Paul's realization that all are equal, that "there is neither Jew nor Greek, slave nor free, male nor female, for you are all one in Christ Jesus" (Gal. 3:28), became a first-century battle cry for breaking down the social walls that divided and destroyed human worth and dignity. The apostle to the Gentiles acknowledged civil authority as God ordained and worthy of respect and obedience (Rom.

13:1–7); however, his life reflected the words of Peter that God always comes before the will of the state (Acts 4:18–20).

How do these biblical teachings and theological understandings relate to the ethical conduct of clergy in society today? Some ministers may have the same hesitation as a seminary student who raised the question, "If neither Jesus nor early Christianity attacked the institution of slavery in the Roman world, why should we today be involved in social action?"

Two responses come to mind. First, as a result of Jesus' life and teachings, the early church did create a slave-free community. One of the first acts of slave owners, after becoming Christians, was to hold a service of manumission in which their slaves were freed, since masters and slaves were now "brothers and sisters in the Lord." Christian cemeteries of that era also made no distinction between the burial plots of slaves and free, as was normally done.[7]

A second reason for a lack of social involvement on the part of the early church was its lack of effective social and political influence. The world of Caesar was pagan, immoral, and hostile. Christianity was initially a very small minority sect, composing less than 1 percent of the population. Trying to exert Christian influence on an Empire that was already persecuting followers of Jesus would have been futile indeed.

In light of the teachings of the Bible and the witness of Christian tradition, modern disciples cannot withdraw from the arenas of politics and economics by saying that the world is too wicked for Christians to get involved. Neither can Christians turn their backs on the brokenness in society and say there is no need for the church to minister to any but its own.

At the same time, as moral leaders of the church, Christian ministers must be the first to admit that the way of the world is not the way of the cross. The Christian witness in the community must always be Christian. Whenever the church gets in a position of influence, because of its own economic wealth or political power, it is then most vulnerable to the twin temptations of greed and pride.

In short, the church is to be in the world, where God put it. Conversely, the world of material and spiritual resources is in the church, also because God put it there. Every minister, therefore, faces a basic ethical question in regard to social ministry and action: How can I be salt and light in the community without losing my savor and radiance?

Community Service

Clergy often have the competence and the professional freedom to engage in community service beyond the demands of the congregation. Public ministry can be a very satisfying but also seductively time-consuming enterprise.

A minister should never neglect pastoral duties to serve the general public. At the same time, a church usually affirms a minister's unique opportunity to benefit the community. A wise pastor will make sure that church duties never take a backseat to community service.

A minister can serve a community in numerous ways. From fund-raising to civic speeches, a church leader has the opportunity to represent the church and the Lord of the church in the community. The motive should always be love of neighbor and selfless service in the name of Christ. If a moral issue emerges, the pastor who has been involved in a positive way in community service will have greater credibility in supporting public morality.

Should a minister join a civic organization? What pastor has not felt the pressure from parishioners to become a member of the Lions, Kiwanis, or Civitan? Certainly advantages, both personal and professional, come with membership in a service club. Yet this decision remains largely a personal matter. Membership in a civic club is time-consuming, but it is often a good outlet for the semi-cloistered minister. Ultimately, no parson should ever join a group just to please parishioners.

How should a preacher respond to an invitation to serve on a public board, council, or agency? Unpaid service on a public advisory commission or city council is appropriate service. There is an important distinction, however, between volunteer positions and paid positions. A minister's power and influence should be used in the interest of the public as a whole, not just a preferred few. A minister should never be among those who are working to gain public advantage for vested interests. Public service for the clergy means commitment to the ethical principle of justice.[8]

Quite commonly, a minister is asked to pronounce an invocation at a public gathering. In such cases, a minister should recognize the religious pluralism of the audience and plan a prayer that is sensitive to all religious convictions.

Gaylord Noyce points out that in several respects, the clergy serve as "chaplains" to the society at large. As ministers invoke God's blessing and offer grace at meals, let them guard against that bland "civil religion" that implies God's acceptance of all things American, from labor unions to the Ku Klux Klan. It may be wise to turn down some invitations.[9]

As a religious authority, a minister is sometimes called on to teach in the public sector. Public schools and universities may invite the clergy to explain religious beliefs, discuss ethical values, or speak to a contemporary social issue. With the renewed interest in teaching moral values to students, ministers will probably have more opportunities to address groups about ethics. Again, a minister must respect the religious diversity in the audience and refrain from any hint of sectarianism.

Political Involvement

A remarkable increase in political involvement by clergy began in the 1960s. During the civil rights movement, many local pastors packed their bags and headed to Selma or Jackson or Washington, D.C. Some sought approval from their congregations; some did not. More than a few ended up in jail. The antiwar movement followed, receiving much of its verve and method from the civil rights marchers. By and large, the ministers who took part came from mainline denominations of a more liberal political persuasion. Conservative ministers criticized this effort as a "social gospel," claiming that the true gospel of Christ focuses on changing hearts, not society.

The movements of the 1960s and 1970s to effect social change were partially rooted in the social gospel movement of the late nineteenth and early twentieth centuries. Rapid industrialization in the late 1800s brought thousands to already overcrowded cities. Factory workers were exploited. Low wages, long hours, and horrendous working conditions increased poverty. Crime, prostitution, alcohol abuse, and subhuman living conditions infested urban slums.

Preachers in England and America cried out against these social ills. Religious leaders worked in the political arena to enact legislation to improve working conditions and protect the weak from economic exploitation. Although the social gospel movement was naive about human nature and utopian about society, it was a genuine attempt to get the church involved in applying the ethical teachings of Christ to modern society.[10]

In more recent times, evangelist Billy Graham upset many conservatives by refusing to tolerate segregated audiences in his crusades, as well as being a foremost advocate for nuclear disarmament and a response to world hunger. In the latter half of the twentieth century, a growing number of evangelicals became concerned about political responses to social needs, forming organizations such as JustLife, Sojourner Community, and Evangelicals for Social Action. Denominational social action committees, usually more progressive than their churches, have often been on the cutting edge of social issues.

An amazing turnaround occurred in the 1980s. Led by Jerry Falwell's Moral Majority, conservatives reversed the older evangelical opposition to political social action. A new force called the Religious Right brought fundamentalist American Christianity into politics. Although this movement was weakened by its penchant for civil religion and its tendency to baptize all conservative political views as "Christian," it did get conservative ministers involved in the political process.

A prime example of the political involvement of ministers during the latter half of the twentieth century is Martin Luther King Jr. On April 16, 1963, from a Birmingham jail, the Baptist minister wrote a letter to eight white clergymen who had declared his strategy disturbing and his tactics inflammatory.[11]

Martin Luther King, Jr., began his reply with "My Dear Fellow Clergymen." His closing remarks opened with "I hope this letter finds you strong in the faith." In between he explains why he has come to Birmingham from Atlanta, saying that as Paul went out from Tarsus, "I too am compelled to carry the gospel of freedom beyond my particular hometown. Like Paul, I must constantly respond to the Macedonian call for aid."[12]

King wrote that his greatest disappointment was with the leadership of the white churches. Among them, as ministers of the gospel, he had hoped to find his strongest support. Instead, he found the country "moving toward the exit of the twentieth century with a religious community largely adjusted to the status quo." He reported traveling through the South, admiring "her beautiful churches with their lofty spires pointing heavenward," but he mused, "Over and over again I have found myself asking, 'What kind of people worship here? Who is their God?' . . . Yes, I see the church as the body of Christ. But, oh! How we have blemished and scarred that body through social neglect and fear of being nonconformists." King concluded:

> If I have said anything in this letter that is an overstatement of the truth and is indicative of an unreasonable impatience, I beg you to forgive me. If I have said anything in this letter that is an understatement of the truth and is indicative of my having a patience that makes me patient with anything less than brotherhood, I beg God to forgive me.[13]

With this historical overview in mind, what can be said about the ethical obligations of a minister in regard to politics? Many ministers refuse to participate in politics for fear of corrupting their ministry. But Scripture has no such negative view. The word *politics* comes from the Greek term *politeusthe* and is quoted by Paul when he wrote, "Let your citizenship [*politeusthe*] be worthy of the gospel of Christ" (Phil. 1:27, author's translation).

At the level of Christian citizenship, the ethical church shepherd certainly will obey the law, pay taxes, pray for public officials, and participate in supporting good government. Beyond these basic duties to government, how politically active should a minister be? The public sometimes reacts to ministers "meddling" in community issues by appealing to the separation of church and state. Scripture does teach, by implication, that the two institutions should be separate (Matt. 22:21). Neither church nor state should be controlled by the other or dependent on the other. Yet that does not prohibit each from being open to the other's views so that respect and influence may flow between them. The First Amendment doctrine as articulated by Thomas Jefferson was never meant to separate God from government, nor does it mean that religion should have nothing to do with politics.[14]

Can a pastor run for public office or become actively involved in a political campaign? A tombstone in a cemetery in Palestine, Texas, reads, "J. D. DuPuy,

December 13, 1853–December 19, 1927. He loved relatives, friends and country; was fond of games and sports; believed in God and Christianity, but denounced political preachers."[15]

Partisan politics is definitely a high-risk avocation for a pastor. Noyce contends, "Style is part of the answer. The minister cannot [be partisan], if his or her way of politicking is primarily to condemn the other side as evil, un-Christian, or vicious."[16] The Vatican has written against all public office for its clergy. Historically, Protestant ministers have served in appointive or electoral office without losing their ministerial standing.

An active political life is the right of all citizens. At the same time, a minister must remember that the line separating personal life from vocation is blurred for the professional. The life of the church pastor is even more open and available to "clients" than that of other professionals, so much so that a member of the congregation on an opposing political side may take offense at a pastor's stance.

Many ministers focus on issues that are clearly moral rather than on partisan politics. Most congregations will support a pastor who takes a courageous stand on the basis of moral convictions. At the same time, the fear of disagreement among church members should never lead a minister to shirk ethical convictions in the name of church harmony. In the late 1930s, Martin Niemoller, a German Protestant minister, confessed his own failure:

> In Germany they came first for the communists, and I didn't speak up because I wasn't a communist. Then they came for the Jews, and I didn't speak up because I wasn't a Jew. Then they came for the trade unionists, and I didn't speak up because I wasn't a trade unionist. Then they came for the Catholics, and I didn't speak up because I was a Protestant. Then they came for me, but by that time, no one was left to speak up.[17]

Ministers who are active in politics should be careful about promoting civil religion. Richard Pierard defines the term as "the use of commonly accepted religious sentiments, concepts and symbols by the state for its own purposes . . . a blurring of religion and patriotism and of religious values with national values."[18]

A renowned television minister who is pastor of a church in Florida preached a patriotic sermon from the Book of Nehemiah. His message asserted that just as Israel was God's hope for the world, the United States is God's hope for the world today. The walls modern believers must help build are the Star Wars defense systems. To oppose funding for Star Wars is to oppose God's will for the protection of Christian America, he preached.

The modern minister must beware of confusing God and country. Civil religion is dangerous because it assumes that the United States is a Christian nation and Americans are God's chosen people. The temptation is to align

Americanism and Christianity with a certain political point of view. The modern prophet of God, like Nathan of ancient Israel, must always keep a healthy distance from the king in order to say, "You are the man!" (2 Sam. 12:7).

Should a minister be involved in organized protests and civil disobedience? In a pluralistic democracy such as ours, books will be written, films produced, and laws passed that offend Christian moral values. As citizens, we can protest in many ways: private and public conversation, letter writing, contacting public officials, picketing, boycotting, and civil disobedience. With such a range of options, how does a minister determine what is acceptable and what is best?

In an editorial in *Christianity Today*, Terry Muck urged Christians to ask four vital questions before joining an organized protest:

1. How serious is the issue?
2. How reasonable and clear are the goals of the protest?
3. How effective will the protest be and with what side effects?
4. What will be the long-range consequences?[19]

Christian social action often fails because these questions are never raised.

For example, television reporters asked abortion protestors in front of a clinic why they were staging a sit-in. Answers ranged from "rescuing babies" to "changing abortion laws" to "raising public consciousness" to "closing down the clinics" to "helping mothers seek other alternatives." Obviously, confusion over the purpose of a protest limits its effectiveness. Muck asks, "Will the public perception of what we are doing through the protest so poison people's perceptions of Christians that the cause of Christ will be hurt?"[20]

Beyond these initial questions about the practicality and prudence of organized protests is a larger one. Is civil disobedience ever right for Christians? On the one hand, the Bible instructs believers to obey the government (Rom. 13:1) and to "accept the authority of every human institution" (1 Peter 2:13 NRSV). Scripture teaches that God instituted government for society's good—to maintain order, punish evil, and provide services to the citizenry (Rom. 13:1–7). A Christian is to be a supportive citizen (1 Tim. 2:2). At the same time, the Word of God lauds people who were not submissive: Rahab (Josh. 6:22–25), Hebrew midwives (Exod. 1:16–22), Daniel (Daniel 6), and Peter and John (Acts 4; 5:12–42).

How should ministers reconcile these seeming contradictions? If the state requires obedience to a law that clearly violates the higher law of God, then it may be God's will to resist. Those who become lawbreakers in the name of God do so in various ways by blocking access to abortion clinics, withholding income tax as a protest against militarism, offering sanctuary to political refugees, and interfering with environmental polluters. Civil disobedience is always a strategy of last resort and can be justified only if the following criteria are met:

- The law being resisted is clearly unjust and contrary to God's will.
- Legal means to change the law have been exhausted.
- The act of civil disobedience is public, not clandestine.
- There is some likelihood of success.
- Participants are willing to accept the penalty for breaking the law.[21]

Civil disobedience is different from revolution. True civil disobedience affirms the authority of the state by emphasizing nonviolent resistance and by submitting to arrest.

> It is inconsistent for the civilly disobedient, after breaking the law to make their point, to then flee arrest, jump bail, hide from the authorities, or harbor personal bitterness as the state proceeds with its vocation to order.[22]

A minister should always work for justice. Civil disobedience may be permissible in unique circumstances, but even then it is an exception to the norm of lawful obedience to government. The purpose of such law breaking should be to raise public consciousness, educate, and focus public concern on an unjust law.

Is it ever appropriate for a minister to endorse a political candidate? In a particularly passionate presidential election, a nominee visited the worship services of the largest church of a leading Protestant denomination. After the service, the renowned pastor stood on the front steps of the church and endorsed the candidate for president. The minister defended his actions, stating that outside the sanctuary he had the right as a private citizen to support whomever he chose. The newspapers, however, did not identify him as a private citizen but as the pastor of the church on whose steps he stood.

Political candidates yearn to list the names of local pastors among their supporters, for religious leaders garner widespread support among their constituency. Ministers often find it difficult not to give public support to politicians who are good candidates and who take a strong stand on crucial moral issues.

In private conversation, a minister is free to share political convictions if he or she so chooses. Public endorsement, on the other hand, is rarely (if ever) the right thing to do. It alienates members who disagree and is undoubtedly a misuse of a pastor's position of power and influence. The conscientious prophet of God must continue to speak to moral issues, but he or she must resist undue entanglement with a particular politician or party. This guideline will protect the cleric from present pressures and future embarrassments.

Given a 1992 ruling,[23] churches and other tax-exempt charitable organizations should think twice before endorsing or opposing political candidates. To maintain tax exemption, churches must not support or oppose candidates for public office. Individual ministers and employees may become involved in campaigns as long as no resources, personnel, or facilities of the organization are involved and as long as the individual makes it clear that he or she is not acting on behalf of the organization.[24]

Public Morality

Richard John Neuhaus is alarmed about what he calls "the naked public square" in America. By that he means "the result of political doctrine and practice that would exclude religion and religiously-grounded values from the conduct of public business."[25] If Neuhaus is correct in his belief that public policy has been divorced from religious belief, what should the contemporary clergy do to influence public morality?

Prophetic Proclamation

One obvious way ministers contribute to public morality is through prophetic proclamation. Being prophetic involves more than vigorous preaching, angry denunciation of social vices, or a therapeutic venting of frustrations over the sinful conditions of society. The biblical prophet spoke for God, delivering a proclamation of God's concern for the unborn and the aged, the poor and the powerful, the environment and the economy, health care and racial equality, personal morality and social righteousness.[26]

Not many years ago, while one of us served as pastor of a downtown Baptist church in a large metropolitan city, a community crisis arose. Unknown to the business and professional leaders, a state senator secretly met with the president of the chamber of commerce and his executive committee to get their support for legislation he was sponsoring. Two days later, the senator introduced a bill that would legalize casino gambling in this community bordering Mexico. Rumors spread that organized crime was involved, for this urban sprawl of over two million people would be an ideal international location for money laundering.

Immediate response from the religious community was vital. Within a few hours, ministers representing several major Protestant denominations, a Jewish rabbi, and an envoy from the Roman Catholic archbishop met at First Baptist Church to construct a joint statement. Before the day was over, a press conference was called for the purpose of reading a statement prepared and signed by all the clergy. The religious community in this city unified to oppose a threat to the moral and social well-being of its citizens.

The next seven days were hectic. On the Sunday following the state senator's surprise legislation, the pastor of First Baptist preached a televised sermon on this moral issue. A large audience from the community listened and joined the opposition to the gambling legislation. The *El Paso Times* claimed that the unified response of the religious community, coupled with the televised sermon, which was widely quoted in the media, were among the major reasons this legislation was quickly defeated.

Prophetic preaching on ethical issues builds a foundation for Christian involvement in community moral issues. A minister may be hesitant to address moral issues in sermons because of their variety and complexity. The potential negative reaction of the congregation is another obstacle. In spite of these difficulties, the faithful proclaimer of God's Word will preach on ethical issues because of the needs of people, the demands of the gospel, and the example of the prophets and Jesus.

Before a minister preaches on ethical issues, a certain amount of preparation is required.[27] A prophet who speaks for God must know and understand God's character, for ethical preaching must be rooted in the moral nature of Jehovah. The proclaimer must also be an ethical model who correctly applies and interprets the teachings of Scripture.

Those who declare a message from God on a moral issue must also know their limits. Because most ethical issues are extremely complicated, thorough research is a must. A preacher may discover that some subjects require more time and study than is available. Ministers should also remember that not every moral problem requires a pastoral comment.

Three Greek words summarize the theological principles on which ethical preaching stands: *kērygma* (gospel message), *koinōnia* (fellowship), and *kairos* (time). The first word defines what to preach from: the Christian *kērygma*, the good news of the gospel. Focusing on the biblical story gives a preacher spiritual vision and corrects cultural blind spots. The second word defines whom to preach through: the Christian *koinōnia*, the people of God. A pastor speaks not only to the church but also for the church as God's moral witness to the world. The last word, *kairos*, indicates to a minister when to preach. Ethical preaching requires a fine sense of timing. One pastor listed five key ethical preaching moments: when the issue is (1) in the canon, (2) on the calendar, (3) before the congregation, (4) an imminent crisis, or (5) a deep conviction.[28]

Charles Swindoll once recalled the words of Wilbur Reece, which may express our generation's reluctance to face the demands of discipleship and the ethical implications of the gospel:

I would like to buy $3 worth of God—not enough to explode my soul or disturb my sleep, but just enough to equal a cup of warm milk or a snooze in the sunshine. I don't want enough of God to make me love a black man or pick beets with a migrant. I want ecstasy, not transformation. I want the warmth of the womb, not a new birth. I want about a pound of the eternal in a paper sack. I would like to buy $3 worth of God, please.[29]

Organized Participation

Another way a church prophet addresses public morality is through organized participation in addressing community needs. Why were the churches and ministers mentioned earlier able to unify the city against the threat of casino gambling? One of the major reasons for their success was the involvement of the ministers and their churches in the community before the crisis arose. For years, the churches had sponsored ministries in the city and responded to a host of social needs. Downtown churches had developed a comprehensive benevolence program that included counseling, food assistance, shelter, job assistance, and literacy classes. Along the international border, churches sponsored medical clinics where doctors and nurses gave of their time to minister to the sick. Several churches sponsored an orphanage in Mexico. During winter months, clothes, blankets, and medicine were donated and taken into Mexico for distribution. Pastors who led their churches to minister to social needs in the community earned the right to be heard when a new moral issue arose.

The first contact of Christian love with social action is what John Stott calls a "simple uncomplicated compassion," which spontaneously serves wherever need arises.[30] The story of the good Samaritan (Luke 10:25–37) could have had a second chapter. Suppose that every time the Samaritan walked the road from Jerusalem to Jericho he found injured people who had been robbed by bandits. If he did nothing to prevent the robberies along this highway, would his love have been perfect?

Genuine love often motivates a person to engage in social action. Ernst Troeltsch argues that this is what happened in the ancient church. Though primarily concerned with social problems affecting its own life, the early church soon realized that those problems (such as slavery and injustice) had to do with social institutions that were part of the state. Thus, the church was forced to confront the state with the demands of the gospel of Jesus Christ.[31]

Moral Leadership

A key ingredient in a church's response to public morality is the moral leadership of its minister. The issues are seldom simple. The pastor may hear two voices when faced with an issue of public morality. One voice is that of the prophet, who calls for a faithful witness; the other is the pastoral voice pleading for church unity. An ethical pastor never backs away from controversy, but he or she also has a mandate to nurture the growth of a congregation—growth in faith, in compassionate concern, and in prophetic witness.[32]

According to Richard Bondi, the minister as a moral leader must live on the edge but remain connected to the center. In a sense, a church leader is "suspended" between center and edge.

> The edge and the center are paired in a difficult bond. There is movement and vitality on the edge, but power and stability at the center. Leaders who live only at the edge can become detached from their communities and unable to lead, whereas leaders who commandeer the center can end up protecting its interests from the dangerous opportunities of the edge. Nonetheless, trying to live always at the center is the more dangerous temptation, for stability without movement leads to stagnation and eventual collapse.[33]

Pronouncements from a denomination can support a pastor's moral leadership. A church should be a community of moral discourse and, as such, should study and deliberate convention resolutions and statements by church groups on ethical issues such as abortion, nuclear arms, ecology, homosexuality, and the AIDS crisis.[34]

Ultimately, for a pastor-prophet to lead a church into community ministry and social action, certain essentials are needed.[35] First, there must be a free pulpit. Though this freedom to preach God's message is assumed when a pastor is called, it must often be clarified by the clergy. The Spirit must be free to speak through God's messenger, or else the people will perish in the wilderness for lack of manna from God. At the same time, a minister as a moral leader is part of a covenant community and always represents that larger body. A prophetic, public ministry should never be isolated from dialogue with the company of believers, whose counsel and support is vital. This reality creates several obligations. The minister must give pastoral care of the congregation top priority. The basis for social action must always be theological; it should not be based on the latest political or social fad. The pastor needs to recognize that he or she may not have all the answers and that laypersons have moral convictions worthy of respect. Often their insight may be superior to that of the clergy. Denominational pronouncements must be seriously received. Finally, the needs of people in the community have a claim on a pastor, as they did on Jesus when he announced his ministry:

> The Spirit of the Lord is on me,
>   because he has anointed me
>   to preach good news to the poor.
> He has sent me to proclaim freedom for the prisoners
>   and recovery of sight for the blind,
> to release the oppressed,
>   to proclaim the year of the Lord's favor.
>
>   Luke 4:18–19

Legal Responsibilities

A prominent minister in northern Florida was arrested as he stepped off the plane after vacationing in the Caribbean. His crime—failing to report a confidential conversation with one of his parishioners. A church member reported to the pastor that her son had been molested by the church janitor. Because he had only a few hours before leaving the country, the pastor counseled the woman to wait until he returned before doing anything. He would have time to investigate the matter after his return.

After a few days, the woman decided to go to the authorities. Because failure to report incidents of child abuse is a crime in that state, investigation of the incident included arresting the minister. Lawsuits against the church were also pending. The affair was so alarming to local churches and ministers that the Baptist Health Care Center in Pensacola arranged a two-day conference titled "Clergy and Ethical Dilemmas: Ethics, Law, and Care" that featured law enforcement officials, lawyers, and an ethics teacher from a nearby seminary. Needless to say, the conference was well attended by ministers from throughout the region.

Ours is an increasingly lawsuit-prone society. Gone is the day when churches and preachers were immune to legal action. Government agencies are scrutinizing churches for infractions of tax laws. Clergy malpractice suits are increasing. Such suits usually involve allegations against ministers and churches in one of five areas: counseling, sexual misconduct, defamation, breach of confidentiality, and child care issues. The term *malpractice* means falling below the established standards of conduct for a particular profession.

Counseling

Oliver Thomas, former counsel for the Baptist Joint Committee on Public Affairs (BJCPA), noted that clergy malpractice "is one of the most challenging legal concepts to face church and state in recent years."[36] In a paper presented to the University of Virginia Law School, Thomas discussed a number of key issues related to clergy malpractice suits.

The watershed Nally case in 1980 involved the suicide of a bright young student who told his minister-counselors (none of whom were trained therapists) that he intended to commit suicide. The counselors neither informed the family nor tried to get Nally to a psychiatrist. The parents sued, alleging both clergy malpractice and outrageous conduct. Ultimately, the appeals court decided that it was wrong for the court to interfere in the counseling activities of the church; setting standards of competence and of training for church counselors would be excessive entanglement of church and state.

The Supreme Court of Colorado has similarly ruled against clergy malpractice, stating that the tort (alleged crime) is fundamentally flawed on two counts. First, upholding this lawsuit would secularize various forms of sectarian religious counseling entitled to constitutional protection. Second, it would deter some ministers, priests, and rabbis from engaging in marriage counseling in order to avoid liability.[37] With one exception, numerous other state courts have rejected the clergy malpractice theory, namely, that any minimal standard for clergy can be set.

The Ohio Court of Appeals, however, has indicated that clergy malpractice suits may be filed against pastoral counselors. The case involved a couple who sought marital counseling from a Seventh-Day Adventist pastor who induced the wife to engage in sex with him against her will. Thomas observed:

> When a couple is in marriage counseling and the counselor begins having sex with one of the counselees, the counselor should expect to be held liable. The fact that the counselor happens to be a minister is irrelevant. These cases, however, should not be termed "clergy malpractice."[38]

Should a church pastor give up counseling for fear of litigation? Ministers who have had little formal training in the field should certainly question their ability to counsel parishioners adequately. Mistakes are sometimes made because a pastor knows neither the basic techniques of counseling nor the legal and ethical obligations.

In this era of specialization, it seems wise for the average minister to refer all serious counseling needs to a trained professional. If a minister plans to specialize in church-related counseling, he or she should receive training in the discipline from a seminary, university, or accredited entity. It is just as unethical to assume competence in counseling when one has no training as it is to exploit a person in counseling.

Sexual Misconduct

As Thomas noted, ministers are not immune from all criminal liability, nor should they be.[39] The rash of lawsuits involving sexual improprieties in recent years should not be defended on First Amendment grounds, for no bona fide religious organization holds beliefs that allow seduction, rape, or other sexual misconduct.

For nonconsensual acts committed by a minister, sexual assault or sexual battery is a possible charge. For consensual acts, ministers have been held liable in three ways: alienation of affection,[40] breach of fiduciary duty or confidential relations,[41] and intentional infliction of emotional distress or outrageous conduct.[42]

In 1999, a minister of students at a large Baptist church in Austin, Texas, was charged with two counts of sexual assault of a child and indecency with a child, both second-degree felonies. He was later convicted and is now serving a prison sentence. The church and its pastor were sued by the parents for failing to prevent this abuse "after being warned of a similar incident involving the minister at another church."[43]

Defamation

Second in frequency to claims of sexual misconduct by ministers are those involving the publication of false or defamatory statements, usually arising out of church disciplinary proceedings.[44] Like the press, churches and clergy enjoy a qualified privilege in regard to defamation, if the communication is made in the exercise of ministry and without malice. The privilege can be lost if a minister's statements concern nonmembers or former members[45] or if defamatory statements are made outside or beyond the membership of the church, as in the *Gorman v. Swaggart* appeal between two Louisiana evangelists.[46]

Confidentiality and Privacy

A fourth type of ministerial misconduct suit involves the disclosure of confidential communications and other private facts.[47] A pastor should inform all counselees that confidentiality may be broken if doing so (1) would prevent a person from harming himself or herself, (2) would prevent a person from harming others, (3) would prevent a crime, or (4) is required by law.

All fifty states now grant a statutory privilege for certain information communicated to clergy, which in most states cannot be breached except by waiver from the communicant or a special law. (Some states, for example, require ministers to report incidents of suspected child abuse even if the information is received through confidential communications.)

Several limitations apply, however. Only a select group of persons are protected by the privilege, usually those who have been licensed, commissioned, or ordained by a religious body. In addition, only certain communications are privileged, such as those in which the congregant is seeking spiritual advice. Casual conversations or business discussions are not covered. The duty of confidentiality may also be limited by (1) statutory provisions, (2) the doctrine and practices of the religious organization involved, and (3) the common law duty to warn third parties of imminent bodily harm. In some places, ministers are given the discretion to decide if and when the privilege applies.

Violation of privacy is a second claim in confidential information lawsuits. Three types of privacy violations apply to clergy: unreasonable publicity given to another's private life, unreasonable intrusion upon another's seclusion, and publicity that places another in a false light.[48] The first violation is the one most likely to be filed against a minister and simply requires (1) public disclosure, (2) private facts, and (3) a matter that is highly offensive and objectionable to a reasonable person. Truth is not a defense.

In the case of Marian Guinn involving church discipline proceeding from alleged sexual misconduct, the church insisted on bringing the matter before the entire congregation. The facts were also publicized to area churches. Although liability was imposed on the Church of Christ at Collinsville for statements about the plaintiff publicized after her resignation from the church, the Supreme Court recognized that the church was shielded from liability by the First Amendment as long as she was a member. By joining the church, Guinn consented to the church's discipline.[49]

As in the case of defamation, a minister's privilege to disclose private facts is not absolute and may be lost if the minister intends harm to the plaintiff, publicizes the information to people outside the church, or continues to publicize the information after the plantiff has resigned membership.

Unreasonable intrusion upon another's seclusion does not require publicity but only an invasion of privacy that would be considered highly offensive to a reasonable person. One minister who entered a plaintiff's home under the guise of helping the family through counseling, when his true motive was to harm the couple through information obtained, was held liable.[50] To avoid liability a minister should make sure that permission is obtained before entering a house or private area and that the purpose of the visit is neither underhanded nor secretive.

The final type of privacy violation likely to affect ministers is publicity that places a person in a false light. Conviction in such cases requires (1) that the publicity be highly offensive to a reasonable person and (2) that the minister acted intentionally or with reckless disregard for the truth. Making false accusations about a person in a sermon is not only unethical but could also result in a day in court.

Child Care

Child care is a sensitive area in the courts today. A mother brought suit against a Memphis church and its staff, claiming that her child had been sexually molested in the church day care center. An aggressive prosecutor spearheaded the case, which dragged on for over five years. The church was finally exonerated of all charges, but the legal fees alone cost the congregation over $500,000.

Churches must know the law, do proper background checks, screen all who work with children, and carefully supervise all child care programs. Church ministers are obligated to be familiar with the law. Many states, for example, have strict regulations about reporting any evidence of child abuse discovered by a teacher or caregiver. A church is also responsible for all its organizational activities involving children: Sunday school, youth meetings, outings, and study groups. If violations occur, the burden of proof is on church leaders to prove they did everything humanly possible to protect the young and the vulnerable from mistreatment.

Attorney William Colbert told participants in the Church and the Law Conference at Stetson University that church leaders are not helpless in today's lawsuit-prone society. He listed several preventive measures as examples:

- Churches should have written policies to guard against charges of inadequate supervision.
- Churches should be alert to hazards and do adequate maintenance to guard against grounds and building liability.
- Churches should use common sense when planning activities. Parent-consent and waiver-of-liability forms ensure that parents know what their children are doing, but they do not absolve the church of responsibility.
- Churches should have church-owned vehicles inspected often and kept in top condition. Drivers should be licensed and have good driving records and insurance coverage.
- To guard against employee negligence, churches should check references and arrest records, use a written application, have job descriptions, and dismiss any employee not doing the job.
- In sexual harassment cases, it is not what is actually said or done but how the victim perceives it.
- To guard against inadequate insurance coverage, churches should (1) know what their assets are and what replacement costs would be, (2) identify potential liabilities, (3) be sure everyone is covered, (4) add a rider covering ministerial counseling liability, personal property on church premises, and special needs such as disability and accident risks.[51]

Even if all precautions are taken, church officials should be aware that lawsuits are increasingly common against ministers and churches.[52] At the present time, professional liability insurance for ministers is inexpensive, while the costs of litigation can be enormous. Adequate church insurance includes professional liability insurance for every staff minister.

The church is in the world. The modern minister cannot make his church into a medieval monastery where he busies himself with spiritual exercises. The biblical mandate from Christ is to be salt and light, to penetrate society with the purifying and illuminating gospel. As both pastor and prophet, the contemporary cleric must be involved in the human community, which was created for God's glory. Life in community for the called of God will probably include community service, political participation, legal responsibility, and promotion of public morality. In every one of these areas, a minister's ethical practice will be tested. Involvement in the community is risky—some would see it as a threat to ministry. The minister, however, has a unique opportunity to bring salt and light into a decaying and darkened world.

An old Scottish professor liked to say that there were just three qualifications for the ministry: the grace of God, knowledge of Scripture in the original languages, and gumption. The first, he said, is available if we pray for it; the second can be ours if we work for it; but the last is a gift of nature. Neither prayer nor labor could produce it.[53] For the minister to be ethically involved in the community in which he or she lives and serves requires ample grace, adequate knowledge of Scripture, and no small amount of gumption.

We have now arrived at our final transition. The first two chapters established the minister's vocation as a called-of-God profession and the importance of a cleric's character, conduct, and moral vision in making good moral choices. With this foundation we then explored the ethical obligations of the church minister in relation to his or her personal life, congregation, colleagues, and community. The final two chapters examine a critical problem in ministerial ethics, clergy sexual abuse, and introduce a practical possibility—that of applying all that has been learned thus far in a ministerial code of ethics.

Suggested Reading

Gushee, David P., ed. *Christians and Politics: Beyond the Culture Wars.* Grand Rapids: Baker, 2000.

Jerisild, Paul T., and Dale A. Johnson, eds. *Moral Issues and Christian Response.* New York: Holt, Rinehart, & Winston, 1998.

Mott, Stephan Charles. *Biblical Ethics and Social Change.* New York: Oxford University Press, 1982.

Niebuhr, H. Richard. *Christ and Culture.* New York: Harper & Row, 1951.

Smedes, Lewis. *Mere Morality.* Grand Rapids: Eerdmans, 1983.

7

A Major Ethical Issue

Clergy Sexual Abuse

The sexual abuse of parishioners by clergy is a major ethical problem. One example, recorded by Marie Fortune, is the story of Peter Donovan, pastor of First Church Newburg (names and places have been changed). Formal charges were lodged against the minister by six women. Donovan's misconduct included sexual abuse of counselees and employees, misuse of the pastoral office to manipulate members, verbal threats to intimidate victims, and rape. He abused as many as forty-five women.[1]

Incidents such as this one have become all too common. Numerous studies during the past two decades support the research of pastoral counselor G. Lloyd Rediger, who contends that 10 percent of clergy are guilty of sexual malfeasance, and another 15 percent are approaching the line of misconduct.[2]

In 2002, the Religion Newswriters Association named the abuse scandal that shook the Catholic Church the top story of the year and Cardinal Bernard Law the top newsmaker. He resigned following a year of controversy regarding clergy sexual abuse. The American Catholic hierarchy also received the association's "Into the Darkness Award," a designation given to organizations that try to hide information from the public.[3]

The wave of sex scandals engulfing the Roman Catholic clergy during 2002 touched nearly every American diocese and involved more than twelve hundred priests. These priests are known to have abused more than four thousand minors during the past six decades, according to an extensive *New York Times* survey of documented cases of sexual abuse by priests.[4]

The Roman Catholic sexual abuse scandal sent the public's view of clergy to its lowest point ever in 2002, 12 points lower than the previous year's Gallup rating. Asked to rate the honesty and ethics of twenty-one professions, just 52 percent of Americans gave high marks to clergy, down from 64 percent in 2001.[5]

The problem of clergy sexual abuse is not just a Catholic issue—the problem extends to Protestant denominations as well. Studies have shown no differences in its frequency by denomination, region, theology, or institutional structure. Mainline Protestant denominations have generally taken the earliest and most aggressive measures to prevent it and fundamentalist churches the least, according to Gary Schoener, a Minneapolis psychotherapist who has handled more than two thousand cases of clergy abuse during the past ten years.[6] The crisis among clergy has revealed an uneven record of response that ranges from the Episcopal Church's aggressive and detailed policies to the Southern Baptist Convention's widespread lack of written standards.

The Roman Catholic response has varied dramatically, partly because each of the 195 American dioceses operates independently. Among Protestants, a landmark case in Colorado involved a woman who accused the Episcopal diocese and the presiding bishop of covering up the sexual misconduct of her priest. In 1991, when the jury found the church liable and ordered church leaders to pay her $1.2 million, "that changed the Protestant game completely," says Schoener, "because it opened the door for higher-ups to be responsible." After the Colorado case, national Episcopal church officers were told by their insurers to develop policies on misconduct and to complete initial training in sexual abuse prevention by 1993.[7]

National policies regarding clergy sexual misconduct have been adopted by most mainline denominations, including Methodists, Presbyterians, and Lutherans. Reformed and Conservative Judaism has recently developed policies, while Orthodox Judaism has moved slower.

Decentralized denominations such as the Southern Baptist Convention and many evangelical bodies have no national policies, leaving each individual church to establish its own guidelines.[8] Sexual misconduct is routinely covered up in these settings. Dee Ann Miller, a victims' advocate and author of books on the topic, has recorded complaints from victims in thirty states, half of them involving minors. Church officials largely have not been responsive.[9]

Through numerous interviews within his own profession, psychologist Peter Rutter has brought to light the power dynamic often at work in abusive relationships. This connection to power makes misconduct mainly a male problem. Rutter asserts that 96 percent of sexual exploitation by professionals is by a man in power who capitalizes on a woman's trust.[10] The focus of this chapter, therefore, is the sexual exploitation of females by male ministers.

Naming professional sexual abuse the "forbidden zone," Rutter defines misconduct as any sexual contact that occurs within the framework of a professional relationship of trust (such as that involving a counselor or a pastor). Thus, such abuse includes any contact or action intended to arouse erotic interest, whether there is touching or not.[11]

Seminary professors Stanley Grenz and Roy Bell assert that sexual misconduct in the pastorate is a grave betrayal of trust that operates in two directions.

> It is a violation of a sacred sexual trust, marring the beautiful picture God has given of the relationship of Christ and the church. And it is a violation of a power trust, abusing the privilege of the pastoral position with which the ordained leader has been endowed by the church and its Lord.[12]

Sexual exploitation ordinarily occurs in an atmosphere of enforced silence. This silence is maintained not only by the participants but also by colluders who are unwilling to breach the dictated censorship. The director of an organization for survivors of clergy abuse writes that the initial response of church officials is to hush the victim and cover up the sexual abuse, which often continues unchecked for years.[13] Rutter insists that this "code of silence" must be broken.[14] A major step toward breaking the silence is understanding the nature and the extent of the problem.

The Scope of Clergy Sexual Abuse

For years, congregants and the wider community assumed that ministers were persons of integrity who were worthy of respect and trust. Yet from King David's abuse of Bathsheba to televangelist Jim Bakker's mistreatment of Jessica Hahn to Rev. Jesse Jackson's admission of adultery and a child born out of wedlock, the reputation of spiritual leaders has been tainted by sexual scandal.

Most ministers begin their vocation with good intentions. Yet as they face sexual temptation and the enticement of power, some succumb. When they fall, they land hard and injure others.

During the past two decades, the media has profiled case after case of ministers, priests, televangelists, and other religious leaders who were guilty of clergy sexual abuse. Ethical failure in ministry has become so prevalent that insurance companies are reevaluating their coverage of clergy, sometimes excluding coverage altogether.[15]

Clergy sexual abuse is not new. The Old Testament records the story of the sons of the priest Eli who misused their position to engage in sexual exploitation: "They slept with the women who served at the entrance to the Tent of

Meeting" (1 Sam. 2:22). In the first century of Christianity, the apostle Paul warned church leaders about the dangers of sexual sin (1 Cor. 6:9–20; Eph. 5:3; 1 Thess. 4:3; 1 Tim. 3:2). Early church leaders such as Jerome, Tertullian, and Augustine instructed pastors about sexual misbehavior.

Today, the problem is especially acute for the Roman Catholic Church, which not only has struggled with scandal and lawsuits but has also lost almost one-fourth of its active priests due to sexual and marital reasons.[16] Protestants are in no way immune to the problem. Therapists and some of the nation's foremost authorities, such as Gary Schoener and Ellen Leupeker of the Walk-In Counseling Center in Minneapolis, confirm that Protestant victims far outnumber Catholic victims.[17]

The first and most important element in addressing the problem is to admit that this evil happens. To deny or minimize the sexual exploitation of parishioners by ministers is to give tacit approval. Statistical studies are necessarily limited by the willingness of anonymous participants to report honestly, but even so, the numbers are alarming.

Two seminal studies in 1984 reported that 12 percent of ministers had engaged in sexual intercourse with congregants. Thirty-seven percent in one study and 39 percent in the other acknowledged sexually inappropriate behavior.[18] In addition, one of the two reports that surveyed clergy in four denominations (Presbyterian, Assembly of God, Methodist, Episcopal) found that over 76 percent knew of a minister who had engaged in sexual contact with a church member.[19]

In 1988, *Leadership* magazine was commissioned by Christianity Today to do a survey that was published under the title "How Common Is Pastoral Indiscretion?" Of three hundred pastors who responded to the inquiry, 18 percent admitted to having had some sort of sexual contact with someone other than their spouse. Of that number, 17 percent admitted to having had sexual contact with a counselee, 5 percent with a ministerial staff member, 8 percent with a church staff member, 9 percent with a church member in a teaching/leadership role, and 30 percent with "someone else in the congregation."[20]

In 1993, the *Journal of Pastoral Care* reported the results of a survey of senior Southern Baptist pastors designed to identify factors contributing to sexual misconduct. From fifteen thousand churches in six southern states, one thousand were randomly selected. The number of individual pastors who had engaged in sexual behavior "inappropriate for a minister" (judged by the individual pastors) was 14.1 percent. Roughly 70 percent had knowledge of other ministers who had engaged in inappropriate sexual contact with members, and 24.2 percent of the group reported that they had counseled a woman who claimed to have had sexual contact with a minister.[21]

More recent surveys by religious journals and research institutes continue to support these findings. The *Journal of Psychology and Theology* reported in 1995 that incidents of sexual abuse by missionaries can be found in almost every country in which missionaries are working.[22] *U.S. News & World Report* cited a nationwide study that found that "1 in 4 members of the clergy reported having some kind of sexual contact with someone other than their spouse, and more than 1 in 10 said they had committed adultery."[23] A disturbing aspect of all research is that the rate of incidence of abuse among clergy generally exceeds the client-professional rate for physicians and psychologists.[24]

Reports also reveal long-standing sexual liaisons, homosexual relations, abuse of children, seduction of youth, inappropriate touching, and verbal and nonverbal sexual innuendoes. Rediger identified six specifics of what he calls sexual malfeasance:

1. Sexual intercourse with persons outside a marriage covenant. This includes rape, a consenting adult, children, and incapacitated persons.
2. Oral sex with persons outside a marriage covenant.
3. Unwanted or inappropriate physical touch outside a marriage covenant. This includes genital fondling, foreplay, and any physical contact not appropriate to pastoral ministry or normal friendship.
4. Physical-sensual displays of the body or titillation of senses in ways suggestive of inappropriate sex.
5. The use of pornography, individually or with others, in ways intended to stimulate erotic fantasies of inappropriate sexual behavior.
6. Verbal and visual contact with another person that implies or demands inappropriate sexual response.[25]

The Nature of Clergy Sexual Abuse

Most people are astounded by the scope of clergy sexual abuse—it has reached horrific proportions. Equally astounding is the nature of the problem. In most cases, well over 90 percent, sexual abuse in the Protestant church occurs between a male minister and a female parishioner.[26] When a clergyman exploits his privileged position for personal sexual satisfaction—whether by seemingly innocent innuendoes, obnoxious harassment, or actual physical contact—he has strayed into the "forbidden zone."

Clergy sexual misconduct is a violation of the integrity of the pastoral office, a betrayal of ordination vows. It is also a betrayal of trust between a pastor and parishioners that involves both an abuse of sexuality and an abuse of power.[27]

Betrayal of Sexual Trust

God created boundaries for sexual expression that reveal and support the intended purpose and meaning of human sexuality. Only within the context of heterosexual marriage can sexual intercourse express the proper intent of the sex act: unconditional, covenantal love. Sexual expression is meant to be both a symbol of mutual commitment and a celebration of the "one flesh" marital relationship (Matt. 19:4–6).

The sex act also carries meaning when practiced outside the context of marriage, but not the meaning God intends. Extramarital sexual relations lack unconditional commitment and all too easily become an expression of self-gratification, exploitation, and infidelity. Outside the boundaries of the marriage covenant, sex actually works to deny the intended meaning of the act. In such cases, sexual intercourse becomes bonding without permanency, a nonbinding covenant, and a false declaration about the depth of the relationship.[28]

For a married pastor, the basic commitment must be to marital fidelity. For a single minister, sexual faithfulness begins with an equally important commitment to sexual abstinence before marriage. Some have tried to put a positive face on certain extramarital sexual activities, but any intentional sexual contact outside the boundaries of marriage violates the marital bond and constitutes adultery (Matt. 5:27–28).

Thus, sexual misconduct by clergy is a distortion of human sexuality—a betrayal of sexual trust. For an offending pastor, whether single or married, the betrayal is a violation of God's intention for humanity from the beginning (Gen. 2:18–25).

Betrayal of Power Trust

Clergy sexual exploitation is not primarily about sex. It is an abuse of power expressed in a highly destructive sexual manner. One writer concludes that the problem "is less about sex and more about power. It has less to do with sexual misconduct such as adultery, and more to do with exploiting one's professional position for personal gain."[29] Only when the power aspect is accepted can the church stop engaging in denial and collusion and become a place of authentic power and healing.

Every minister is a symbol of religious authority. By virtue of the pastoral office, a minister interprets religious truth, the meaning of life, the way of faith, and even the reality of God. When the power of a pastor's presence through ministry is added to that status, the special influence a minister holds among his or her congregants becomes evident.

For example, in pastoral counseling, a female church member brings her intimate, wounded, vulnerable, or undeveloped parts. Often the problems are closely tied to her sexuality. Whatever the cause of her wounds, she comes to her minister seeking acceptance, self-worth, and emotional support. Ultimately, she seeks healing. A special bond of trust develops between her and her pastor, which may lead to more openness and more vulnerability. Peter Rutter notes that "even a woman with a firm sense of sexual boundaries often stops guarding them in order that her inner self may be seen and known by this healer."[30]

Motivated by his own needs, a minister may move this relationship into the sexual sphere, seeking his own "healing." Whatever the motive, through sexual contact a pastoral counselor exploits a congregant's vulnerability, violates her trust, and meets his own needs at her expense. Karen Lebacqz and Ronald Barton accurately note that this sexual contact "revictimizes her, repeating patterns from her past, and keeps her from recognizing and claiming her own strength apart from a man."[31]

While this scenario describes a typical case of clergy sexual abuse, at times the sexual contact is initiated by the congregant. Or perhaps the sexual contact is by mutual consent. Most male ministers have encountered seductive behavior in unstable members, and the story of a colleague who has left his spouse because of sexual involvement with a church member is not uncommon. Yet most authorities insist that any sexual contact between a minister and a congregant involves an abuse of power. Whatever the circumstances, sexual behavior by a minister (who always occupies the position of power) is inherently exploitive of a member's trust. Even a woman's advance does not excuse a minister from his responsibility to maintain boundaries.

Types of Abusive Ministers

Sexual misconduct by clergy takes many forms: voyeurism, exhibitionism, incest, child molestation (pedophiles and ephebophiles),[32] homosexual liaisons, and rape. Clergy sexual abuse usually begins with acts or statements intended to arouse erotic interest. When pastoral power is used to manipulate a congregant to engage in sexual relations, the results are devastating.

There are many ways to classify abusers. Observers of clergy abuse list as many as seven profiles.[33] Recognized authority Marie Fortune has made a major distinction between predators and wanderers, to which Grenz and Bell have added a third type: the lover.[34]

The predator is a person who actively seeks opportunities to abuse women sexually. Targeting his prey, the predator pretends to be a caring pastor but uses his power and position to manipulate his victims. The pastoral predator is

manipulative, coercive, controlling, predatory, and sometimes violent. He may also be charming, bright, competent, and charismatic. He is attracted to powerlessness and vulnerability. He is not psychotic, but is usually sociopathic; that is, he has little or no sense of conscience about his offending behaviors. He usually will minimize, lie, and deny when confronted. For those offenders, the ministry presents an ideal opportunity for access to possible victims of all ages.[35]

In contrast to the predator, the wanderer is not violent, not premeditative in his sexual abuse, and generally less successful personally and professionally. Because he is a vulnerable and inadequate person, the wanderer easily becomes emotionally and sexually involved with a congregant or counselee. According to Fortune, the wanderer "has difficulty maintaining boundaries in relationships and attempts to meet private needs in public arenas."[36] The catalyst for his sexual misbehavior is usually an equally needy woman who holds her minister in high regard, almost to the point of adoration.

The growing intimacy between pastor and parishioner usually culminates in an emotional moment when inhibitions are cast aside and the two engage in an episode of sexual intercourse. Once the passions have subsided, both begin to feel anxiety, shame, guilt, and a sense of betrayal. The two express regret and swear themselves to secrecy. Although things may seem to return to normal, a trust has been violated, and a shadow falls over their lives and relationships.

The lover is a third type of minister who enters the "forbidden zone" with a parishioner. This spiritual shepherd becomes infatuated with one of his flock. Though a sexual transgressor like the other two, he is motivated neither by the desire to conquer nor by the need to overcome personal inadequacies.

Although there is no stereotypical perpetrator of clergy sexual abuse, the distinction between predator, wanderer, and lover is insightful. The predator offender moves from conquest to conquest, leaving a trail of victims. The wanderer minister yields to temptation in a moment of crisis and immediately feels remorse over his failure. The romantic minister is drawn to a church member when his passion convinces him he is in love.

Not all agree with these distinctions. Many victims of clergy sexual abuse believe that all ministers fall into the first category and will continue to victimize if not apprehended and removed from ministry. Perhaps these victims have never observed a wanderer, whose offense is normally a once-in-a-lifetime mistake and who ordinarily admits his failure and seeks professional help. A counselor of ministers who developed a restoration process for fallen ministers shared in a meeting that in his years of work not once did a predator come to him for help. On the other hand, he witnessed scores of wanderers who benefited from his recovery program.

Understanding the nature of clergy sexual abuse raises other important questions. What is its impact on churches, victims, and the families involved? Are there ways to prevent the abuse? How should churches and denominations respond to the malady?

The Impact of Clergy Sexual Abuse

In ten years, the congregation of a middle-class church in the suburbs of a large metropolitan area grew to over one thousand members. When the only pastor most members had known accepted the call to a church in another state, the congregants were deeply distressed. Only a few lay leaders knew why Brother Jim (not his name) was leaving. He had become intimate with three married women in the church while counseling them about family problems.

Pastoral care was Jim's strong suit. He was a charismatic leader who invested much of his time in counseling members. When deacon leaders confronted the pastor with evidence of his sexual involvements, he admitted his errant behavior. The relationships were not planned, he explained. But during counseling, these needy women "fell in love" with the first man in their life who listened, cared, and gave them emotional support. He realized his sin, vowing never to let it happen again. The decision to move to another church was Jim's way of making a clean start.

Rumors that Brother Jim had been intimate with several women began to make the rounds about the time a new pastor came. The reactions of members of the congregation varied. Some believed the charges and in their anger left the church. Others disbelieved the rumors, claiming they were concocted by enemies of the former pastor or by the new pastor. Many who stayed in the church were so hurt and disappointed that they vowed never again to trust a minister.

The impact on church members was widespread and devastating. Young people who had admired their lifelong pastor were crushed. Parents struggled to explain to their children how a minister could be guilty of clergy sexual abuse. Families of the victims felt cut off from their church, as many blamed the abused women of being the culprits in the sexual affairs. To complicate the matter, within two years evidence surfaced that a part-time counselor and a youth minister were also guilty of sexual abuse. For the next five years, the new pastor spent much of his ministry working to rebuild trust and credibility.[37]

Baptist counselor Roy Woodruff, executive director of the three-thousand-member American Association of Pastoral Counselors, is concerned about the frequency of sexual abuse among clergy. "According to informed estimates, about 15 percent either have or are violating sexual ethical boundaries. I don't think I would use the word 'epidemic' . . . but I suspect the number of incidents is increasing."[38]

Although sexual abuse scandals in the Roman Catholic priesthood make the headlines, no religious group has escaped the malady. Leaders who work across denominational lines see no pattern. Sexual misconduct has invaded big-city megachurches and small-town pastorates, liturgical churches and charismatic congregations, and both ends of the theological spectrum.

When clergy sexual misconduct interrupts the life of a congregation, what impact does it have? As a whole, the church body tends to follow certain predictable patterns in their reaction to ministerial abuse that range from secrecy and silence to blame and excuse. The clergy perpetrator normally fails to anticipate the severe problems that descend on him and his family as a result of his transgression. Often overlooked is the effect on the abused woman and her family.

Impact on the Church

The initial response of church leaders to Brother Jim's admission of clergy sexual abuse was to avoid a public scandal and to protect Jim's reputation. A "code of silence" was pledged by the few who knew the facts. However, the enforced secrecy about Jim's infidelity was a mistake.

Clergy sexual misconduct is often a secret of church life that is concealed from public scrutiny. Most people are content to deny or ignore an incident, but this is destructive. Breaches of pastoral ethics must not be dismissed.

A church contributes to the conspiracy of silence when it cajoles the victims to remain silent and attempts to conceal the facts. Denominational officials often join the attempted cover-up by recommending the minister for another location without addressing his misconduct.

Concealing sexual exploitation compounds the problem and augments the damage. Breaking the code of silence is a major step in dealing with the issue. Only as clergy sexual abuse is dealt with honestly and openly will healing, health, and safety be available to the church, the perpetrator, and the victim.

Concealment, however, continues to be the main response of churches that deal with clergy sexual abuse. If preserving the secret fails, a second strategy usually follows. Church leaders direct their energies toward protecting the church's good name and the pastor's reputation.[39] Often the victim is blamed and the pastor is excused. The only eyewitness is thus demonized, for she is "the seductress who took advantage of our pastor in a moment of human weakness!"

It is also not uncommon for a church to blame the pastor's wife. If she had met his sexual needs adequately (so runs the argument), he would not have been vulnerable. Thus, the abuser (the pastor) becomes the victim, and the victims (the abused and the wife) are blamed as the real perpetrators of this tragic event.

In addition to misrepresenting the facts, this second reaction perpetuates the problem and creates additional negative responses. To excuse the pastor encourages him to deny his responsibility and to postpone confronting his behavior. Until a minister acknowledges that he is accountable for his conduct, little can be done to restore him to wholeness. Ministerial colleagues may join this charade, which pictures the pastor as the innocent victim of a seduction.

In a discussion of therapists who have sexual liaisons with their patients, psychiatrist Glen Gabbard observed:

Incest victims and those who have been sexually exploited by professionals have remarkably similar symptoms: shame, intense guilt associated with a feeling that they were somehow responsible for their victimization, feelings of isolation and forced silence, poor self-esteem, suicidal and/or self-destructive behavior and denial. Reaction of friends and family—disbelief, discounting, embarrassment—are also similar in both groups.[40]

Applying this insight to the pastorate, Fortune writes that the church functions as a family. The family image, with God as Father and fellow believers as siblings, suggests a relationship of trust, intimacy, caring, commitment, and respect, which are the bases of family life. Viewed from this perspective, clergy sexual abuse may be likened to spiritual incest. "When the irresponsible pastor does engage in sexual activity with parishioners, the result is incest in the church family; the parallels to incestuous abuse are disturbing."[41]

One such comparison of clergy sexual abuse to incest by David Brubaker reveals five common traits:

1. social isolation
2. blurred boundaries
3. the paradoxical feelings of inadequacy and perfectionism
4. the "no talk" rule, which distorts communication
5. unequal power[42]

Spiritual incest is a violation of trust. Because a minister represents God and the church, to be violated by a man of the cloth is to feel violated by God and the church.

Clergy sexual misconduct impacts the church in other ways as well. In the wider society, the church's reputation is seriously marred. The pastor's action will likely create public embarrassment, diminishing the credibility of the church throughout the community. In our increasingly litigious society, legal difficulties may be added to the long list of problems created by a pastor's misconduct.

Equally devastating is the turmoil created within the congregation. As news of the pastor's sexual conduct becomes known, the event polarizes the congregation. Members of the church may feel shame, anger, resentment, or empathy. Some may become vindictive. The end result is usually strife and division within the church body. Those who were significantly helped by the pastor's ministry will be deeply hurt and confused by the sexual misconduct. People on all sides of the debate may lose faith in the church leadership.

The debilitating effect of internal strife and external embarrassment is a loss of morale. Instead of utilizing its resources for witness and service, the congregation finds itself dissipating its energy on the internal crisis. Growth is stymied, attendance drops, and many families decide to join another church.

Like Solomon's razed temple, once the church has been damaged by clergy sexual abuse, it may be unable to regain its past influence.

"Whenever a pastor is accused of inappropriate sexual conduct within a church," conclude Lebacqz and Barton, "the bonds of trust between that pastor and the congregation are stretched to the breaking point. The focus of attention within the congregation shifts from the worship of God and the mission that flows out of that worship and begins instead to concentrate on the behavior of the pastor and of church members."[43]

Inevitably, the church moves from ministry and worship to crisis management. Dealing with this requires the energy, time, and focus of the church. Often, outside expertise and assistance are needed. A body of literature is developing to assist churches and "after pastors" in dealing with the many problems that confront a congregation for years after the abuse incidents.[44]

Impact on the Minister

Sexually abusive behavior has devastating consequences for the professional life of the abuser. The sexual misconduct undermines the integrity of his ministry, for it is a denial of all he has claimed to be and all he has taught others to be. Once reputation and credibility are lost, a minister's vocation is in serious jeopardy. Legal liabilities and financial pressures add to the turmoil.

Equally serious is the collateral damage done to the minister's colleagues, his church, and his denomination. Like waves from the wake of a passing ship, clergy sexual abuse washes muddy waters across the reputation of ministry at large. An incident of clergy sexual misconduct breeds a loss of faith in all ministers and ministry.

Impact on the Perpetrator's Family

The impact of clergy sexual abuse moves beyond the pastor and the congregation. The transgression also touches the minister's spouse (normally the wife) and family.

An immediate reality is the loss of income. A common reaction by church leaders to a pastor's sexual misconduct is to demand an immediate resignation. At best, this usually means no more than two to four weeks of severance pay. If the family is living in the church parsonage, it is not abnormal for the church to request that the manse be vacated within a few weeks. In their haste to deal with a difficult situation, church leaders often overlook the financial effect of their decisions on the pastor's wife and family.

Financial instability is a serious reality, but it is not the most devastating issue faced by the minister's spouse. Her husband is guilty of marital infidelity. If the sexual misconduct went on for months without her knowledge, the deceit is devastating. The emotional pain and confusion felt by the spouse are captured in the comment of one minister's wife: "It is impossible to describe the mental and physical pain—if he dies before me, he will have died twice."[45]

Along with an immediate loss of trust and intimacy, the minister's wife often begins to feel a sense of shame, guilt, and personal inadequacy. The incident raises in her mind typical questions about her adequacy as a sex partner, a marital companion, a mother, and a pastor's wife.

Whatever the outcome of the clergy sexual misconduct for her husband, she herself will face profound changes in her entire way of life. She is denied her sense of calling as a pastor's wife. Most of her church friends will disappear. Often the job of explaining "Daddy's problem" to the children will fall on her shoulders. If the couple decides to rebuild their relationship, it will take years of hard work.

The losses faced by the children are similar to those confronting their mother. They too will be cut off from church friends, lose face among their peers, and feel the financial pinch of a family lacking reliable employment. Should their father's sexual misconduct lead to a divorce, the children will experience the trauma of separation.

In the aftermath of clergy sexual abuse, the family members of the minister are innocent bystanders, immediately affected and most often overlooked. Disillusionment at the deepest level often permanently alienates the spouse and children from the church and fellow Christians. Family members may wonder if God also has left them.

Impact on the Abused Woman and Her Family

None of these consequences seem to equal the havoc experienced by the victim of pastoral sexual abuse. Most victims never come forward. Generally, the vulnerable survivor who does bring allegations disappears from the story early on, as few people truly care about her or reach out to her.

Grenz and Bell observe that a woman exploited during counseling (about one in five of those abused) often faces triple jeopardy. In the beginning, personal problems led her to seek her pastor's care. Needing personal healing, she found instead sexual violation from a man she trusted. Once the incident is public, her church rejects and abandons her. In this wounded condition, the victim who sought help instead found further injury from her family, her pastor, and her church family.[46]

The personal repercussions of clergy sexual abuse on a woman are similar to those experienced by abuse victims of other caregiving professionals. Often they are caused not by the abuse but by the collusion that comes later. Physical disorders are common. Health problems ranging from back pain to nervous disorders appear. Emotionally, the victims of clergy sexual abuse may experience anxiety, fear, panic, depression, mood changes, guilt, anger, loss of trust, problems with sexual intimacy, and thoughts or attempts of suicide. Socially, the victim may find it difficult to maintain close relationships, which may lead to social withdrawal and alcohol and drug abuse.[47]

The impact on the abused woman's family is just as devastating as on the perpetrator's. Marriages often end in divorce. Normal children may become rebellious and turn to antisocial behavior such as drugs, crime, and illicit sex.

Once the victim realizes she has been led into sexual abuse by a trusted caregiver, this awareness can cause grave damage to her view of herself as a woman. Coming to her pastor for healing from former hurts (sometimes incurred in earlier abusive relationships), she found instead someone who violated and used her, like a commodity to be exploited.

Pamela Cooper-White summarizes the impact of clergy abuse on the victim:

> The pastoral relationship can and should be a sacred trust, a place where a parishioner can come with the deepest wounds and vulnerabilities. . . . By modeling appropriate boundaries and healthy responses, the pastor can begin to empower her to heal those wounds. The harm done when this is exploited is no less than a violation of sacred space, which further ruptures and destroys the woman's boundaries, devastating her mental health and her sense of self.[48]

Thus, abandoned by her church, betrayed by her pastoral counselor, unaided by her dysfunctional family, and devastated by physical and emotional disorders, the abused woman suffers from guilt, isolation, and humiliation. Her mood deepens from shame and self-blame to despair and desperation. She may ponder or even act on thoughts of suicide. Inevitably, she faces a crisis of faith. If all those who represent God have betrayed her, she may feel betrayed by God also.

Prevention of Clergy Sexual Abuse

If two decades of research is accurate, 10 to 12 percent of ministers engage in sexual relations with members of their church, and 25 to 35 percent of clergy admit to sexually inappropriate behavior with parishioners. What can be done to prevent this destructive behavior? Why do some ministers fall and others do not? Are there protective measures that can help ministers and churches avoid this breach of power and trust?

Clergy sexual abuse is seldom an isolated action. Rather, it is a complex problem involving a confluence of circumstances and motivations, especially the twin dynamics of sexuality and power.

Some offer a straightforward solution to the problem: The church should weed out those who are likely to harass or abuse. Certainly, ordination and ministerial placement should be limited to persons of the highest spiritual maturity and moral integrity (1 Tim. 3:1–13). No one disagrees with that principle.

However, clergy sexual misconduct is very difficult to predict. As Christian psychologists Jack Balswick and John Thoburn confirm, "No one factor in and of itself can be identified as the reason why a given minister succumbs to a sexual temptation. In most cases, a combination of factors contributes to their behavior."[49]

Adding to the difficulty of predicting abuse is the fact that comparatively little has been written about the factors that make a person vulnerable to victimization. Even less is available on what makes an individual in the institutional church vulnerable to colluding.[50]

A better approach for preventing clergy sexual misconduct is to equip ministers and churches to understand negative influences and to encourage positive resistance. Clergy and churches must refuse to succumb to the demons of denial, ignorance, and minimization, which usually foster secrecy and collusion.[51]

Research indicates that ministers who withstand sexual temptation understand their own personal susceptibility, recognize the danger signals, and build strong support systems. Churches assist in prevention by perceiving the dynamics of the clergy role, encouraging methods of accountability for ministers, and developing wise policies.

Personal Awareness

For perpetrators, victims, and colluders, the first step in the prevention of clergy abuse is a personal recognition of the problem. An inadequate approach is to ask, "Who's at fault?" The blame game usually misreads the situation and offers little help for prevention. Some blame the minister who profanes his calling by taking advantage of a vulnerable church member. Some blame the church that puts its pastor under pressure to perform. Some identify the culprit as a seductive female or an inadequate wife.

Sex abuse expert Fortune insists that most offending ministers violate ethical sexual boundaries long before they commit vocational suicide. However, it's not about sex. It's a misuse of power. Fortune observes that church members want to excuse the pastor and often slip into denial, but it is not fair to the pastor or the congregation to ignore the real problem. "We need to say, 'Look, it was wrong. It was unethical behavior.'"[52]

The ministry is an attractive profession for anyone who is looking to exploit vulnerable people, claims Roy Woodruff. "The average parish pastor has no one he reports to or is supervised by. And he has a lot of needy people coming for help. A pastor who could be needy himself can exploit the needs of others."[53]

Awareness of the dynamics of clergy sexual abuse is basic to all prevention strategies. Every minister needs to realize that he is at risk of crossing the boundary into the forbidden zone every day. The male pastor is not exempt from sexual attraction to congregants. He must be aware of his feelings and honestly acknowledge the sexual urges he senses.

In addition, as a professional caregiver, a minister may have difficulty accepting his limitations, especially in counseling members of the opposite gender. Pastors who see themselves as rescuers may create a codependent relationship that is dangerous. A rescuer-healer minister is susceptible to sexual misconduct because he may cross healthy boundaries to fulfill his own personal needs.[54]

A minister must be aware of personal susceptibilities that make him more prone to sexual abuse. Deep-seated insecurities, which easily surface as sexual and power needs, often fuel misconduct. Unresolved questions relating to a pastor's own sexuality, especially destructive experiences from the past, can contribute to the exploitation of others. Sexual addiction has a critical influence on some abusers.

Pastoral counselor Woodruff contends that sexually abusive ministers usually fit one of two profiles: the prima donna or the depressed pastor.[55] The prima donna pastor operates out of a desire for power and control, loses touch with boundaries, overdirects people's lives, and develops a sense of "I can do no wrong." Central to this person is the idea of entitlement—that he is entitled to certain behavior that others are not. The highly publicized televangelist scandals and the sexual failure of many contemporary megachurch pastors illustrate this type.

At the other extreme is the depressed pastor whose judgment becomes cloudy because of low self-esteem and a growing inability to function as a minister or as a man. Thus, he becomes vulnerable to relationships that provide gratification. The high-profile pastor and the despondent minister share one fatal weakness: isolation.

What lessons can be learned from this summary of factors related to clergy sexual misconduct? First, male ministers inclined to harass or abuse urgently need personal therapy. For them, the personal and professional risk of ministering to women is too great. For pastors who do not sense a vulnerability toward abusing parishioners but do recognize the reality of sexual temptation, the dynamics of the pastor/congregant relationship may offer another lesson. Peter Rutter observes, "Every forbidden-zone relationship in which sexual tension appears also presents an opportunity to heal."[56] The male minister holds the power to move the arousal of sexual feelings from temptation to an opportunity for the healing of deeper wounds. He alone can turn an impending disaster into a life-giving moment.

Warning Signs

Knowing the warning signs of clergy sexual abuse can aid the prevention of it. Ministers should be aware of their boundaries and always seek to maintain them. "Even if the boundaries for sexual intimacy are the same for pastor and lay person, the responsibility for maintaining those boundaries falls to the professional person."[57]

Ministers need a warning system that will alert them when they are approaching unacceptable levels of intimacy with parishioners. Lebacqz and Barton have proposed a checklist of signals that warn ministers when they are headed for trouble:

- the publicity test: What would others think?
- physical arousal—one's own or the other's
- inordinate sexual fantasy
- sexual gestures or body language
- intuition, instinct, or not feeling right
- wanting to share intimacies that are not called for
- a parishioner wanting too much time or attention
- wanting to shift the focus to sexual subjects[58]

Fortune has developed a list of questions to which affirmative answers suggest the possibility of sexual misconduct:

- Is the minister doing a lot of counseling beyond his or her scope of responsibility?
- Is the minister not taking care of himself or herself, canceling vacations, neglecting time with family?
- Does the pastor tend to sexualize conversations?
- Are mechanisms of accountability being ignored?
- Is lay leadership discouraged?
- Does everything in the church focus on the pastor?[59]

Grenz and Bell offer six warning signs that indicate boundaries are being violated:

1. The conversation becomes increasingly personal, as the pastor talks unduly about himself.
2. The pastor's physical contact has moved beyond greetings to inappropriate pats and hugs.

3. The pastor fantasizes about a sexual relationship with the congregant.
4. The pastor offers to drive the congregant home.
5. The pastor arranges meetings with the congregant outside the normal counseling time.
6. The pastor increasingly hides his feelings for the parishioner and his meetings with her from his accountability systems, especially his wife.[60]

Support Systems

One of the best ways to ensure responsible sexual behavior is for a minister to build strong support systems. Accountability relationships offer a crucial antidote for misconduct.

A good marriage reinforces sexual faithfulness in many ways. It provides the context for wholesome sexual expression. Marital intimacy also facilitates honest communication while reminding the married church leader that he is accountable to his partner. The research of Balswick and Thoburn revealed, "Over one-fourth of the pastors cite their relationship with their wife as the most important reason for sexual fidelity." The study concluded, "Marital dissatisfaction coupled with work boredom is the kind of situation that has been conducive to the most fantasy and openness to actual liaisons."[61]

Colleagues and personal counselors provide another support group. A pastor should not hesitate to seek personal counsel from trusted friends or professional advice from a qualified therapist when he needs inner healing and emotional health.

Another important support group is composed of models and mentors. Many pastors belong to accountability groups whose members meet regularly to develop trust, offer encouragement, and hold one another morally accountable.[62] One group of ministers in Phoenix meets weekly, and members ask one another a series of questions, beginning with, "Have you had any sexual thoughts about women in your congregation since we last met?"

The greatest role model for ministers is Jesus, who ministered to women without moral compromise. He viewed each woman he encountered through God's eyes, not as objects for selfish gratification or pawns to be controlled but as persons with deep needs and spiritual aspirations. As disciples of Christ, pastors are to minister to women as Jesus did.

Professional Safeguards

Ideally, prevention safeguards for ministers should be established during preparation for ministry. Seminary students and new ministers need information about and clarification of ethical standards for ministry. Many denominations have begun developing educational and training resources for their clergy and laity.[63]

> [Ministers] need to understand the nature of the power and authority of their role and the responsibility that goes with it. They need to learn how to maintain boundaries in relationships with parishioners and counselees. They need to learn to care for their own emotional and sexual needs in appropriate ways.[64]

Seminaries may be the first line of defense in protecting church members from sexual abusers. Although there is no reliable test for identifying abusive applicants, seminaries do rely on essays, recommendations, applications, and psychological tests to screen prospective students.[65]

Individual churches share some responsibility for prevention. Churches should have policies about standards of conduct, screening procedures, supervision guidelines, adequate insurance coverage, honest pastoral references, and procedures for handling allegations of sexual misconduct by ministers.[66]

Safeguarding potential victims from perpetrators is made more difficult by the common practice of abusers moving from one state to another, one institution to another, and one denomination to another. The structure and practice of autonomous churches make them more vulnerable to traveling abusers. As a result, they need to do a thorough background check on every potential minister. One denominational group has recently recognized its responsibility to assist churches in identifying past abusers, even though the churches are autonomous.[67] If a past history of sexual abuse is discovered in a candidate, the church body should be informed.

Most professionals operate under an accepted code of ethics developed and enforced by their peers. However, clergy face three major problems in writing a code of ethics: authorship, instruction, and enforcement.[68] In addition, congregational-type churches have been reluctant to accept a standard code of ethics for all ministers.

Nevertheless, a growing number of church leaders believe a ministerial code of ethics is possible and necessary. For the first time in its 118-year history, a Baptist state convention is writing a code of ethics for ministers to be approved at its annual convention in 2004.[69] Chapter 8 addresses this issue.

People need to know their church is a safe place. Denial is deadly. As long as a church ignores the problem of sexual misconduct or cajoles victims to remain silent, the problem persists. Ignorance compounds the issue and augments the damage sexual abuse perpetrates. To ignore clergy sexual misconduct is to become a colluder, one who joins the perpetrator in victimizing the vulnerable and their families. Prevention, therefore, is the responsibility of everyone.

Responding to Clergy Sexual Abuse

The phone rings. With anguish, a female victim of clergy sexual abuse tells you her story and then asks the question, "What can we do?" A second call comes from a lay leader in the church of the minister abuser and his victim. He confirms the allegations and then asks the same question: "What can we do?"

When a minister is accused of sexual misconduct, those involved are perplexed about what to do. Victims are embarrassed and ashamed. Should they keep quiet or report the incident? Family members cope with several levels of disruption. Where do they turn for help? Not knowing what else to do, church leaders may join the perpetrator in a denial of the accusation.

A common scenario is as follows: Secrecy is urged by church leaders for the sake of the church and the families involved. As news of the incident spreads, many blame the female victim, assuming she is guilty of seducing the minister. Others suggest that the pastor's wife may be at fault—if she had been an adequate partner, he would not have strayed! Whether the allegations are true or not, church leaders usually choose one of two options: They either support the pastor and try to keep the charges undercover, or they force the pastor to leave through resignation or termination.

Why do most churches and their members fail to respond appropriately to reported clergy sexual abuse? Two major reasons emerge: (1) a lack of understanding of the nature of the problem and (2) a failure to have well-defined policies and procedures in place.

The first reason was addressed by defining the nature of clergy sexual abuse, its impact, and various prevention strategies. Addressing the second reason involves outlining appropriate and practical ways the church and other entities involved can respond to pastoral sexual misconduct.

Ensuring Justice

When allegations of sexual abuse by a minister come forth, protecting the good name of the church or salvaging the pastor's ministry may become the highest priority. If that is the case, the victims of clergy abuse suffer injustice. True concern for the victimized congregant and her family means the church, first and foremost, must ensure justice through due process.[70]

Justice means just treatment of all persons involved. Justice means no cover-up or whitewashing of evil. Justice means giving a fair and impartial hearing to the allegations of the congregant and to the response of the accused. Justice means refusing to make assumptions or reach conclusions before all the evidence is heard. Justice means launching a formal accountability process immediately. If the charges prove to be true, justice may include removing the abusive pastor from office so that he cannot victimize others. Fortune explains why this is crucial:

> When a minister like Donovan [the guilty pastor in her story] behaves unethically and the authorities merely express concern and issue a warning, he is likely to be more discreet in the future but not likely to change his behavior.[71]

The process of ensuring justice is often difficult and painful. The goal of the process is not to resolve a conflict between two persons but to advocate for those who have been harmed and to hold the offending party accountable.[72] Therefore, when it becomes clear that clergy sexual abuse has occurred, the attention and energy of those in charge must be directed toward ensuring justice.

Interpersonal Resolution

The 2002 Southern Baptist Convention adopted a resolution calling for churches and civil authorities to hold ministers guilty of sexual abuse accountable. Thus, the largest non-Catholic flock acknowledged that sexual misconduct among spiritual leaders is a problem that Baptists face. The resolution, however, contained a fatal flaw: It "called for Southern Baptist churches to discipline those guilty of sexual abuse by the pattern provided in Matthew 18."[73]

Some in the church argue that any dispute between two Christians should be resolved between them. Did Jesus not provide detailed instructions that apply to every interpersonal problem in the church, including sexual misconduct (Matt. 18:15–17)? Indeed, the first step outlined by Jesus is a face-to-face encounter between the accused and the accuser (18:15).

At first this approach seems reasonable and biblical. However, a closer examination of the text reveals that the situations involved were private, personal matters. The sexual exploitation of a parishioner by a minister, though personal, is never merely a private matter. Furthermore, this passage describes two people who have a peer relationship. Two believers are advised about reconstructing a marred relationship between equals. Sexual abuse by a minister does not fit this description. In addition, requiring a victimized congregant to confront her abuser privately could actually work against Jesus' intent that victims receive justice. An offending pastor could use the confrontation to silence his victim or even to persuade her that she is responsible for the event.

A study of women who attempted to confront their offender revealed: (1) they were met with strong denials; (2) church members and leaders were reticent to believe their story; and (3) when the victims were heard, they were under intense pressure to bypass the biblical mandate calling for public confrontation ("tell it to the church" [Matt. 18:17]).[74] The call of church leaders "to forgive" replaced the clear call to bring the matter to the congregation.

To dispense with justice in the name of forgiveness becomes a simple way for churches to resolve a "messy problem."

Response of the Church

In her story of Rev. Peter Donovan and First Church Newburg, Fortune raised the question, "How could a credentialed, highly regarded, well-liked pastor in a mainline, middle-class Protestant church do such things and get away with it for so long?" The abuse expert identified three primary factors that leave churches unprotected against pastoral offenders:

1. The church is myopic about the problem of abuse by clergy.
2. The power of the pastoral role is seldom acknowledged, especially in denominations with a strong congregational polity.
3. The familial model of congregational life is assumed, which makes incest a possibility.[75]

Acceptance of responsibility is the necessary first step in dealing with clergy sexual abuse. Since the church called the minister, the church must hold the minister accountable. At the same time, the church must also accept its share of responsibility.[76]

The first responsibility of a church is to develop guidelines for ministry to victims and their families. The previous discussion under the heading "The Impact of Clergy Sexual Abuse" explains the needs of those victimized by abuse and makes suggestions for responding and ministering to their unique needs.

The second responsibility of a congregation is to develop policies and procedures for responding to accusations of clergy sexual abuse. If a church waits until an allegation occurs before developing procedures, it will be too late. Policies need to be in place to ensure justice and due process.

When a report of sexual misconduct by a minister is received, a church must respond immediately. A fair hearing of the victim's account of the abuse needs to be witnessed by an appropriate group without delay, followed by an immediate investigation. Established policies make a speedy response possible.

Every report of clergy sexual abuse must be taken seriously. Church leaders must never be guilty of sweeping charges under the rug or denying their significance. Claiming that the matter is a personal problem between two people or practicing a code of secrecy compounds the problem and escalates the damage. Wise policies and procedures will ensure that a church's response is fair, sensitive, and serious. A procedure for responding to charges of clergy sexual abuse may be found in appendix A.

The third responsibility of a church is to develop sound procedures for minister search committees. When a church seeks a minister, it has the responsibility to check a candidate's background and references thoroughly. The editor of the largest Baptist state paper challenged search committees to ask serious questions of people giving references such as, "Would you consider calling this person as pastor of your church?" or, "Is there any reason why you would be hesitant to hire this person to serve your church?" He added, "If you get any hesitancy, check further."[77]

Although there is always a first time for crossing the ethical boundaries into the forbidden zone, research indicates that a large percentage of incidents involve a pattern of sexual abuse. Failing to check thoroughly the background and references of every potential minister invites tragedy.

Ultimately, church leaders and church members must acknowledge the reality of ministerial sexual misconduct, understand the nature of this behavior, and develop a response that ensures justice through due process and ministry to victims. Anything less than this is less than Christ would have us do.

Suggested Reading

Grenz, Stanley J., and Roy D. Bell. *Betrayal of Trust: Confronting and Preventing Clergy Sexual Misconduct.* 2d ed. Grand Rapids: Baker, 2001.

Kroeger, Catherine Clark, and James R. Beck. *Healing the Hurting: Giving Hope and Help to Abused Women.* Grand Rapids: Baker, 1998.

Laaser, Mark, and Nancy M. Hopkins, eds. *Restoring the Soul of a Church: Healing Congregations Wounded by Clergy Sexual Misconduct.* Collegeville, Minn.: Liturgical, 1995.

8

A Ministerial Code of Ethics

Help or Hindrance?

In a particular church, a complex situation erupted that raised several ethical questions. Over a period of many months, a single college student made homosexual advances to several church youth, all under sixteen years of age. To further complicate the matter, the college student also served as a part-time minister on the church staff.

After one young person told his parents of an episode, the family confided in an associate minister. Other incidents soon came to light. Finally, two staff ministers went to the student with the revelation. When confronted with the facts, he broke down emotionally and admitted his guilt. Although he expressed deep sorrow over the pain he had caused, he refused to accept advice or seek counseling, stating again and again that his problem was "incurable." Immediately, he moved to a distant city, where he soon found employment as a student minister in another church.

This crisis posed several questions in regard to ministerial ethics. First, there was the issue of confidentiality. One youth confided in the minister of music, who was unsure how to handle the situation. Should he tell the parents? The pastor? The youth minister? How far does confidentiality extend, and under what conditions can a promise of confidentiality be broken?

A second question concerned obligations to colleagues. What responsibility does one minister have to another, especially if that other is his or her supervisor? A difficult decision came in relation to the student after he moved. After much discussion, the church ministers decided to inform the student's new pastor of the incidents, both to protect against recurrences and to open the door for ministry to the student.

Another ministerial ethics question concerned the congregation. How much information should be shared? How would it affect the parents of the youth? Should anything be shared with the church youth, especially since some of them knew of the encounters?

Certainly, there were legal obligations to the community at large. The laws of most states require that any act of sexual abuse involving minors be reported.

Most ministers have never reasoned through a professional dilemma such as this one or developed guiding principles. Ordinarily, church leaders simply respond to problems as they happen, hoping their ability to think clearly will carry them through. This approach sometimes works, particularly if the minister is mature, experienced, and well trained. Too often, however, tragic mistakes are made that create vocational headaches and personal heartaches.

Is there a way for clergy to be prepared for the ethical questions inherent to their profession? Are there obligations that are basic to the role of the ordained? Can a code of ethics for ministers be developed that guides and motivates them as they make decisions in their professional life?

Chapter 1 noted that almost all functional definitions of *professional* include self-regulation, usually in the form of a code such as the Hippocratic Oath or the Code of Professional Responsibility of the American Bar Association.[1] Virtually every profession has a written code of ethics to guarantee moral performance in the marketplace.

It seems enigmatic that in the one profession expected to model morality, very few codes of ethics can be found. Although some religious denominations have written codes for their clergy, the number of codes decreased in the last century. Nolan Harmon's classic text on ministerial ethics contains sample codes adopted by five major denominations between 1926 and 1944 (appendix B), but none of these is in current use.[2] A recent search among these same five denominations uncovered only two with contemporary standards, the Disciples of Christ and the Unitarian Universalist (appendix C). Occasionally, a smaller group of ministers will develop a written code.[3]

As shown in earlier chapters, the call to Christian ministry leads to many ethical dilemmas. The complex role of the modern minister and the structure of the contemporary church make it difficult for a minister to maintain ethical integrity. The contemporary cleric often feels like a person driving through a large city who makes one wrong turn on the freeway and gets horribly lost. After several detours and dead-end streets, the traveling cleric searches for a map.

One possible road map to assist ministers in their professional conduct is a code of ethics. Although such codes by themselves cannot create an ethical person, they can give guidance. Codes promote personal responsibility by encouraging a minister to think seriously about ethics in ministry.

At his daughter's graduation ceremony, Arthur Becker heard the class of veterinarians pledge compliance to a code of ethics. The Lutheran teacher wondered why something similar does not exist for ministers. "I think we need to have underscored for us the fact that being a professional in large part means being accountable to a set of values which guide our behavior as ministers."[4]

The credibility of church shepherds is contingent on their ability to control their own ethical conduct. James Allen Reasons, in his thorough study on the role of codes in ministerial ethics, states, "It is crucial that the minister be able to discern the ethical difficulties unique to his profession and act on them in a biblical manner."[5] In a recent book dealing with sexual exploitation in the pastoral relationship, Marie Fortune calls for "the establishment of clear ethical guidelines concerning clergy misconduct by each denominational body" and urges church leaders to develop "unequivocal policies and procedural safeguards."[6]

Yet the question remains, Is a ministerial code of ethics a help or a hindrance? A second question follows: Is it possible to write such a code for ministers? Some clergy oppose a written code for theoretical and practical reasons. Liberal clergy may feel that the strong deontological bent of professional codes inevitably leads to legalism.[7] Conservative clerics may fear that a denominational hierarchy will use the code as a club to keep disloyal ministers in line and out of significant churches. Ministers of every stripe are nervous about a document that could threaten their pastoral autonomy.

Developing a code of ethics for any professional group poses three major problems: authorship, instruction, and enforcement.[8] First, who should write the code: the professionals, the clients, or third parties? Second, who should teach the code: someone outside the profession or a colleague from within? Third, who should enforce the code: the professionals themselves or others?

There are lesser problems. What subjects should be addressed in a code? Should the document consist of rules, principles, or both? How should the code be distributed? What sanctions are fair? What process should be used to enforce the code? To lead a group of ministers through that wilderness of questions might require another Moses!

Although developing and implementing a code of ethics for ministers is an arduous task with many risks, it is a worthwhile endeavor. It will not be a panacea for every ministerial problem, nor will it automatically ensure safe passage through the moral maze of ministry. Nevertheless, a written code of ethics can serve as a guide and a goal; it can both teach and inspire.

Let us now explore that possibility. First, we want to look at how codes function in the secular professions. The way doctors, lawyers, and other professionals utilize codes can reveal their potential for ministers. This overview will prepare us to address the heart of this chapter: the value of a ministerial code of ethics. A related task, how to write a code of ethics, is a third major concern. One practical result of this study can be for you, the reader, to write your own personal code of ethics.

Codes in the Professions

Visiting professor Amitai Etzioni thought he was overprepared to teach ethics to a group of MBAs at Harvard Business School. He had just completed a book on ethics after thirty years of teaching at Columbia, Berkeley, and George Washington Universities. He soon discovered, however, that these business-leaders-to-be were not easily swayed. In one class period, after presenting a case study, the professor asked, "Is that ethical?" One student responded, "I'm not sure there is such a thing as the subconscious."

Later the subject of binding moral duties was introduced with the sentence, "I would *like* to go to a movie but *ought* to visit a friend in the hospital." The students challenged the ethical dilemma, saying, "The real reason for your moral quandary is that you are just trying to impress your friends." In the minds of the students, there were no noble acts in human behavior; moral goodness was always a result of baser motives such as self-interest.

The teacher noted that these MBAs were joining an age-old tradition called reductionism by denying the existence of morality. In so doing, they were also diluting its significance. While indicating that his teaching was not a complete failure, Etzioni did confess that he "had not found a way to help classes full of MBAs see that there is more to life than money, power, fame and self-interest."[9]

Since the 1990s there has been a growing concern about the ethical values of professionals. Blatant moral misbehavior has erupted at the New York Stock Exchange, among corporate CEOs, in Congress and the White House, throughout the health care system, and among religious leaders.

As noted in chapter 1, this crisis in professional life has been caused primarily by a loss of common values. Alasdair MacIntyre thinks discussing professional ethics in a pluralistic society is impossible because of this lack of shared moral values.[10] Three major movements in Western culture have precipitated the crisis: secularization, pluralism, and relativism. Like a trio of termites, these cultural trends have eaten away the foundation of professionalism.

Many professionals today lean in the direction of self-interest and away from altruistic service and moral commitments. Countering this tide are two trends: a surge of interest in professional ethics and the reintroduction of ethics studies in schools of law, medicine, business, and other professional institutions.[11]

Not everyone is convinced this will help. When it comes to the use of professional codes, many professionals are skeptical, believing codes are basically self-serving and contribute to unethical conduct. Michael Bayles strongly disagrees, stating that professionals engage in unethical behavior for the same reasons others do: financial gain, fame, the desire to benefit clients or employers, and the simple failure to reflect on the ethical import of one's conduct.[12]

The Purposes of Professional Codes

Why should professionals have codes of ethics? In the broad sense, these codes specify the moral role of the professional and the special obligations understood by the profession. "They tell professionals how to act *as a professional*, as understood by the professional group."[13]

Specifically, written codes of professional ethics have four major purposes. First, they spell out guidelines accepted collectively by peers.

> The ethic of the professional is to be found in the dialectical interaction between the conscience of the individual professional and the collective conclusions of the profession as a whole, and the formulations of the "Professional Code," always provisional and continually being revised.[14]

Having guidelines protects professionals from possible errors and "keeps us from reinventing the wheel every time we make a decision."[15]

Second, codes of ethics protect a profession from incompetent practitioners. Standards are established to protect the medical profession from quacks and the legal profession from shysters.

> Although it is not a virtue, competence is probably the most crucial of a professional's characteristics. Professionals have an ethical responsibility not to hold themselves out to do or accept work they are not competent to handle.[16]

Third, codes support and protect individual members.[17] The existence of a code protects a professional from social pressures to violate the code. An engineer can refuse to reveal corporate information simply by saying, "Sorry, my professional code of ethics forbids such disclosures." It also reminds a professional that personal actions represent to society the ethical convictions of colleagues and of the entire profession.[18]

Finally, a professional code defines the nature of a profession.[19] Codes help to define the moral values of a group. Individuals considering entrance into a profession know from its written code what the ethical tone of that particular vocation is.

Karen Lebacqz has observed that if codes are simply guidelines for specific behavior in certain circumstances, then they rapidly become either too vague to be helpful or too rigid to adapt to change. She makes this proposal: "Rather than looking for specific guidelines for *action* in professional codes, they might be better understood as statements about the *image* of the profession and the *character* of professionals."[20]

Understood this way, codes are not simply rules for action. They identify the moral stress points within a profession and present a model of a "good" professional.

The Nature of Professional Codes

Professional ethics usually takes the form of a code, contract, or covenant.[21] A contract involves a promise between people in which an obligation to perform is expected, followed by a reward when the action is accomplished. The covenant approach involves both codal and contractual elements but is based on a gift between two parties, resulting in a covenant promise and a change in the covenanted people because of this relationship (Gen. 17:1–22). The code approach is the most common for evaluating professions, professionals, and their conduct. It involves listing the obligations a professional has in regard to clients, colleagues, and the community.

In their classic study of the professions, A. M. Carr-Saunders and P. A. Wilson note that most professional codes are characterized by positive prescriptions and negative sanctions.[22] These codes usually try to balance the ethical concerns of the professionals, their clients, and the general public.

Do professionals live by different moral standards than the rest of society? Some say that they do, believing that higher standards give professionals a sense of mission to act appropriately. Others just as vigorously contend that they do not. Two sets of standards breed elitism, confuse the public, increase distrust of professionals, and put nonprofessionals in a vulnerable position.

A better understanding involves a combination of these two points of view. Ordinary morality governs all members of society, including professionals, but a profession's special ethical obligations are reflected in a professional code. These codes do not promote a unique system for an elite group "but rather . . . utilize societal values to give the professional useful, specific direction."[23]

The Structure of Professional Codes

Professional codes have a long history. The earliest known code was a medical code found on a stone pillar dated 2250 B.C. Attributed to Hammurabi, the code dealt mainly with the physician-patient relationship. Hippocrates of Greece (350 B.C.) wrote the most famous medical oath (which bears his name) to separate medicine from magic. Also called the "Doctor's Oath," it established a formal code of conduct for physicians who treated disease. In the Middle

Ages, Maimonides, an Egyptian who practiced medicine (A.D. 1135–1204), wrote ethical guidelines that obligated a physician to treat any patient needing care, regardless of financial status.

Codes of ethics vary considerably in content and structure. The majority tend to include certain basic categories of duties. The key ingredients of professional codes are:

- private or personal obligations
- responsibilities to clients and special interest groups
- obligations to colleagues and to the profession
- responsibilities to the community or society as a whole

C. S. Calian surveyed eight codes from various professions and developed a list of fifteen items of commonality. Six of the fifteen items are personal obligations the professional assumes: a sense of calling, the value of knowledge and skill, the need for continuing education, the derivation of primary income from the profession, the need to reduce conflicts of interest, and the need to maintain good health.[24]

A second major area covered by professional codes of ethics relates to obligations between the professional and the client. Calian's list includes questions about confidentiality, the primacy of service over remuneration, the duty to know one's limits and consult others, and the attitude of respect for the worth of every individual.

A third area of responsibility contained in most professional codes concerns obligations individual professionals have in regard to their profession and their colleagues. In the eight codes Calian reviewed, one item relating to fellow professionals made his list of fifteen: the need to cooperate with colleagues. Three specific obligations professionals have in regard to one another are to offer respect, to provide information concerning the competence and character of applicants to the profession, and to bear their fair share of the work in the profession's social role.[25]

Finally, what are the obligations professionals have in regard to their community or society at large? Calian listed three: to be sensitive to consumers' rights and well-being, to be discrete in publications and solicitations, and to exemplify good citizenship.

A professional's responsibility for public good has at least three other facets. First, there is the role of social leadership, such as service to charitable organizations or governmental boards and agencies. A second facet of responsibility for public good is the improvement of professional knowledge and skills. A third facet is to preserve and enhance the social role of the profession, which ultimately benefits society.[26]

This brief overview of the structure of professional codes reveals something important for the formation of a ministerial code of ethics. Secular codes typically outline the kinds of ethical dilemmas professionals encounter, the loyalties expected of them, the duties they perform, and the conflicts their role creates. These obligations are not simply codes for action but statements that project the character of the professional.[27]

The Enforcement of Professional Codes

Before we leave the subject of professional codes of ethics, it is necessary to explore one other issue, enforcement. Historically, professional groups have been self-regulating, which most believe is the best approach. The traditional method for ensuring compliance has been selective admission and discipline of members, mainly through sanctions. Some ethicists believe a focus on sanctions is a mistake because there is no evidence that adequate sanctions (whether blame or loss of license) deter misconduct by others.[28] William May strongly denounces using a code to solve the problem of professional discipline, preferring an approach that seeks to be remedial and inclusive rather than codal and exclusive.[29]

The enforcement of codes of ethics poses many problems.[30] The basic problem of distribution is often overlooked. The regular distribution of a written code to members is not sufficient to ensure compliance. On the other hand, simply posting an organization's code on a bulletin board will almost certainly encourage noncompliance. The assignment of accountability is also vital to enforcement. Experts contend that enforcement committees should be composed of both professionals and laypersons to prevent in-house protectionism.

The enforcement of standards is chiefly dependent on the willingness of colleagues and the public to report violations. Once guilt has been determined, disciplinary action usually takes one of three forms: censure, suspension, or termination.

The Limitations of Professional Codes

What then can be said about professional codes of ethics as they apply to ministerial ethics? Do they benefit the professions today?

Many people feel uncomfortable with a rules approach to morality, which professional codes appear to be. This deontological bent seems to downplay the role of character and overlook the complex question of motives and consequences. As many note, the inner integrity of a professional may be assumed, but it is seldom encouraged in the codal approach to professional ethics.

Another concern regarding traditional professional ethics is the failure to consider the nature of social roles. Codes of ethics fail to recognize the "power gap" between professional and client. It is also difficult to translate the ethical ideals of justice and liberation into codes of ethics.[31]

A third concern could be labeled self-interest. Lisa Newton attacks professional codes as "a code of Professional Manners oriented toward a Professional Image for the protection of Professional Compensation."[32] Her scathing critique notes that codes limit advertising, suppress competition, and forbid contradiction of professional judgments, which she calls "gentlemanly etiquette." Yale professor Gaylord Noyce agrees, stating that the codes of professional groups "are shot through with collusive self-interest."[33]

No doubt, codes also have a serious problem with accountability. Because the authorship, instruction, and enforcement of codes generally take place within each professional organization, the perception is that professionals are more concerned with self-interest than with ethical conduct. This obstacle is best overcome by including nonprofessionals, who have no vested interests, in all aspects of the code process.

In spite of these limitations, professional organizations continue to depend on codes of ethics to ensure standardized behavior. A report by the Business Roundtable found that 84 percent of Fortune 500 companies has a code of ethics.[34] Professional codes communicate the basic ethical expectations within an association of professionals. Codes of ethics will serve professionals, their clients, and society at large for some time to come.

A Ministerial Code of Ethics

According to some, a code of ethics for ministers seems about as necessary as Reeboks for a jaguar. "After all, ministers live and breathe morality, don't they? Their job is *upholding* a community's ethics, isn't it? So why a code for pastors?"[35]

In the earliest days of the settlement of Texas, a historian wrote of the organization of a "Committee of Vigilance" in May 1837. It was composed of six Protestant ministers "to prevent imposters from securing the confidence of the people, in the exercise of ministerial functions."[36] This must have been one of the earliest attempts to codify ministerial ethics.

A discussion of standards for ministers appeared in 1928 titled *Ministerial Ethics and Etiquette: The Minister's Own Manual of Conduct—Practical Guidance for Specific Situations.* Like so many early ministerial codes, "it is interesting as a period piece—but it is minimalism in ethics."[37] The book contains some discussion about relationships with colleagues, a denomination, and a community, but most of the lengthy admonitions concern personal life, finances, conducting worship, appropriate dress, and professional etiquette.[38]

Since these words were penned, expectations for an ethical ministry have increased greatly. In recent days, moral lapses among the clergy have alarmed parishioners and aroused the public. Church leaders in every denomination are calling for a thorough study of ethical issues involving the clergy and seeking ways to increase moral accountability in the ministry. Concerned that denominations and local churches are not holding pastors to high moral standards, Focus on the Family in 2003 asked fifty thousand pastors to adopt a "Shepherd's Covenant" for greater accountability.[39]

After a Colorado district court awarded $1.2 million in damages to a woman who had an affair with an Episcopal cleric, Bishop Peter Lee of Virginia warned his priests:

> Laity and others who turn to the clergy for pastoral counsel and prayer have every right to expect their most painful secrets to be safe, their most confusing thoughts to be heard, their hopes and their aspirations to be received with respectful concern. But some persons expect their clergy to provide the permanent tenderness of intimacy they missed as children or that eludes them now as spouses.[40]

His letter also cautioned priests against offering themselves as "substitute objects" for the longings of their parishioners. Absent from the bishop's communiqué, however, was any acknowledgment of clergy vulnerability or any plan for prevention.

This episode highlights one of the difficulties ministers share with the secular professions. They are self-protective.

> Jurgen Moltmann reminds us that clergy protect the *status quo*. We fear we have much to lose if we examine our practice as clergy in the context of new understandings about our responsibilities; if we find ourselves wanting, we will have to change. We may have to give up established ways.[41]

As already observed, professional groups have traditionally regulated themselves (though not always with success), utilizing codes of ethics and disciplining boards. The professions regularly examine their responsibilities to their constituencies, evaluate their behavior, compare codes, and work to improve ethical practice.

Should there be equivalent accountability among the clergy? It is indeed startling that these concerns are so seldom raised by the ordained. Some believe ministers do not need ethical reflection because ministry is a moral work and therefore self-correcting. Others claim it is demeaning to approach ministry as one would a secular profession.

A major reason codes of ethics for ministers are so rare, claims Paul Camenisch, is the clergy's dedication to "atypical moral commitment." Such a commitment is a significant part of the self-image of the minister and the public's expectations.

> I would suggest that one reason the clergy has been slower than the other major professions to develop its own distinctive ethic is that this atypical moral commitment was assumed to be so central to the profession that many thought it insulting to suggest that specific rules and guidelines were needed to require it.[42]

Because of the separation of church and state in the United States, the public sector ordinarily does not regulate the standards of clergy as they do those of other professionals, except in two areas: performing marriage ceremonies and counseling.[43] From an ethical perspective, this should be no problem. Clergy standards should always be higher than legal codes, which are only society's baselines. In spite of this or any other variation, the question remains, "Does this difference free us from the accountability we expect of sisters and brothers working in other vineyards?"[44] We cannot presume that just because preachers proclaim justice, righteousness, and morality that they will be just, righteous, and moral.

Ministers are accountable for their behavior not only because of professional expectations but also because of their commitment to Christian ethics. Being a moral example in ministry is a biblical expectation.[45] Ethical conduct based on theological convictions is the very soil in which the clergy work.

A ministerial code of ethics is supported by biblical principles, theological conclusions, professional standards, and practical considerations. That is why a clergy code of ethics, properly developed, clearly written, and appropriately enforced, is needed.

Unlike other professionals, ministers will probably never be driven by outside forces to begin this task, nor should they be. Their own moral convictions and vocational expectations should motivate them to seek the highest ethical standards for ministry. Their calling from God, personal character, and commitment to Christian ministry will allow them to do no less.

The Purposes of a Ministerial Code

The overarching purpose of a ministerial code of ethics is accountability. Ministers sometimes resist codes and regulations because they want to be answerable to no one except God. When questioned about financial accountability, televangelist Paul Crouch of Trinity Broadcasting Network declared publicly that "the Almighty [was] his only watchdog." An editorial in *Christianity Today* responded that eventually we all get what is coming to us, but "in the meantime it helps to have structures that encourage us to behave."[46]

Professional codes are usually written to specify the moral obligations of the professional, as understood by the professional group. Likewise, a code of ethics for ministers should reflect how the ordained of God should conduct their ministry, as understood by their fellow ministers. In other words, a Christian minister is accountable not only to God but also to other members of the clergy. Codes are usually developed over many years and represent the combined experience of many people. Writing an adequate code, therefore, is more than a personal enterprise.

The four major purposes of professional codes also apply to clergy codes. The first purpose of a ministerial code is to provide guidelines that reflect the values of ministry. Clergy ethics affirms that to be a Christian minister means assuming certain basic obligations common to all clergy. These norms guide those called to serve toward an ethical ministry and stress the areas in which ministers are uniquely vulnerable.

Archibald Hart of Fuller Seminary describes a strange paradox in Christian ministry:

> We can be supersensitive to sin and immoral behaviors, but we are often oblivious to the need for ethical boundaries. This partially accounts for the fall of upright, spiritual, and well-intentioned pastors.[47]

Hart concludes that the underlying problem is not so much a lack of morality as a lack of broad ethical guidelines to govern the practice of ministry.

Guidelines for ministers serve three functions.[48] First, they articulate personal ethical standards that are significant. Such standards relate to financial and family responsibilities and classic labor-management issues such as work schedules, study habits, vacations, and sabbaticals. Second, guidelines govern expectations regarding a minister's conduct in relation to colleagues, the congregation, and the community. Third, guidelines express ministerial ideals. Like the best examples from professional codes, clergy norms should stretch toward a higher standard of behavior than is currently being practiced. The Disciples Code reads, "I will seek to be Christlike in my personal attitudes and conduct toward all people regardless of race, class, or creed."[49]

The second purpose of a ministerial code relates to competency. At first we may think this trait applies more to the secular professions than to the ministry. Doctors need to be well trained and to keep up with the latest medical discoveries. People confide in lawyers to protect their legal rights. Physicians and lawyers possess "threatening knowledge" that, if used carelessly or improperly, could be harmful.

Yet ministers also have threatening knowledge in the form of confidential information and the knowledge they possess about God. For a pastor to be competent in the use of this knowledge requires at least two essentials: ministry skills and mental and spiritual health. Most ministerial codes require ministers to grow "through comprehensive reading and careful study and by attending . . . conferences" and to cultivate their personal devotional lives.[50]

Third, a code of ethics can support and protect an individual minister. Under the topic "financial matters," a 1990 Presbyterian code states, "Ministers and church professionals shall not use church funds, accounts, and/or resources . . . [or] parishioner funds, accounts, and/or resources for personal or private advantage."[51] Codified statements such as this one can protect a pastor from behavior that could lead to serious personal or congregational problems.

Hart views morality as the edge of a precipice. On one side is safe ground (non-sin); on the other there is disaster (sin).

> It's only one step from safety to falling off the cliff. A code of ethics is like a fence erected well back from the precipice edge. It warns all those who come close that this is dangerous territory: CAUTION! PASS HERE AT YOUR OWN RISK.[52]

A final purpose of an ethical code for ministers is to define the moral necessities of the ministerial profession. For the person planning to become a minister, as well as for the layperson, a written code explains the ethical expectations of the pastoral vocation.

An association of ministers in the United Church of Christ recently completed a policy on sexual ethics for their group. The document begins by explicitly defining sexual misconduct:

- sexual advances, welcomed or unwelcomed
- requests for sexual favors
- inappropriate affection such as kissing, touching, bumping, patting
- any sexual contact related to terms of employment
- any sexual contact that exploits the vulnerability of a parishioner, client, or employee
- Dating of parishioners by religious professionals is a gray area filled with ambiguity. In such situations, consultation with colleagues is essential.[53]

There should be no doubt among this group of ministers or their congregations what is construed as sexual misconduct.

These four purposes of ministerial codes should not mislead a person to view them as a collection of moral rules to keep ministers out of trouble. In a sense, "a professional code of ethics is simply an intensification of the ethical concerns of normal life, but an intensification needed because of the more specialized role, the intense knowledge in human situations of high risk and vulnerability, which are a part of functioning as an ordained pastor."[54] As such, codes are not merely guidelines for how ministers are to act in certain situations. If so, they would always be too specific or too general to be helpful.

As Karen Lebacqz has so well explained, codes of ethics for ministers are better understood and utilized as statements about the "image of the profession and the character of the professionals."[55] Clergy codes of ethics reflect the virtues and values of the person called to minister in Christ's name. Simply put, a code paints the portrait of a good minister.

The Structure of a Ministerial Code

A growing concern about the spiritual formation of seminary students and their readiness for ministry led the Association of Theological Schools (ATS) to conduct intensive research in the 1970s and 1980s. To develop a profile for ministry, the study group surveyed over four thousand clergy and laity representing all denominations affiliated with the ATS. The results, along with recommendations, were published in the document *Clergy Assessment and Career Development*. One section of the report revealed some serious deficiencies in ministerial morality, which led the researchers to make three proposals: (1) that a more formal code of ethics be established to help regulate ministry relationships, (2) that a pastor set up an accountability system as a prevention strategy, and (3) that a minister know his or her personal limits and vulnerabilities.[56]

Let us assume that a group of ministers took the first charge seriously. What topics should they address in a code? Should the document be composed of principles or specific obligations? In particular, what categories should be covered in a ministerial code?

As a result of the renewed interest in clergy ethics in recent years, a host of new publications have appeared. A survey of the literature reveals several recurring themes, many focusing on the moral character of the cleric. According to these writers, an ethical minister should possess certain fundamental virtues: trustworthiness, prudence, faithfulness, truthfulness, and integrity.

When the conduct of the ordained is specifically described, certain issues rise to the surface. Presbyterian professors Walter Wiest and Elwyn Smith are most concerned with truth telling, especially in relation to plagiarism, letters of recommendation, and theological differences. A philosophy professor writing about "Professional Ethics and the Practice of Religion" suggests that any discussion of the clergy/parishioner relationship should deal with clerical roles, truth telling, confidentiality, paternalism, and behavior control.[57]

Another text analyzes organized religion from a critical point of view. The book begins by looking at three central ethical issues: confidentiality, "risk taking," and "convert seeking." The author seems most concerned with religious groups that endanger the life and health of members or use coercive conversion techniques.[58]

Studies such as these do pinpoint some of the more obvious and crucial issues in ministerial ethics. As might be expected, however, one of the best ways to analyze the structure of clergy codes is to study existing ones.

During the early part of the last century, several mainline denominations developed formal codes of ethics for their ministers (appendix B). In comparison to these early examples, the few denominational codes in use today appear to be extensively updated (appendix C). The present trend is away from denominational documents and toward codes constructed by smaller associations of ministers, usually covering only one area of responsibility, such as clergy sexual ethics or counseling ethics (appendix D).

An analysis of these statements reveals a certain common structure and great similarity in content. One thing that is not apparent is the kind of language that best fits a clergy code. One Christian psychologist acknowledges that "some of the unique roles of the pastor don't easily lend themselves to ethical codes"; therefore, he prefers basic principles.[59] However, if a primary purpose of a code is to serve as a guideline, then specific obligations have to be spelled out in addition to guiding principles.

Another purpose of codes is ensuring competency. This intent does not surface in many of the present or past documents. Theological, pastoral, and spiritual qualifications for ministers need to be clearly defined to endorse skills in ministry.

The practice of ministry also involves many unique roles and responsibilities. Most written codes address the major areas of ministerial vulnerability (such as sex, money, and power), as well as unique pressure points (such as family, confidentiality, and plagiarism). Codal statements that cover these topics serve to support and protect a minister by clearly defining ethical boundaries.

Sometimes a code begins with an introductory paragraph, a preamble affirming a minister's sense of calling to the ministry and commitment to ethical integrity. The Disciples Code begins:

> I am a minister of the Lord Jesus Christ, called of God to proclaim the unsearchable riches of His love. Therefore, I voluntarily adopt the following principles in order that through dedication and self-discipline I may set a more worthy example for those whom I seek to lead and serve [appendix C].

As already shown in this book, a clear definition of pastoral ethics can be given by addressing four areas of a minister's life: obligations to self and family, to the congregation, to colleagues, and to the community. Most clergy codes follow this format in one way or another. To lay the groundwork for a code of our own, let's look at each of these four worlds of the minister.

Normally overlooked in other professional codes are the personal and family responsibilities of the professional. Not so in codes of ethics for ministers. The personal integrity of a servant of God is at the heart of ministry. Guarding that integrity involves such obvious matters as lifestyle, which is why most denominations have written and unwritten codes defining conduct unbecoming a minister. The codes cited in appendices B and C are quite specific: They require a minister to keep physically fit, avoid debts, be scrupulously honest, pay bills before moving, and give ample time to family life. When pastoral needs collide with family needs, a minister must be sure that church duties do not become an idol before which the spouse and children are sacrificed.

The personal integrity of a pastor is important because it affects credibility. As the "medium of the message," the life of the prophet of God must point to the truth of the gospel. Credibility in ministry includes such basic matters as a minister's covenant to cultivate a devotional life, reserve study time, refuse to plagiarize sermons, and keep in touch with the best religious thought.

Ministers are forever pulled by weekly necessities (sermon preparation, newsletter articles, committee meetings), unanticipated ministries (funerals, counseling, visiting the ill), and the need and desire for spiritual development (reading, conferences, spiritual disciplines). Meanwhile, the family waits at the dinner table. The busy church leader desperately wants to keep work and family life in proper balance. A well-written code can help a minister establish priorities and stick to them.

The second area addressed in a ministerial code is the congregation. Most difficult problems for professionals appear in relation to parishioners.

Although the member of a congregation is a "client," several important differences exist between a typical professional-client association and a minister-parishioner relationship.[60] For one thing, the distinction between laity and clergy is not as well-defined as it is for the client and other professionals. The authority of the minister is perceived differently than that of a professional (and it should be). Another major disparity is that a minister's "clients" are an organized group; in fact, in many denominations, the vote of the congregation determines employment, termination, and salary.

This reality imposes a vulnerability on a minister. No doctor worries about a disgruntled patient starting a campaign among clients to have his or her salary frozen. Yet every time a pastor serves an individual member, possible repercussions in the flock must be considered. Why? Misperceptions could erupt into church conflict and cause the pastor's dismissal.

With all this in mind, what ethical obligations do pastors have in regard to parishioners? One shepherding sin is almost universal in codes for ministers. It is "the unethical aspect of what we call 'sheep stealing' or proselytizing members from another community of faith."[61] This practice, perhaps influenced by the competitive nature of American business, undercuts the credibility of the pastoral office.

The limits of confidentiality is another issue with which all professionals wrestle. Many states now have legal codes that carefully prescribe "confessional privilege." Beyond what is legally required, a pastor must carefully consider obligations regarding confidentiality. A minister's obligation is often stated in codes as an absolute principle: "The confidential statements made to a minister by his parishioners are sacred and not to be divulged" (Presbyterian Code). It would be better to word the standard in a way that allows each minister to define the rare circumstances in which information may be divulged.[62]

Other responsibilities involving congregations that are covered in codes include service rather than salary as the primary motivation for ministry, integrity in preaching, fairness in dealing with factions, impartiality in administrative decisions, and the basic obligation to nurture the believing community.

Although ministers have a community of colleagues, they often lack structural unity. Ministry can be a lonely profession. Most ministers confess that they need support from their colleagues, including moral discernment, empathetic understanding, encouragement, ministry resources, and general camaraderie. Too often the relationships among ministers are characterized by competition and conspiracy rather than mutual blessing.

Clergy can find many positive ways to build healthy relationships with other ministers and still uphold ethical standards. Almost all codes emphasize four basic obligations ministers have in regard to one another:

> I will not speak scornfully or in derogation of any colleague in public. In any private conversation critical of a colleague, I will speak responsibly and temperately. [Unitarian Universalist Ministers Association (UUMA) Code]

> It is unethical for a minister to interfere directly or indirectly with the parish work of another minister. [Methodist Code]

> Except in emergencies, ministerial service should not be rendered to the members of another parish without the knowledge of the minister of the parish. [Presbyterian Code]

> If I am to share the ministry of a church with (an)other minister(s), I will earnestly seek clear delineation of responsibility, accountability, and channels of communication before responsibilities are assumed. [UUMA Code]

A variety of other collegial responsibilities appear in some current codes (appendix C). The Disciples Code adds a number of pledges: not to compete with other ministers for pulpits or honors; not to embarrass successors by "meddling in the affairs" of a former church; to show courtesy to predecessors; to show loyal support to a pastor after retirement; and to show respect toward all ministers, regardless of the size or nature of their field.

The Eastern Oklahoma Presbytery Code (EOP) is thorough—twenty-five pages written in a narrative style. Under "Colleague Relationships" the authors present forty-four imperatives in nine categories. Most of these obligations cover the common ground of staff relationships, denominational duties, treatment of predecessors and successors, and the role of retired pastors. The document does plow some virgin soil, however, in two important areas overlooked in other codes: the responsibilities of the "minister-without-pastoral-charge" and proper relationships with other professionals.[63]

Are there limits to clergy collegiality? We all know ministers who destroy healthy congregations. Some are on the way out of ministry. Others are truly incompetent. A few have serious spiritual, moral, and emotional problems that will not change until they receive help. When such pastors fail and are forced to move on, do ministers close ranks behind the flawed colleagues and try to find them another place of service?

Herein is a major ministerial dilemma. How can ministers be supportive of a comrade in the ministry and at the same time honestly fulfill their responsibilities to other congregations? Truthfulness in letters of recommendation and "truth in love" to the guilty colleague is a starting point.[64] One current code reads, "Should I know that a colleague is engaged in practices that are damaging . . . I will speak openly and frankly to her/him and endeavor to be of help" (UUMA Code).

The final statement of the Congregational Code is a principle that summarizes for ministers the responsibility they have to one another: "As members of the same profession and brothers in the service of a common Master, the relation between ministers should be one of frankness, of comradeship, and of cooperation."

The final area usually covered by traditional ministerial codes is a minister's responsibility to the community. This appears to be one of the weaker sections of most written codes. Three of the four early codes were silent on this subject. Only the Unitarian Code spoke to community obligations: The minister is "not under obligations to marry every couple that comes to him to be married," and as a citizen "he should, therefore, be faithful to his public obligations and should respond to reasonable requests for assistance in community work."

More recent codes have more to say on the subject, but most of the counsel centers on the self-interests of the church rather than on service to the community. The concern of the Disciples Code seems to be a fear that the church or its ministers might be corrupted by the world; thus, it warns ministers "to be human . . . but . . . never lower [your] ideals in order to appear 'a good fellow.'" It further cautions its clergy to avoid "funeral or marriage rackets" and to beware of consuming the time of business and professional people with "unimportant matters."

A more positive word about church and community as it relates to the ministerial profession comes from three denominational groups. First is an obligation to be a moral and spiritual leader in the community: "I will maintain a prophetic pulpit, offering to the community religious and ethical leadership" (UUMA Code).

Second is a charge to remember that one's primary calling is to be the pastor of a congregation, a minister's primary community. This means, on the one hand, "I consider that my first duty to my community is to be a conscientious pastor and leader of my own congregation" (Disciples Code). On the other hand, "Ministers may assume outside commitments that do not detract from their pastoral responsibilities" (EOP Code). The Disciples document adds that this primary responsibility to the church should never be used "as an easy excuse to escape reasonable responsibilities that the community calls upon me to assume."

Only rarely do codes direct pastors to step into the community to render beneficial service. Whereas professional codes emphasize that doctors, lawyers, and engineers have an obligation to be social leaders, assume community responsibilities, and work for the betterment of society, this concept is glaringly absent from ministerial codes.

One clergy code prohibits accepting "fees or gifts as payment for business or professional referrals" (EOP Code). Another encourages "sympathetic support to neighboring ministers or other religious bodies" (UUMA Code). The only time the codes of ethics for ministers focus on the needs of the community is when they say, "I will encourage members' participation in efforts to solve community problems" (UUMA Code), and "Ministers shall support efforts to better that community" (EOP Code).

Obviously, this area of a minister's responsibility needs serious thought. If the church is to be salt and light to the world (Matt. 5:13–16), then the moral leaders of the Christian community surely have significant obligations to society.

What have we discovered then about the structure of ministerial codes? First, the language of the codes is dualistic: Both specific norms and general principles are declared. Second, certain key issues, such as confidentiality and truthfulness, appear in most codes. Third, the points at which a minister is most vulnerable ethically, such as sexual temptation and imbalanced work habits, receive a great deal of attention. Finally, most codes for ministers focus on the four major categories outlined above: self and family, the congregation, colleagues, and the community.

The Enforcement of a Ministerial Code

Earlier we noted three major difficulties in developing a code of ethics: authorship, instruction, and enforcement. The first two problems will be discussed when we consider how to write a code. Before us now is the issue of enforcement.

When the National Religious Broadcasters formally established its ethics and financial accountability code in January 1989, the organization told members to comply within three months or they would be dismissed. Before the year ended, officials admitted they had been overly optimistic about implementation and enforcement.[65] The variety of ways church groups have enforced their codes, or failed to do so, indicates the complexity of this issue for ministers as well.

By assumption of the role, a minister vows to abide by certain codes of conduct, whether written or not. Formal clergy codes are based on this account-ability. A ministerial code of ethics, by its very nature, assumes the acceptance of personal responsibility, the reporting of violations, and effective enforcement. Yet this last matter of disciplining code breakers has long troubled churches and denominations.

A Virginia minister who chairs an ethics guidelines committee in his reli-gious body told of a recent dilemma. One of the denomination's prominent pastors became sexually involved with a married parishioner. After he expressed repentance for his failure, the erring cleric's church voted to restore him. Pas-toral colleagues in the Ministers Association felt they also had an obligation to respond, as the group's code of ethics had been violated. After investigation by the association, the group sent a letter of admonition to the clergyman.

When church shepherds break their covenants to God and fail to fulfill their responsibilities to their congregation, what should be done? Should a minister report the sexual abuse of a parishioner by another pastor in the name of col-legial support? What enforcement procedures should churches or denomina-tions follow? What sanctions, if any, are appropriate? How should the laity and clergy relate to a fallen minister who needs healing and restoration?

As noted earlier, professional groups historically have been self-regulating. The importance of including both professionals and laypersons on enforce-ment committees, say the experts, cannot be overstressed. Another essential ingredient is the willingness of colleagues and the public to report problems. Key components in effective enforcement by committees are confidentiality, fair and just representation, and the release of committee members from legal liability.

The most common practice of most groups is to have an ethics committee that decides on all aspects of ethical behavior. As one regulatory board said, "We are the police, we are the prosecution, we are the grand jury, and the petit jury."[66]

Studying the practices of churches and denominational groups in response to ministers accused of unethical behavior is indeed a frustrating exercise. The majority of congregations have no established procedure. Most church groups act in an informal way; they simply deal with offenses as they arise. When a pastor or other staff member is charged with a transgression, an established church authority (deacons, elders, or committee) usually investigates the accusation. They then either exonerate the falsely accused or sanction the guilty.

There is no end to the ways religious bodies respond to ministerial mis-conduct. This obvious inconsistency among churches cannot help but diminish ministerial accountability. Why should the ordained seriously reflect on their ethical obligations if church and denominational expectations are lax or nonexistent?

The ministerial codes written during the first half of the twentieth century (appendix B) contain no instructions about enforcement. The documents seem to assume, with unrealistic optimism, that the ethical ideals contained in the codes would so motivate ministers that no enforcement would be necessary.

The more recent pastoral codes (appendices C and D) are not so naive. "A profession that will not police itself runs the danger of being policed by others," states the EOP Code. Although the newer documents evidence a great deal of diversity, they all contain a procedure for compliance. At the same time, none of them outlines a method of distribution of the code, and only one of them addresses the vital responsibility of reporting infractions.

The United Church of Christ's statement on "Sexual Ethics in the Pastoral Relationship," framed by the Potomac Association (appendix D), is a good example of a code created by a smaller group of ministers dealing with one ethical topic. The opening paragraph alludes to "specific incidents surfacing . . . [of] sexual misconduct of religious professionals" among their congregations. These incidents evidently precipitated the study and the report. More than one-half of the policy specifies procedural responsibilities to ensure compliance to the code.

The Potomac group's Committee on Church and Ministry (composed of laity and clergy) has the primary responsibility for enforcement. The committee investigates allegations, appoints advocates, conducts hearings, and determines actions. Other procedures recommended in the code relate to appeals, timing, negotiated settlements, disciplinary reviews, and preventive strategies.

Two documents that model a more complete procedure for enforcement are the EOP Code and the UUMA *Guidelines*.[67] They are also helpful because of the church traditions they represent—the limited hierarchical structure of the Presbyterians and the congregational ecclesiology of the Unitarian Universalists.

In the EOP Code, a great deal of space is given to defining the responsibility of the governing authorities of the church. Briefly described, the process follows this order:

1. Allegations are brought to an elder.
2. The accused is confronted.
3. The elder takes the accusation to session.
4. The session confronts the pastor and investigates.
5. If the charge is false, the accuser is disciplined.
6. If the allegation is true, the Committee on Ministry (COM) is contacted.
7. The COM may address the problem or assign it to a committee.

8. The investigation is done by a special disciplinary committee, which decides on sanctions.
9. The presbytery may initiate its own investigation without a request.

The EOP report also includes a policy regarding the immoral or unethical behavior of "Potential Members of Presbytery." This "front door" regulation determines the moral fitness of ministers who seek membership in the Presbytery.

Although the doctrines of the Unitarian Universalist denomination are significantly different from those of most Christian churches, its government is basically congregational, which is similar to that of Baptist and Congregational denominations, as well as that of many evangelical churches. UUMA ministers are called and ordained by a local congregation. If they plan to move to another church, they need to receive ministerial credentials from the Fellowship Committee, which is the gateway to membership in the Ministers Association.

An accusation against a UUMA minister is first handled by the local church. The *Guidelines* explain procedures for dismissing a faulty minister by vote of the congregation and the conditions of termination. Charges of immoral behavior can be taken to the Fellowship Committee, which can investigate the allegations. The Ministers Association may also initiate investigation, usually at the request of colleagues. A minister determined to be guilty by either group faces six possible sanctions: three levels of censure (caution, admonition, or reprimand) and three severe sanctions (probation, suspension, or removal from UUMA membership).[68]

To their credit, professional codes of ethics over the years have developed carefully worded procedures that prescribe enforcement of their standards. To their detriment, ministerial codes of ethics seldom deal with compliance. With rare exception, the few that do seldom go beyond a few words of counsel about the censure or termination of ministers. Parachurch group codes are only slightly better.

What lessons can we learn from these limited attempts at enforcement of ethical standards by denominations, associations of ministers, and other Christian groups? Obviously, ensuring compliance to a code is a difficult task with many risks. Perhaps that is why enforcement procedures are so rare among clergy codes. Nevertheless, since ministerial codes are based on accountability, there must be some group to which a minister is accountable.

This brief overview also reveals the importance of having a system for reporting violations that is free from intimidation or coercion. Perhaps the most difficult aspect of enforcement is the one assigned to an authoritative group: the responsibility to investigate charges, determine actions, and apply sanctions. A committee adequate for this task must represent all involved, both laity and clergy.

To make certain that enforcement procedures are just and complete, a well-thought-out and clearly written policy is imperative. Of course, the church polity of a person's denomination will significantly influence the entire process.

This discussion of a ministerial code of ethics has made known the purpose, nature, and structure of codes, as well as their enforcement. Other professional ethics models have revealed the strengths and the weaknesses of clergy codes in general. Now the discussion becomes more specific. As we approach the final assignment, that of writing a code of ethics suitable for today's minister, we will seek to apply what we have learned thus far.

How to Write a Code of Ethics

Voices from many sectors of the religious community are calling for a reconsideration of the value of a written code of ethics for ministers. "Many groups, especially mainline Protestants, have elaborate books of order or discipline governing the conduct of their clergy. Even evangelicals have come to realize in recent years that there must be some way to guide ministerial conduct in matters that are not made explicit in Scripture."[69]

A study by the Association of Theological Schools attempted to assess the correlation between readiness for ministry and seminary training. The published report contained many recommendations. In a section stressing the importance of personal growth for clergy, the authors noted with regret that ministers are "currently only loosely bound by a moral code that is subject to differing interpretations." Therefore, they proposed that "a more formal code of ethics be established to help regulate ministry relationships."[70]

Over a decade ago, the growing problem of pastoral abuse of women was the subject of an article in the *Christian Century.* One solution suggested by the alarmed author was the creation of "a new ethical code that accurately names and recognizes the problem."[71]

Another voice supporting codes of ethics for ministers is that of a psychology professor. H. Newton Maloney observed that clergy malpractice issues are increasing, and ministers have no agreed upon statement of ethics to which they can subscribe and by which they can be judged. He added:

> A recent national survey concluded that there is a dearth of concern for professional ethics among church bodies. . . . This lack of overt concern, coupled with denominational protectionism and the separation of church and state, leads me to say that the statement that there is no agreed upon code of ethics for clergy across denominations is not an exaggeration.[72]

Ministers, unlike other professionals, have no central organization or single code of ethics to which they can turn for support. Even among religious denominations, as we have just seen, there are relatively few statements of ethical guidelines for clergy. It is alarming that in the two major sources that contain more than two hundred professional codes, not a single code for ministers can be found.[73]

This void may be due partly to the nature of the ministerial profession and partly to the existence of religious pluralism in the United States. American religious diversity, however, does not prevent religious denominations or groups of ministers from creating a code for their own constituency. Most certainly it does not hinder an individual minister from reflecting on his or her own moral obligations and writing a personal code as a guide for ethics in ministry.

Certainly, a written code of ethics by itself does not guarantee satisfactory moral performance. A Notre Dame law professor notes, "Such guiding codes are thus at one and the same time absolutely necessary as a first level in establishing the ethics of the profession and also a serious, if unrecognized danger when they serve to reduce moral inquiry and wrestling to a merely literal conformity devoid of moral argument."[74] Nonetheless, a clear statement of ministerial ethical standards, adequately authored, properly developed, and appropriately implemented, can go a long way toward strengthening ministerial integrity.

Authorship—The Who Question

Who should author codes, individuals or groups? Should authorship come from within the profession or from without? As late as the nineteenth century, leaders in professions did serve as the sole authors of codes. Today, virtually no professional code has a single author; "codes by committee" is the norm.[75]

The most common practice is for the members of a profession to write a code themselves. This is the pattern used for most medical, legal, and business codes. The obvious problem with this method is that the document may be written in the self-interest of the members with little regard for the clientele or society.[76] Proponents of internal authorship believe, however, that members of a profession can best determine what policies are in society's best interest and that members are in a better position to relate them to society than a third party.

Those who argue for external authorship do so from one of two perspectives. One group believes that codes should be written entirely by outside sources. Since professions depend on society's willingness to promote them, only society can "provide a sufficient moral foundation."[77]

A second theory, and one that seems to be the best option, is that professionals should write codes in conjunction with laypersons. To do otherwise is to place too much importance on the work of either group. This cooperative effort also provides credibility at a later time if people question certain practices.

How do these trends apply to the ministerial profession? The best code, the most comprehensive code, and the one most free from self-interest is undoubtedly the one produced by a committee composed of both laypersons and clergy. Since parishioners are the ones most affected by ministries, they should be included in defining ethical standards and supervising implementation. The committee chosen to author a clergy code should also be inclusive, representing male and female, young and old, and all ethnic groups within the larger body.

Does this mean a personal code authored by an individual minister is obsolete? Not at all. Writing a personal code of ethics is a good exercise in developing one's own ethical standards in ministry. Every minister should at some time think through his or her own ethical conduct in ministry. What better way than by writing a personal code of ethics? Such a document should allow for evaluation and updating. As ministers grow in ethical sensitivity, they should expand and adjust their moral guidelines. A personal code of ethics written by a minister could also be shared with the cleric's own congregation. Most churches would be pleased to learn of their spiritual leaders' ethical standards. Shared codes serve two main purposes: They support ministers in clearly defining ethical intentions, and they hold ministers ethically accountable to a larger group, which is a central purpose of all ethical codes.

Procedure—The How Question

When a denomination, a church, or a group of ministers decides it needs a code of ethics, how should those involved proceed? A typical approach might be as follows. A church approves a resolution authorizing a code committee to go to work. A representative committee is selected and begins by reviewing past and present clergy codes, comparing the recent codes of similar organizations, and studying helpful resources in the field of ministerial ethics. A preliminary draft of the new code is circulated to all members for feedback. When the responses have been assimilated, the committee puts the code in final form and sends it to the entire membership for study. The church then ratifies and adopts the document, and implementation begins.

A minister who is writing a personal code of ethics would follow a similar procedure. After wrestling with the key questions of ministerial ethics, the pastor would reflect on the basic areas of clergy ethics to be covered by the code (see the worksheet at the end of this chapter). After writing a preamble, he or she would compose statements of obligation in regard to self and family, the congregation, colleagues, and the community. The first draft could be reviewed by another minister and a layperson to provide perspective, as well as to prevent serious oversights. The final draft would become a working document as the pastor matures in ministry.

Content—The What Question

We have come now to the "meat and potatoes" of a clergy code, the content. What subjects and statements should be included in an ethical code for ministers? Before we can unravel that question, a preliminary distinction must be made.

Professional ethics scholars have called attention to differences between present and older codes. Modern Generation I codes, products of the early twentieth century, dealt with the etiquette of relationships—"Do not speak ill of a colleague." Since the 1980s, complex ethical questions have led to the era of Modern Generation II codes, which "deal with dilemmas rising out of new knowledge, new technology, and new social attitudes."[78]

In like manner, the older clergy codes in appendix B reflect Modern Generation I codes. The content of contemporary codes (appendix C) reveal a more complex ministry in an increasingly complicated world—Modern Generation II codes.

One way to address the what question of ministerial codes is to use a threefold division first introduced by the Christian apologist C. S. Lewis. His approach focuses on the major areas of the moral life itself: What do the codes have to say about the inner moral life of the practitioner, the relationships between individuals, and the purpose of human life as a whole?[79]

Whereas other professional codes pay scant attention to the inner life of the practitioner, ministerial codes focus on the moral character of the clergy, as well they should. Clergy codes are not just Talmudic collections of rules to guide action. Laws will do little to promote ethical conduct unless the ministers to be guided are persons of character. Integrity is central to ministry; it is not an option. A car may lack air conditioning and still be a good car. Not so for a minister and moral character. "Losing integrity is like having your lungs cave in," writes Lewis Smedes. "Everything else goes out with them."[80]

Those composing guidelines for ethics in ministry must underscore the centrality of character. Ministerial codes of conduct should point to the inner life of the one called of God to be an overseer of the church. Paul reminded Timothy that a pastoral overseer must be "blameless" (1 Tim. 3:2 NKJV). In personal life, family relationships, and spiritual leadership, the person set apart to minister must be "above reproach" (1 Tim. 3:1–7). Solomon, possibly reflecting on his father's thumbprint on his own life, wrote, "The righteous walk in integrity—happy are the children who follow them!" (Prov. 20:7 NRSV).

The shortcoming of most codes is that a set of rules fails to instill internal character. Many professional codes assume the integrity of their members and do not attempt to develop the inner life, which is the Achilles' heel of professionalism. Writers of codes for ministers must not make this mistake. Though all pastors should be persons of good character, a code should contain statements that harmonize the inner life of church ministers with their personal ethical standards.

Far more coverage is given in the ministerial codes to the second area of the moral life, relationships between individuals. The codes in the appendices discuss duties in regard to parishioners, fellow ministers, and people in the community. Insofar as the clergy codes spell out in detail a cleric's obligations to others, they encourage enablement and discourage exploitive relationships.[81] Writers of codes need to pay serious attention to stress points in the congregation, between colleagues, and among persons in the community in relation to the church minister.

Self-interest is often overlooked. Ministers are no different from other professionals, who often use their power to promote their own interests. One illustration of this is seen in procedures outlined for reporting ministerial misconduct (EOP Code). A layperson is immediately disciplined if the accusation cannot be substantiated; a minister rightly charged is given numerous levels of appeal and a wide assortment of lesser sanctions. The system is weighted against the lay accuser.

In the third area of ethics outlined by C. S. Lewis, that of the purpose of human life, most codes receive a low score. Many older codes, from that of Hippocrates in the fourth century B.C. to that of Florence Nightingale in the nineteenth century, were explicitly religious. Modern American pluralism and secularism have put an end to that.

Codes of ethics for ministers should express in clear language a worldview based on Christian belief. The preamble is an appropriate place to state basic convictions about God, Jesus Christ, the church, the world, and the cleric's call and commitment to ministry. The code should also contain statements of ministerial ideals, which represent a higher standard of behavior than most are practicing.[82] These ethical principles point to the moral will of God and provide a theological framework for clergy ethics.

The word that sums up the content of a ministerial code is the same word that characterizes ministerial ethics: *integrity*. A clergy code envisions an integrated moral life. The Hebrew word for integrity is *tōm* and means "whole," "sound," "unimpaired." Modern dictionary definitions of *integrity* define it as "soundness," "adherence to a code of values," "the quality or state of being complete or undivided."

In reality, no human being has arrived at wholeness. The important thing, however, is direction, not destination. A code of ethics for ministers is intended to guide them on that journey. As Lewis Smedes states:

> We have to check our intentions regularly and see whether we are still moving on the journey or whether, at some shadowed station, we left the train and went off to nowhere. For without integrity, anywhere is nowhere.[83]

Implementation—The When and Where Questions

The mere existence of a professional code is no guarantee of ethical performance. Darrell Reeck observed that the code of the American Bar Association did not prevent lawyers surrounding President Nixon from committing unethical and illegal acts.[84] The question now raised is this: What programs for implementing the code will make a difference?

A primary component of implementation is distribution. The first responsibility of any group producing a clergy code is to get copies printed and into the hands of every member. Simply publishing the code in a denominational journal is not enough. Every minister in the group must personally receive a copy.

A lack of instruction is a common weakness in all professions. A ministerial code of ethics is merely a document to frame and hang on the wall unless responsible leaders provide training. Either someone within the group who worked with the code committee or, better, an ethics authority from outside the profession could serve as a teacher.

Immediately after a code is ratified, instructional meetings should be scheduled. From that point forward, regular training sessions should be provided both to teach new ministers about the code and to help longtime clergy maintain a working knowledge of their ethical guidelines. These regular gatherings would also provide a forum for dialogue, updating, and adaptation of the guidelines to changing needs.

A third responsibility of implementation is organization. Once the code is approved, what ongoing structure is needed to ensure distribution, instruction, reporting, and enforcement? By assumption of the ministerial role, a church shepherd obligates himself or herself to abide by the group's code of ethics. This first means personal responsibility, but it also means accountability to all members of the ministerial association, for misbehavior brings criticism to the entire body.

The best insights from other professions reveal that a ministerial group should elect or appoint a standing committee to oversee enforcement, instruction, and other organizational responsibilities. As was true of the original code committee, this board should evidence gender, age, and ethnic diversity.

Concerning reporting and enforcement, the standing committee should develop methods that encourage both colleagues and the public to share information about violations. Enforcement is dependent chiefly on the willingness of people to report infractions. As discussed at length in the previous section, the enforcement of a code is one of three major difficulties in developing a code. The enforcement committee could be a separate council, but for several practical reasons, one standing committee would probably be adequate for most ministerial groups.

The toughest problem any denomination or association of ministers faces is prescribing disciplinary action that is appropriate, fair, legal, and redemptive. The three most common options are censure, suspension, and termination, although the latter two may have to be enforced by a local congregation in denominations with autonomous churches.

The Value of a Ministerial Code of Ethics

In sum, then, does the writing of a clergy code of ethics, along with its implementation, enhance ministerial behavior? This limited survey of past and present efforts suggests that the clergy profession has much work to do to make codes a vital part of daily practice. Compared to ethical guidelines of other professions, codes for church leaders suffer many deficiencies in authorship, procedure, content, and implementation.

Despite this apparent failure, a code of ethics for ministers has many positive values. The mere existence of a ministerial code radiates an unseen influence. The fact that a church minister receives a copy and reads it at least once, and perhaps in times of crisis refers to it for guidance, suggests a subtle but real influence.[85]

At the beginning of this chapter, two questions were raised: Is a code of ethics for ministers a help or a hindrance? Is it possible to write such a document? By now it should be clear that the answer to both questions is positive. Writing such a code is not only possible but imperative! Ministers need the guidance and support a code gives. Laypersons need to understand the ethical commitments of their clergy. Ministers need to be accountable to one another.

Addressing the serious problem of sexual misconduct among the clergy, a female associate minister concluded her appeal with several suggestions:

> [T]he most efficacious approach is clearly to work at prevention. Churches should encourage mutually supportive clergy marriages; develop clear professional ethical guidelines spelling out procedures and consequences for sexual misconduct; set limits on time, place, and circumstances of pastoral visits and counseling sessions; decrease pastoral stress factors . . . ; and put into place ministerial accountability (to the congregation, to denominational officials, and primarily, to God).[86]

We share this conviction about the need for guidelines and accountability. We also share a dream that reaches beyond this book. From our perspective, the purpose of this book is not fulfilled until each reader possesses an ethical code to guide him or her in ministry. At the primary level, this means developing a personal code of ethics. That is the reason for the worksheet at the close of this chapter. At a second level, it means initiating a code of ethics for a group of ministers to which he or she belongs, such as a local ministerial association.

The denominational level is admittedly the most difficult. This is especially true in denominations with strong convictions about congregational government and local church autonomy. At the same time, is it not possible for such bodies, who traditionally have produced confessions of faith that are accepted as doctrinal guides (although they may have no binding authority on the churches), to develop a code of ethics for ministers? Further, could not each local church in those denominations adopt and support a denominationally approved code or write one of its own?[87]

Why do we dream such dreams and see such visions? We believe, as the biblical prophets did, that such hope for integrity in ministry is not in vain. We pray that others agree.

Phillips Brooks, the renowned pastor of Holy Trinity Church in Boston, lived an exemplary and contagious Christian life. There was a saying that on gloomy days in Boston, when Brooks appeared in public, the sun came out. One day Josiah Royce, a Harvard philosopher, was asked by a student, "What is your definition of a Christian?" Royce walked to the window, peered over the campus, and pondered the question. After a moment of silence, he replied to the freshman, "I do not know what is the definition of a Christian, but there goes Phillips Brooks."[88]

Brooks preached by example, and so do ministers. May their codes be their lives, and may their lives illustrate their codes.

Suggested Reading

Bayles, Michael D. *Professional Ethics.* 2d ed. Belmont, Calif.: Wadsworth Publishing, 1989.

"Integrity and Ethics." *Leadership* (winter 2003): 1–58.

Reasons, James Allen. "The Biblical Concept of Integrity and Professional Codes of Ethics in Ministerial Ethics." Ph.D. diss., Southwestern Baptist Theological Seminary, Fort Worth, Texas, 1990.

Reeck, Darrell. *Ethics for the Professions: A Christian Perspective.* Minneapolis: Augsburg, 1982.

Theology Today 59 (October 2002): 329–450.

Ministerial Code of Ethics Worksheet

Preamble

Section 1: Personal and Family Relationships (see chap. 3)

Section 2: Congregational Relationships (see chap. 4)

Section 3: Collegial Relationships (see chap. 5)

Section 4: Community Relationships (see chap. 6)

Appendix A

A Procedure for Responding to Charges of Clergy Sexual Abuse

Constructing a deliberate and methodical response to allegations of ministerial sexual abuse is a serious task.[1] A clearly stated process is needed to ensure that everyone involved is fully heard, adequately defended, and justly treated. Once an acceptable procedure is approved, a church must instruct its ministers and the congregation about the process and provide a clear definition of clergy sexual abuse. In addition, churches must be aware of all legal requirements, such as reporting any sexual abuse involving minors. The following is a broad outline that may serve as a guide for churches. Each church will have to adapt it in light of church policies.

Step 1: Hearing the Accusation

1. The church appoints and trains a specific committee, containing both men and women, to hear all complaints of clergy sexual misconduct. People on this committee must be trustworthy, compassionate, and spiritually mature. Since this committee investigates and possibly charges ministerial staff, staff members should not serve on this committee. Also, staff could be prone to a prejudicial view and may be needed as witnesses.
2. A complaint from a congregant is heard immediately by the committee, which assesses the veracity and the seriousness of the alleged offense.

3. A written summary of the charges is recorded and outlined in a clear, specific, and reasonably documented manner. Both the complainant and the accused should have access to this document and be given an opportunity to respond orally or in writing.
4. The committee explains the process to the complainant, stressing the intent of the church to address the charges without delay.
5. All parties maintain strict confidentiality.

Step 2: Confronting the Accused Minister

1. A meeting between the accused minister and the committee follows immediately. Since public trust is at stake, consideration should be given to placing the minister on administrative leave at the conclusion of this meeting. Suspension in no way assumes guilt.
2. Before this meeting, the committee prepares by: (1) reviewing the factual details of the complainant's story, (2) understanding the dynamics of the minister's possible responses (disbelief, anger, denial, evasion, panic, shame, or even confession), and (3) committing themselves to the same fairness and compassion as was given to the complainant.
3. The committee explains the purposes of the meeting to the accused minister: (1) to hear the allegation of clergy sexual abuse, (2) to assure the minister of the committee's intent to ensure justice through fair and impartial hearings, and (3) to allow the minister to respond to the charges.
4. If the minister denies the charges, the committee determines if further investigation is needed, if the members can reach a decision concerning guilt or innocence, or whether the complaint should be taken to the church.
5. If the minister admits the truth of the accusation, the committee must resist the temptation to accept his resignation and avoid scandal by keeping the incident from the church. This hasty "solution" derails the process designed to remove offenders from leadership and to bring healing into the lives of all persons involved, including the church membership. If the pastor resigns, the committee should still complete its investigation and report to the church.
6. The committee outlines for the minister the process that follows.
7. A written summary of the meeting is recorded, focusing on factual information. As before, the minister and the complainant may read the document and respond to it.

8. After deciding whether further investigation is needed, the committee composes its report and recommendation to the adjudicating body (for autonomous churches, the congregation).

Step 3: Preparing for the Formal Hearing

1. If the church follows congregational polity, the committee calls a meeting of the membership to inform the church of the charges and to explain the hearing process.
2. The church must follow due process in accordance with the church's code of ethics (written or assumed) and its procedure for dealing with disciplinary matters.
3. A formal hearing is scheduled immediately following the conclusion of the investigation. Public access to this meeting supports the church's quest for justice in both the hearings and the verdict.
4. The congregation may consult someone who has expertise in clergy sexual abuse to assist in the process.
5. The church may consider getting legal advice concerning specific matters.

Step 4: Conducting the Formal Hearing

1. Church leaders such as elders, deacons, or members of a personnel committee appoint a moderator who is highly respected and fair-minded and is capable of maintaining order, decorum, and a spirit of mutual respect.
2. The committee reads to the church the charges brought against the minister, a summary of the interviews with the complainant and the minister, and any additional relevant information discovered by the committee.
3. The committee answers appropriate questions from the congregation.
4. The committee recommends to the church one of the following actions:
   a. If the charge is considered false, the minister is exonerated and the church acts to restore the minister's reputation. The complainant receives appropriate discipline and/or counseling and ministry from the church.
   b. If the accusation is considered true, the committee recommends possible sanctions according to the nature of the offense.

Levels of censure can range from admonition to severe sanctions such as probation, suspension, or termination of employment.
5. If the minister is a sexual predator who refuses to admit wrong-doing and evidences a pattern of manipulation, coercion, and control, the church takes whatever action is necessary to keep him from doing further harm to the membership, other churches, or the community at large.
6. If the minister is a first-time offender, acknowledges his abuse, and is genuinely remorseful, the church assists the minister in enrolling in a supervised program of professional counseling designed for clergy sexual abusers.

Step 5: Ministering to the Victims of Clergy Sexual Abuse

1. The church offers support to the complainant and the family. This may include providing counseling, emotional support, financial assistance, and pastoral care to enable them to deal with the personal and family problems resulting from the clergy sexual abuse.
2. The church reaches out to members of the minister's family, who feel isolated and rejected as they deal with vocational, relational, and marital disruptions. They may need professional counseling, financial assistance, emotional support, and pastoral care.
3. Denominational leaders and officials are notified of the church's action so that a perpetrator is not able to continue victimizing the vulnerable in other churches or institutions.
4. A final action of the committee may be to recommend that the church employ a consultant or an interim minister who can help church members deal with the internal turmoil (hurt, confusion, anger, resentment, shame, or even empathy) experienced in the aftermath.

An allegation of sexual misconduct by a minister is a serious matter. If the charge proves to be true, the consequences can be enormous. Marriages may be severed, homes divided, children hurt, churches split, and ministries ruined. The lives of those involved are never the same again. Chronic depression and even suicide attempts are not unusual. A healthy response to clergy sexual abuse can aid the healing of both the church and individuals.

Appendix B

Early Denominational Codes

The Congregational Code

I. The Minister and His Work

1. As a minister controls his own time, he should make it a point of honor to give full service to his parish.
2. Part of the minister's service as a leader of his people is to reserve sufficient time for serious study in order thoroughly to apprehend his message, keep abreast of current thought, and develop his intellectual and spiritual capacities.
3. It is equally the minister's duty to keep physically fit. A weekly holiday and an annual vacation should be taken and used for rest and improvement.
4. As a public interpreter of divine revelation and human duty, the minister should tell the truth as he sees it and present it tactfully and constructively.
5. It is unethical for the minister to use sermon material prepared by another without acknowledging the source from which it comes.
6. As an ethical leader in the community, it is incumbent on the minister to be scrupulously honest, avoid debts, and meet his bills promptly.
7. The minister should be careful not to bring reproach on his calling by joining in marriage improper persons.

II. The Minister's Relations with His Parish

1. It is unethical for a minister to break his contract made with the church.
2. As a professional man the minister should make his service primary and the remuneration secondary. His efficiency, however, demands that he should receive a salary adequate to the work he is expected to do and commensurate with scale of living in that parish which he serves.
3. It is unethical for the minister to engage in other lines of remunerative work without the knowledge and consent of the church or its official board.
4. The confidential statements made to a minister by his parishioners are privileged and should never be divulged without the consent of those making them.
5. It is unethical for a minister to take sides with factions in his parish.
6. The minister recognizes himself to be the servant of the community in which he resides. Fees which are offered should be accepted only in the light of this principle.

III. The Minister's Relations with the Profession

1. It is unethical for a minister to interfere directly or indirectly with the parish work of another minister; especially should he be careful to avoid the charge of proselytizing.
2. Ministerial service should not be rendered to the members of another parish without consulting the minister of that parish.
3. It is unethical for a minister to make overtures to or consider overtures from a church whose pastor has not yet resigned.
4. It is unethical for a minister to speak ill of the character or work of another minister, especially of his predecessor or successor. It is the duty of a minister, however, in flagrant cases of unethical conduct, to bring the matter before the proper body.
5. As members of the same profession and brothers in the service of a common Master, the relation between ministers should be one of frankness and cooperation.[1]

Methodist Ministers' Ethical Code

When a Methodist minister becomes a member of the conference he promises to employ all of his time in the work of God. We again call attention to the fact that he is thus honor bound to give full service to his parish.

Part of the minister's service as a leader of his people is to reserve sufficient time for serious study in order thoroughly to appreciate his message, keep abreast of current thought, and develop his intellectual and spiritual capacities.

It is equally the minister's duty to keep physically fit. A weekly holiday and an annual vacation should be taken and used for rest and improvement.

As a public interpreter of divine revelation and human duty, the minister should tell the truth as he sees it and present it tactfully and constructively.

It is unethical for the minister to use sermon material prepared by another without acknowledging the source from which it comes.

As an ethical leader in the community, it is incumbent on the minister to be scrupulously honest, avoid debts, and meet his bills promptly.

The minister should be careful not to bring reproach upon his calling by joining in marriage improper persons.

As a professional man the minister should make his service primary and the remuneration secondary. This implies a salary, paid regularly, and adequate to the work he is expected to do and commensurate with scale of living in that parish where he serves.

The confidential statements made to a minister by his parishioners are privileged and should never be divulged without the consent of those making them.

In the making of conference reports, it is unethical for a minister to report other than the actual salary received.

The minister recognizes himself to be the servant of the community in which he resides. Fees which are offered should be accepted only in the light of this principle.

It is unethical for a minister to interfere directly or indirectly with the parish work of another minister; especially should he be careful to avoid the charge of proselytizing.

Ministerial service should not be rendered to the members of another parish without consulting the minister of the parish, or by invitation from him.

It is unethical for a minister to speak ill of the character or work of another minister, especially of his predecessor or successor. It is the duty of a minister, however, in flagrant cases of unethical conduct, to bring the matter before the proper body.

It is unethical for a minister on leaving a charge to leave the parsonage property in other than first-class condition, with all dirt, rubbish, etc. removed. Common courtesy to his successor demands the observance of the Golden Rule.

As members of the same profession and brothers in the service of a common Master, the relation between ministers should be one of frankness, of comradeship, and of cooperation.[2]

The Presbyterian Code

I. Personal Standards

1. As a minister controls his own time, he should make it a point of honor to give full service to his parish.
2. Part of a minister's service as a leader of his people is to reserve sufficient time for serious study in order to thoroughly apprehend his message, keep abreast of current thought, and develop his intellectual and spiritual capacities.
3. It is equally the minister's duty to keep physically fit. A weekly holiday and an annual vacation should be taken and used for rest and improvement.
4. It is unethical for a minister to use sermon material prepared by another, without acknowledging the source from which it comes.
5. As an ethical leader in the community, it is incumbent on the minister to be scrupulously honest, avoid debts, and meet his bills promptly.

II. Relations with the Parish

1. In accepting a pastorate, a minister assumes obligations which he should faithfully perform until released in the constitutional manner.
2. As a professional man, the minister should make his service primary and the remuneration secondary.
3. A minister should not regularly engage in other kinds of remunerative work, except with the knowledge and consent of the official board of the church.
4. The confidential statements made to a minister by his parishioners are sacred and not to be divulged.
5. As a minister is especially charged to study the peace and unity of the church, it is unwise as well as unethical for a minister to take sides with any faction in his church, in any but exceptional cases.
6. The minister is the servant of the community and not only of his church and should find in the opportunity for general ministerial service a means of evidencing the Christian spirit.

III. Relations with the Profession

1. It is unethical for a minister to interfere directly or indirectly with the parish work of another minister; especially should he be careful to avoid the charge of proselytizing from a sister church.

2. Except in emergencies, ministerial service should not be rendered to the members of another parish without the knowledge of the minister of the parish.
3. A minister should not make overtures to or consider overtures from a church whose pastor has not yet resigned.
4. It is unethical for a minister to speak ill of the character or work of another minister, especially of his predecessor or successor. It is the duty of a minister, however, in cases of flagrant misconduct to bring the matter before the proper body.
5. A minister should be very careful to protect his brother ministers from imposition by unworthy applicants for aid and should refer such cases to established charitable agencies rather than send them to other churches.
6. A minister should be scrupulously careful in giving endorsements to agencies or individuals unless he has a thorough knowledge and approval of their work lest such endorsements be used to influence others unduly.
7. As members of the same profession and brothers in the service of a common Master, the relation between ministers should be one of frankness and cooperation.[3]

Unitarian Ministers' Code of Ethics

I. The Minister and His Task

1. The minister should always place service above profit, avoiding the suspicion of an inordinate love of money, and never measuring his work by his salary.
2. He should be conscientious in giving full time and strength to the work of his church, engaging in avocations and other occupations in such a way and to such a degree as not to infringe unduly upon that work unless some definite arrangement for part-time service is made with his church.
3. The minister should count it a most important part of his work to keep in touch with the best religious thought of his day and should make it a point of honor to set aside sufficient time for reading and study.
4. It is the minister's duty to keep himself in as good physical condition as possible.
5. The minister should set a high moral standard of speech and conduct. He should be scrupulous in the prompt payment of bills and careful in the incurring of financial obligations.

6. The minister should never speak disparagingly of his church or his profession.

II. The Minister and His Church Officials

1. The minister's relation to his parish is a sacred contract, which should not be terminated by him, or broken by his resignation, without at least three months' notice, except by special agreement.
2. The minister is the recognized leader of the parish, but he should not assume authority in church affairs which is not expressly granted to him by the terms of his contract, or the usage of his office, or the vote of his church.
3. The minister rightfully controls his own pulpit, but he should not invite persons into it who are not generally acceptable to the parish, and he should be ready to accede to all reasonable requests by responsible church officials for its use.

III. The Minister and His Parishioners

1. The minister should remember that he is pastor of all his people. He should avoid the display of preferences and the cultivation of intimacies within the parish which may be construed as evidence of partiality. He should not attach himself to any social set either in the church or in the community. He should not allow personal feelings to interfere with the impartial nature of his ministrations.
2. In the case of parish controversy, the minister should maintain an attitude of good will to all, even when he himself is the subject of controversy.
3. It is unethical to divulge the confidences of parishioners without their consent.
4. Professional service should be gladly rendered to all, without regard to compensation, except for necessary expenses incurred.

IV. The Minister and His Brother Ministers

1. It is unethical for a minister to render professional service within the parish of another minister, or to occupy another minister's pulpit, without the consent of that minister, whenever obtainable, and this consent should be given readily.
2. He should be very careful not to proselytize among the members of another church.

3. He should discourage all overtures from a church whose minister has not yet resigned.

4. He should always speak with good will of another minister, especially of the minister who has preceded or followed him in a parish. It may be his duty, however, to bring to the attention of the responsible officials of the fellowship any instance of gross professional or personal misconduct that may injure the good name of the ministry.

5. The minister should be very generous in responding to reasonable requests for assistance from his brother ministers and his denominational officials, remembering that he is one of a larger fellowship.

6. It is his duty to show a friendly and cooperative interest in his brethren, attending the group meetings of the ministers, assisting his brother ministers with labors of love, defending them against injustice, and following them with kindly concern in their hours of need or distress.

7. He should never accept from a brother minister fees for professional services at christenings, weddings, and funerals.

V. The Minister and His Community

1. The minister is not under obligations to marry every couple that comes to him to be married. The power of refusal, however, should be exercised with great discretion.

2. The minister's responsibility to the state is that of a citizen. He should, therefore, be faithful to his public obligations and should respond to reasonable requests for assistance in community work.[4]

Appendix C

Contemporary Denominational Codes

The Disciples Code

My Ministerial Code of Ethics

I am a minister of the Lord Jesus Christ, called of God to proclaim the unsearchable riches of His love. Therefore, I voluntarily adopt the following principles in order that through dedication and self-discipline I may set a more worthy example for those whom I seek to lead and serve.

I. My Personal Conduct

I will cultivate my devotional life, continuing steadfastly in reading the Bible, meditation, and prayer.

I will endeavor to keep physically and emotionally fit for my work.

I will be fair to my family and will endeavor to give them the time and consideration to which they are entitled.

I will endeavor to live within my income and will not carelessly leave unpaid debts behind me.

I will strive to grow in my work through comprehensive reading and careful study and by attending conventions and conferences.

I will be honest in my stewardship of money.

I will not plagiarize.

I will seek to be Christlike in my personal attitudes and conduct toward all people regardless of race, class, or creed.

II. My Relationship to the Church I Serve

I will dedicate my time and energy to my Christian ministry and will maintain strict standards of discipline.

In my preaching I will exalt the Bible and will be true to my convictions, proclaiming the same in love.

I will maintain a Christian attitude toward other members of the church staff and will not expect the unreasonable of them.

I will not seek special gratuities.

In my pastoral calling I will have respect for every home I enter, for I am a representative of Christ and the Church.

In my administrative and pastoral duties I will be impartial so no one can truthfully say that I am pastor of only one group in the church.

I will strive with evangelistic zeal to build up my church but will maintain a Christian attitude at all times toward members of other religious bodies.

I will under no circumstance violate confidences that come to me as a minister.

I will strive to strengthen the congregation when leaving a pastorate regardless of the circumstances.

III. My Relationship to Fellow Ministers

I will refuse to enter into unfair competition with other ministers in order to secure a pulpit or place of honor.

I will seek to serve my fellow ministers and their families in every way possible and in no instance will I accept fees for such services.

I will refrain from speaking disparagingly about the work of either my predecessor or my successor.

I will refrain from frequent visits to a former field and if, in exceptional cases, I am called back for a funeral or a wedding, I will request that the resident minister be invited to participate in the service.

I will never embarrass my successor by meddling in the affairs of the church I formerly served.

I will be courteous to any predecessor of mine when he returns to the field and will be thoughtful of any retired minister.

I will, upon my retirement from the active ministry, give my pastor loyal support.

I will not gossip about other ministers.

I will hold in sincere respect any minister whose work is well done, regardless of the size or the nature of the field he serves.

I will consider all ministers my co-laborers in the work of Christ and even though I may differ from them I shall respect their Christian earnestness and sincerity.

IV. My Relationship to the Community

I will strive to be human in all my relationships to the community but will never lower my ideals in order to appear "a good fellow."

I will not be a party to funeral or marriage rackets.

I will be considerate of the working hours of business and professional men and will not consume their time with unimportant matters.

I consider that my first duty to my community is to be a conscientious pastor and leader of my own congregation, but I will not use this fact as an easy excuse to escape reasonable responsibilities that the community calls upon me to assume.

V. My Relationship to My Communion

I will at all times recognize that I am a part of a fellowship that has made large contributions to my church, my education, and my ministry. In view of this fact I acknowledge a debt of loyalty to my communion and will strive to fulfill my obligations by cooperating in its efforts to extend the Realm of God.[1]

VI. My Relationship to the Church Universal

I will give attention, sympathy and, when possible, support to the Ecumenical Church, recognizing that my church is a part of the Church Universal.[2]

Code of Professional Practice as Revised at the UUMA Annual Meetings of June 1987 and June 1988

Statement of Purpose

We, the members of the Unitarian Universalist Ministers Association, give full assent to this code of professional life as a statement of our serious intent and as an expression of the lines and directions that bind us in a life of common concern, shared hopes, and firm loyalties.

1. Self

Because the religious life is a growing life, I will respect and protect my own needs for spiritual growth, ethical integrity, and continuing education in order to deepen and strengthen myself and my ministry.

I commit myself to honest work, believing that the honor of my profession begins with the honest use of my own mind and skills.

I will sustain a respect for the ministry. Because my private life is woven into my practice of the ministry, I will refrain from private as well as public words or actions degrading to the ministry or destructive of congregational life.

As a sexual being, I will recognize the power that ministry gives me and refrain from practices which are harmful to others and which endanger my integrity or my professional effectiveness. Such practices include sexual activity with any child or with an unwilling adult, with a counselee, with the spouse or partner of a person in the congregation, with interns, or any other such exploitive relationship.

Because the demands of others upon me will be many and unceasing, I will try to keep especially aware of the rights and needs of my family and my relation to them as spouse, parent, and friend.

2. Colleagues

I will stand in a supportive relation to my colleagues and keep for them an open mind and heart.

I will strictly respect confidences given me by colleagues and expect them to keep mine.

Should I know that a colleague is engaged in practices that are damaging, as defined in our Code of Professional Practice, I will speak openly and frankly to her/him and endeavor to be of help. If necessary, I will bring such matters to the attention of the UUMA Board.

I will not speak scornfully or in derogation of any colleague in public. In any private conversation critical of a colleague, I will speak responsibly and temperately.

I will inform my colleague in advance of any public engagement I may accept in his or her community or church, which might bear upon local issues or policies. I will accept no request for my services in the office of the ministry within my colleague's congregation without his or her explicit invitation or permission. I will inform my colleague of any request for advice or counsel from members of his or her congregation, and I will consider with respect any objection to my meeting such a request. When in doubt I will err on the side of deference to the prerogatives of my colleague's call.

If I am to share the ministry of a church with (an)other minister(s), I will earnestly seek clear delineation of responsibility, accountability, and channels of communication before responsibilities are assumed. I will thereafter work in cooperation and consultation with them, taking care that changing roles and relations are renegotiated with clarity, respect, and honesty.

If I am a member of a colleague's congregation, I will in all ways honor the priority of his or her call to the ministry of that congregation, and I will carefully shun inappropriate influence which other members may tend to yield to me. I will be generous toward a colleague who is a member of my congregation.

I will share and support the concerns of the Unitarian Universalist Ministers Association, especially as reflected in these Guidelines.

I will keep my collegial relationships alive by attending UUMA Chapter meetings whenever possible and by thoughtfully considering matters of mutual professional interest.

3. Congregation

I will uphold the practices of congregational polity including both those of local self-government and those of counsel and cooperation within our Association. I will only serve regularly a congregation(s) issuing a call in the manner prescribed by the Bylaws of the congregation(s) or under a program instituted by the UUA or its member groups. Throughout my ministry I will teach the history, meaning, and methods of congregational polity, recognizing informed and faithful adherence to these practices as the bond preserving and reforming our free corporate religious life.

I will respect the traditions of the congregation, enriching and improving these in consultation with the members.

I will hold to a single standard of respect and help for all members of the church community of whatever age or position.

I will respect absolutely the confidentiality of private communications of members.

I will remember that a congregation places special trust in its professional leadership and that the members of the congregation allow a minister to become a part of their lives on the basis of that trust. I will not abuse or exploit that trust for my own gratification.

I will not invade the private and intimate bonds of others' lives, nor will I trespass on those bonds for my own advantage or need when they are disturbed. In any relationship of intimate confidentiality, I will not exploit the needs of another person for my own.

I will not engage in sexual activities with a member of the congregation who is not my spouse or partner, if I am married or in a committed relationship. If I am single, before becoming sexually involved with a person in the congregation, I will take special care to examine my commitment, motives, intentionality, and the nature of such activity and its consequence for myself, the other person, and the congregation.

I will exercise a responsible freedom of the pulpit with respect for all persons, including those who may disagree with me.

I will encourage by my example an inclusive, loyal, generous, and critical church leadership.

I will take responsibility for encouraging clear delineation of responsibility, accountability, and channels of communication for the minister(s) and other staff.

I will take responsibility for encouraging adequate and sensible standards of financial and other support for minister and staff.

Prior to sabbatical or other leave, I will clearly negotiate a minimum amount of time to serve as minister to the congregation upon my return before making myself available as a candidate for another pulpit.

I will inform the Board of the congregation immediately when I have accepted a call to another position.

4. Movement and Association

I will encourage the growth of our congregations and the spread of the ideals of the Unitarian Universalist tradition and fellowship.

I will participate and encourage lay participation in meetings and activities of our Association.

I will encourage financial support of the Unitarian Universalist Association and its associated programs.

I will inform myself of the established candidating procedures of the Unitarian Universalist Association, and I will strictly observe them.

I will make myself a candidate for a pulpit only with serious intent.

5. Community

In word and deed I will live and speak in ways representing the best Unitarian Universalist tradition and leadership in the larger community.

I will maintain a prophetic pulpit, offering to the community religious and ethical leadership.

I will encourage members' participation in efforts to solve community problems.

I will offer sympathetic support to neighboring ministers of other religious bodies.[3]

The Pastor's Code of Ethics (United Church of Christ)

As a minister of the Lord Jesus Christ, called by God to proclaim the Gospel of his love, I subscribe to the following principles in order that I may set a more worthy example for those whom I seek to lead and serve:

My Personal Conduct

I will observe times of quietness for reading the Scriptures, meditation, and prayer.

I will endeavor to keep physically and emotionally fit.

I will remember my obligations to the members of my family to give them the time and consideration to which they are entitled.

I will endeavor to be a student at all times, through comprehensive reading and study and attendance at conferences and institutes.

I will be honest and responsible in my stewardship of money.

I will seek to be Christlike in my attitudes and conduct toward all people.

My Relationship to the Church I Serve

I will remember that a minister is also a servant. I will love the people I serve with the love of Christ, exercising conviction with patience, guidance with understanding.

In preaching, I will be diligent in my preparation, scriptural in my presentation, speaking the truth in love.

I will be diligent in the discharge of my responsibilities as pastor, preacher, and teacher, observing proper work habits and responsible schedules.

I will strive with evangelistic zeal to build up the church I serve but will not proselytize the members of other religious groups.

I will not violate confidences which come to me as a minister.

I will not seek special gratuities or privileges as a clergyman.

My Relationship to My Fellow Ministers

I will endeavor to be a brother in Christ to my fellow ministers and to offer and receive counsel in times of difficulty.

I will not speak disparagingly about the work of either my predecessor or my successor, nor encourage members in their real or imagined grievances.

I will refrain from visits to a former field for professional services, such as baptisms, weddings, funerals, and anniversaries, except upon invitation of the resident pastor.

I will, upon retirement from the active ministry, give my pastor my loyal support.

My Relationship to the Community

I will consider my primary duty to be the pastor but will also accept reasonable responsibilities which the community may call upon me to assume.

I will not set aside convictions and ideals to win popular favor.

My Relationship to My Denomination

I will recognize that I am a part of the larger fellowship which is the United Church of Christ and will strive to fulfill my obligations to it, accepting my responsibility both to support and to constructively criticize its efforts to extend the Kingdom of God.

My Relationship to the Church Universal

Recognizing that the United Church of Christ is a part of the Church Universal, I will participate in the work of the Ecumenical Church, supporting, as my convictions and energy permit, whatever measures may be proposed toward the strengthening of the fellowship of Christians everywhere.[4]

The Covenant and Code of Ethics for Professional Church Leaders of the American Baptist Churches in the U.S.A.

Having accepted God's call to leadership in Christ's Church, I covenant with God to serve Christ and the Church with God's help, to deepen my obedience to the Two Great Commandments; to love the Lord our God with all my heart, soul, mind, and strength, and to love my neighbor as myself.

In affirmation of this commitment, I will abide by the Code of Ethics of the Ministers Council of the American Baptist Churches and I will faithfully support its purposes and ideals. As further affirmation of my commitment, I covenant with my colleagues in ministry that we will hold one another accountable for fulfillment of all the public actions set forth in our Code of Ethics.

- I will hold in trust the traditions and practices of our American Baptist Churches; I will not accept a position in the American Baptist family unless I am in accord with those traditions and practices; nor will I use my influence to alienate my congregation/constituents or any part thereof from its relationship and support of the denomination. If my convictions change, I will resign my position.
- I will respect and recognize the variety of calls to ministry among my American Baptist colleagues and other Christians.
- I will seek to support all colleagues in ministry by building constructive relationships wherever I serve, both with the staff where I work and with colleagues in neighboring churches.
- I will advocate adequate compensation for my profession. I will help lay persons and colleagues to understand that professional church leaders

should not expect or require fees for pastoral services from constituents they serve, when these constituents are helping pay their salaries.

- I will not seek personal favors or discounts on the basis of my professional status.
- I will maintain a disciplined ministry in such ways as keeping hours of prayer and devotion, endeavoring to maintain wholesome family relationships, sexual integrity, financial responsibility, regularly engaging in educational and recreational activities for professional and personal development. I will seek to maintain good health habits.
- I will recognize my primary obligation to the church or employing group to which I have been called and will accept added responsibilities only if they do not interfere with the overall effectiveness of my ministry.
- I will personally and publicly support my colleagues who experience discrimination on the basis of gender, race, age, marital status, national origin, physical impairment, or disability.
- I will, upon my resignation or retirement, sever my professional church leadership relations with my former constituents and will not make professional contacts in the field of another professional's church without his/her request and/or consent.
- I will hold in confidence any privileged communication received by me during the conduct of my ministry. I will not disclose confidential communications in private or public except when in my practice of ministry I am convinced that the sanctity of confidentiality is outweighed by my well-founded belief that the parishioner/client will cause imminent, life-threatening, or substantial harm to self or others, or unless the privilege is waived by those giving the information.
- I will not proselytize from other Christian churches.
- I will show my personal love for God as revealed in Jesus Christ in my life and ministry, as I strive together with my colleagues to preserve the dignity, maintain the discipline, and promote the integrity of the vocation to which we have been called.[5]

Signed _____

Code of Ethics for Ordained and Licensed Ministers and Lay Speakers in the Church of the Brethren

We believe that we have been called by God, through the church, to the set-apart ministry in the Church of the Brethren. It is our calling, and our function, to lead and facilitate the church in its mission to obey and serve Christ and to witness to the good news of the gospel. We are committed to fulfilling the trust the church has placed in us by maintaining a high standard of Christian conviction, by sincerity of purpose, by nurturing and sharing our gifts, and by integrity of our character. We are dedicated to upholding the dignity and worth of every person who seeks or is reached by our care and proclamation. In order to uphold our standards we, as ministers in the Church of the Brethren, covenant to accept the following disciplines:

1. We will be true to the Judeo-Christian Scriptures in our preaching, teaching, and conversation.

2. We will be true to Christian convictions as revealed in the Bible and interpreted, taught to, and nurtured in us by the church under the guidance of the Holy Spirit.

3. We will live lives of integrity, upholding the commitments we make to God, to others, to the church, and to ourselves.

4. We will exercise lifestyles consistent with the teachings of Christ, giving serious attention to relevant Annual Conference statements.

5. We will treat members of our family with Christian love and respect.

6. We will not misuse the trust placed in us and the unique power inherent in our function by exploiting in any way those who seek our help or care. We will guard against violating the emotional, spiritual, and physical well-being of people who come to us for help or over whom we have any kind of authority. We will not use our authority to defame, manipulate either individual or congregational decisions, or to create or cultivate dependencies. We will avoid situations and relationships which could impair our professional judgment, compromise the integrity of our ministry, and/or use the situation or relationship for our own gain.

7. We will avoid all forms of sexual exploitation or harassment in our professional and social relationships, even when others invite such behavior or involvement.[6] We will not seek sexual favors from volunteers or employees of the church as a condition of their participation or employment.

8. We will not engage in any form of child abuse, sexual, physical, or emotional.

9. We will not use our office or authority to apply influence upon a parishioner or others in order to get bequests, gifts, or loans that would personally benefit us.

10. We will act with financial integrity in all our dealings, professionally and personally.

11. We will endeavor to manage our affairs in order to live within our income and neither expect nor specify financial favors, fees, or gratuities because of our position.

12. We will be responsible and honest in the management of all resources and funds entrusted to our care in the course of our employment.

13. We will give credit for all sources quoted or extensively paraphrased in sermons and prepared papers. We will honor all copyrights.

14. We will respect the privacy of individuals and will not divulge information obtained in confidence. We will share confidences revealed by others without their consent only where such information may need to be revealed for legal reasons or for professional consultations.

15. We will neither exchange nor tolerate scandalous, malicious, or inaccurate information with or about other persons.

16. We will, wherever possible, maintain a friendly, courteous, and cooperative relationship with other ministers, both within our denomination and in the larger Christian community. We will not proselytize people from other churches. We will not render professional service in the congregation being served by another pastor without the knowledge and consent of that pastor, except in emergencies.

17. We will not perform professional services in former parishes, unless invited to do so by the present pastor. We consider it unethical to be involved in the pastoral affairs of a congregation after leaving it or upon retirement, or to cultivate such relationships with former parishioners as may hinder the ministry of the new pastor.

18. We will assume responsibility for our physical and emotional health and for our spiritual growth and enrichment. We will strive to maintain reasonable expectations for ourselves and not allow others' unreasonable expectations for us to endanger our well-being.[7]

Note: Richard M. Gula concludes his *Ethics in Pastoral Ministry* by noting that pastoral ministers in the Roman Catholic Church have no formal code of ethics; nevertheless, he then proposes a "tentative and limited one, open to revision."[8] Two other contemporary codes that are quite lengthy are the Eastern Oklahoma Presbytery Code (adopted February 13, 1990)[9] and the National Capital Presbytery Code of Ethics for Clergy and Other Church Professionals (approved January 24, 1995).[10]

Appendix D

Ministerial and Parachurch Groups Codes

Potomac Association Sexual Ethics Code

Because of increased awareness of sexual misconduct by clergy and religious professionals in general and because of specific incidents surfacing within the Central Atlantic Conference regarding sexual misconduct of religious professionals, the Church and Ministry Committee of the Potomac Association has been urged to study the procedures for dealing with problems of professional sexual misconduct.

Statement of Policy

In all cases involving complaint, the person charged will be considered innocent until proven guilty *beyond a reasonable doubt.*

Sexual contact as described below is a violation of the trust necessary for effective pastoral care and constitutes unethical behavior.

The professional is *always* responsible for protecting the spiritual, emotional, and physical well-being of those who seek counsel and help. Sexual contact *always* undermines that well-being.

The complainant, the accused, and the church or organization are entitled to fair and just treatment and due process, are to be accorded respect, and are to be assured of the church's intent to seek justice, reconciliation, and healing.

Theological Foundation

Human sexuality is a gift of God given to all creatures as a way by which partnership with God in the development of God's creative intent for human life is enabled. Through human sexuality, love and mutuality are built, our connection and link with the whole created order are affirmed, the continuity of human life is assured, and the development and evolution of new life are empowered.

Because human life has been endowed with freedom, human sexuality can be used to undermine and corrupt God's creative intent. Sexual expression may express hostility and anger as well as love. It may seek to exert dominance and exploit vulnerability as well as express mutuality. It can become an agent of addiction by which meaning and esteem is [sic] sought in an exclusively sexual context. As such, sex is elevated to a level of meaning and importance it is not capable of providing. The result is sexual addiction and abuse of self and others, undermining God's creative intent for us.

When God's creative intent has become distorted our faith reminds us that God calls us to engage in the work of justice, reconciliation, and healing. Justice is, in the eyes of faith, restoring life to its original purpose and intent; it means restoring right relationships, the root meaning of the word righteousness. Repentance, restitution, and restoration are involved in the work of justice. The presence of justice is the foundation for human reconciliation. While a state of absolute justice is impossible to fully achieve, a maximum state of relative justice is essential if reconciliation between people is possible. Reconciliation is the establishment of conditions in which alienated and injured parties have the optimum opportunity to heal personally. Healing occurs when the possibilities of justice and reconciliation are realized.

The purpose in cases of sexual misconduct is to commit ourselves to the work of healing by establishing standards of justice and remaining open to possibilities of reconciliation.

Definitions of Terms Regarding Sexual Misconduct or Inappropriate Sexual Behavior in the Pastoral Relationship

Sexual misconduct is a broad term that includes the following behaviors:

1. sexual advances, welcomed or unwelcomed
2. requests for sexual favors
3. inappropriate affection such as kissing, touching, bumping, patting
4. any sexual contact related to terms of employment
5. any sexual contact that exploits the vulnerability of a parishioner, client, or employee

6. Dating of parishioners by religious professionals is a gray area filled with ambiguity. In such situations, consultation with colleagues is essential.

The term "religious professional" in this document applies to the following people: all licensed, commissioned, or ordained ministers: Directors of Christian Education; church musicians with the exception of paid church soloists and others contracted for limited services; pastoral counselor and others in specialized ministries involving licensing, commissioning, or ordination.

Responsibilities in Dealing with Sexual Misconduct

Investigations of complaints regarding sexual misconduct of religious professionals may be appropriately initiated by local church leaders, the professional, professional colleagues, the ACM or Conference Minister for cause, or the Committee on Church and Ministry of the Potomac Association.

It shall be the responsibility of the initiating party to seek pastoral intervention by the ACM or their designee. The purpose of pastoral intervention is to hear complaints and allegations; to assess need for further action; and to inform complainants and the professional of due process procedures if necessary.

The Committee on Church and Ministry in consultation with the ACM shall appoint advocates for the professional, the complainant, and the church or organization. Advocates will seek to understand their clients' needs, help them through the due process procedures, and provide a nonjudgmental presence through the whole process.

The advocate for the complainant will arrange for the following ministries of support.

1. counseling to meet the initial trauma
2. explanation of the procedures to be used in dealing with the complaint
3. advocacy if fair and just treatment seems questionable
4. determining ways, in cooperation with the church advocates, for complainant's community of faith to understand the complainant's feelings and views
5. referring the complainant to appropriate resources for ongoing treatment and healing
6. advocating before the Association and Conference for a just share of meeting financial expenses incurred

The Committee on Church and Ministry shall determine the necessity for special or disciplinary reviews and conduct all necessary hearings, and make the initial determination of action.

If appeal is made the Board of Directors will review the Committee on Church and Ministry's findings and will confirm or reverse the committee's action.

An ecclesiastical council may be called by the complainant, professional, or church to review actions by the Board. The ecclesiastical council's decision is final.

Procedures

All complaints must be submitted in writing by complaining parties to the ACM.

The ACM informs the Chair of the Committee on Church and Ministry of the complaint and the steps to be taken regarding pastoral intervention. TIME IS OF THE ESSENCE. RESPONSE TO COMPLAINTS SHOULD OCCUR WITHIN 72 HOURS OF RECEIPT.

The ACM or designee will make pastoral intervention. The purpose of pastoral intervention is to determine the depth and dimensions of the problems, to assess the possibility of resolution, to inform all parties of the procedures of due process.

Within two weeks the ACM or designee will report to the Committee on Church and Ministry regarding the results of the pastoral intervention.

The Committee determines whether a negotiated settlement is possible. If so the procedures for Special Review as outlined in the Manual on the Ministry are begun. This involves (1) a meeting individually with the complainant, the professional, and church or other organizational leaders, (2) convening a meeting with all parties to explore options, (3) assessing the possibility of settlement.

If the process of Special Review brings no resolution or if the Committee on Church and Ministry determines negotiated settlement is not possible or desirable, procedures for Disciplinary Review are initiated according to the Procedures outlined in the Manual on the Ministry. It should be noted that in matters of sexual misconduct disciplinary review is almost always necessary.

The following procedures for Disciplinary Review shall be instituted by the Committee on Church and Ministry.

1. Advocates will be assigned to the complainant, the professional, and the church.
2. Charges shall be set out in writing—presented to the professional and to the Committee on Church and Ministry.

3. The Committee will seek response from the professional to the charges.
4. A hearing will be scheduled. It shall be closed and confidential unless otherwise requested by the professional and agreed to by the Committee on Church and Ministry.
5. The hearing will be conducted as follows:
    a. statement of the role of the Church and Ministry Committee
    b. introduction of all persons present and statement of their roles
    c. statement about how the hearing will be conducted
    d. prayer for guidance
    e. reading of the charges against the minister in question
    f. presentation of evidence supporting the charges against the minister in question, generally through the testimony of witnesses or use of documents
    g. presentation of evidence refuting charges against the minister in question, again through the testimony of witnesses or use of documents
    h. opportunity for the presenter to respond to the minister in question's evidence
    i. opportunity for the minister in question to respond to the evidence against him or her
    j. closing statement by the presenter
    k. closing statement by the minister in question
    l. prayer for continued guidance and comfort
6. The Committee on Church and Ministry will determine the outcome.
7. Appeal of the outcome maybe [sic] made to the Board of Directors of the Potomac Association by the church, the complainant, or the professional.
8. Appeal of the decision of the Board of Directors will result in a call for Ecclesiastical Council, whose decision is final.

The office of Church Life and Leadership of the United Church of Christ will act as a consultant in the proceeding as deemed necessary.

Possible Outcomes

1. The charges are unfounded.
2. If the charges are judged unfounded, the Association, through its Committee on Church and Ministry, will make a public declaration both through the mail and at an appropriately called congregational meeting.

3. Educative response is made in situations where nothing unethical has occurred but poor judgment has been shown.
4. Warnings may be given where behavior is inappropriate and unwise but not unethical.
5. Censure may be given where behavior is unethical but consequences are minor.
6. Rehabilitation treatment and supervision may be ordered where unethical behavior is determined.
7. Temporary leaves and removal from pastoral responsibilities may be recommended by the committee for the purpose of treatment.
8. Termination of employment may be recommended.
9. Termination of authorization to practice may be recommended.
10. Termination of ministerial standing may be determined and enacted.

Timing

In case of sexual misconduct, time is of the essence: 1) pastoral intervention should occur within 72 hours; 2) reports of the intervention and determination of further procedures within 2 weeks; 3) disciplinary review and conclusions within 3 months; 4) board review within 5 months; 6) ecclesiastical council within 6 months. In cases where legal procedures have been instituted this time line will need to be revised and extended depending on circumstances.

Appendix: Preventative Strategies

While stress and external pressures cannot be used as an excuse for sexual misconduct by a religious professional, it is believed and substantiated that proper support and education of religious professionals greatly reduces the incidence of such behavior. Therefore, the following preventative steps, while not exhaustive, may serve as guidelines to Conference, Association, and local church leaders in working to prevent incidence of sexual misconduct.

A. Support strategies to religious professionals and their families
1. The role of the Conference and Association in advocating for fair and just professional compensation for all religious professionals should be extended to include more than ordained ministers in parish settings. Fiscal security is both an affirmation of worth and a reducer of stress.
2. Association and Conference leadership need to work with local churches in supporting the religious professionals' need for adequate rest, relaxation, privacy, and both educational and spiritual renewal.

3. The Association and Conference structures need to provide opportunities for professional and personal growth of religious professionals.
4. The Association and Conference need to provide a list of resources available for help to families of religious professionals who face personal and family crisis. Such resources should be separate from Conference and Association connections in order to insure [sic] objectivity and confidentiality.

B. Educational strategies regarding sexual misconduct of religious professionals

1. Seminaries and other training institutions should provide a course in ministerial ethics in general and the dynamics of sexual misconduct in particular.
2. Associations should provide workshops on sexual misconduct and this policy.
3. This policy should be a point of conversation at every periodic review with clergy and should be a point of conversation at every change of pastorate with both clergy and representatives of the calling body.
4. The Committee on the Ministry of the Potomac Association should orient in-care students to the issues of sexual misconduct in general and this policy in particular.
5. The Association should request opportunities to present the issues of sexual misconduct to the leaders and members of each local church in the Potomac Association and to orient them to this policy.

C. Continuing the process

It is quite clear that a policy of such personal and intimate dimensions with such public and social impact needs constant monitoring and adjustment in the light of further experience and changing conditions. Therefore, it is recommended that periodic reviews of this policy be conducted by the Committee on Church and Ministry upon request by the Potomac Association through its Board of Directors.[1]

A Covenant of Clergy Sexual Ethics

Introduction

This Covenant calls Baptist ministers to commit to God and the congregations they serve to be faithful to the biblical sexual ethic of fidelity in marriage and celibacy in singleness. Because sexual integrity is foundational to Christian life and ministry, we encourage ministers and congregations to discuss this or similar ethical covenants in the context of the theological foundations and definitions expressed below, and we urge ministers to sign and adhere to a covenant of sexual ethics. We suggest that signed covenants be kept by ministers with copies given to church officers.

Theological Foundations

Human sexuality is a good gift of God through which we become partners with God's creative intent for humanity (Gen. 1:27, 28, 31). Faithful sexual practice expresses the loving commitment of marriage and embodies the mutual intimacy between husband and wife (Gen. 2:18–25).

When we misuse our sexuality, God's creative intent is supplanted by destructive consequences. Raised to the status of idol, the good gift of sexuality mutates into the power of exploitation, selfishness, anger, and domination.

When sexual sin and abuse occur, Christian practice calls us to engage the work of justice, reconciliation, and healing. The work of justice involves repentance, restitution, and restoration. Justice builds the foundation for reconciliation by establishing conditions in which alienated and injured parties have the opportunity to heal. Healing can occur when the possibilities of justice and reconciliation are realized.

The relationship between ministers and congregants is based upon trust. In difficult times, church members turn to ministers for comfort, support, guidance, and assurance, expecting the minister to act as a pastor, shepherd, counselor, and friend. Church members trust ministers never to take advantage of them or to manipulate them, especially when they are most vulnerable.

The purposes of a covenant of sexual ethics for ministers are threefold: (1) to provide a framework for upholding sexual integrity among ministers, (2) to support and protect ministers by defining ethical norms, and (3) to establish a process for achieving justice, reconciliation, and healing.

Definitions of Sexual Misconduct by Ministers

- sexual relations outside of marriage
- unwanted or inappropriate physical contact
- all other sexually oriented or suggestive behaviors, such as overt and covert seductive speech and gestures
- the use of pornography

Preamble

As a disciple of Jesus Christ, called by God to proclaim the gospel and gifted by the Spirit to minister to the church, I dedicate myself to conduct my ministry according to the ethical guidelines and principles set forth in Scripture and this covenant, in order that my ministry may be acceptable to God, my service beneficial to the Christian community, and my life a witness to the world.

Covenant

As a minister called to serve God and God's people, I commit myself to the following norms of ethical conduct, for which I am accountable to God, to my colleagues in ministry, and to the church in which I serve.

- I will demonstrate sexual integrity in ministry by understanding, respecting, and observing the boundaries of sexual misconduct as defined above.
- I will nurture my physical, emotional, and spiritual health, maintain enriching friendships, and build strong relations with my spouse and family.
- I will develop relationships with God, my spouse, and close friends which encourage accountability and protect against temptation.
- I will recognize the special power afforded me in the pastoral office by never abusing that power in ways that violate the personhood of another human being, by assuming responsibility for maintaining proper boundaries in church staff/church member relationships, and by acknowledging that the congregant is always in a vulnerable position.
- I will avoid all forms of sexual exploitation and/or harassment in my professional and social relationships, even if others invite such behavior or involvement.
- I will not seek or accept sexual favors.
- I will exercise good judgment in professional and private conduct by avoiding situations which create the appearance of sexual misconduct.
- I will assume responsibility to report any reliable evidence of sexual misconduct by another minister to the appropriate person or committee.
- I will submit to the policies and procedures of the church when an allegation of sexual misconduct has been made, recognizing the importance of justice and due process.

Conclusion

As I seek to fulfill my responsibilities as a minister, I will strive to embody servant-leadership in all my relationships and to pattern my life and ministry after the example of Jesus Christ.[2]

Christian Association of Psychologists and Counselors

Applicability of the Code

This Code of Ethics (hereinafter referred to as the "Code") is applicable to all current dues-paid Members and Associate Members of the Christian Association for Psychological Studies (CAPS). While CAPS is not a licensing or accrediting agency, it does desire that members who provide mental health, pastoral, or other personal services do so with highest possible level of Christian and service or ministry ethics, whether professional, layperson, or student. Further, even though CAPS is not a licensing or accrediting agency, it does have the authority to set and monitor qualifications for membership in good standing. Thus, the Board of Directors urges each member to consider carefully and prayerfully the Code and to adopt it personally.

Biblical Foundation

Note: Each of the biblical blocks of the foundation that follows has one or more references. The references are not exhaustive, nor are they meant to be convenient "proof-texting." Rather, the Scriptures cited are meant to be representative of the many biblical references that build the foundation of this Code. The complete foundation is the total message of the Gospel of Jesus Christ. Also, it is recognized that each believer in Christ has the capacity—even the privilege and duty—to explore the depths of God's Word and discover personal guidance for daily living. This Code could not hope to explore all the richness of the Bible as it relates to ethical conduct.

Biblical "Building Blocks" of the Foundation

Conflicts, difficulties, power struggles, trials and tribulations are normal and to be expected, whether one is a Christian or not (Ps. 37:7; John 16:33; Rom. 2:9).

We are to grow and mature through the conflicts, problems, trials and tribulations, and discipline that we experience (1 Thess. 5:18; James 1:2–4).

We are to support and encourage each other (John 13:35; 15:17; Eph. 4:32).

We are to admonish and, if necessary, discipline each other, especially those Christians in positions of leadership and trust. However, such discipline is to be constructive rather than judgmental, done in love, and with caution about our own shortcomings (Matt. 18:15–17; 1 Cor. 5:11–13; Gal. 6:1).

We are to demonstrate the lordship of Christ in our lives by servant-like leadership, a sense of community, and a lifestyle that reflects the will of God (Matt. 20:25–28; John 12:26; Col. 3:12–17; 1 Peter 4:8–11).

We are to reach out to others in love and concern (Matt. 25:31–40; 2 Cor. 1:3–7; Heb. 13:16).

Basic Criteria and Principles of the Code

1. The Code includes a broad range of morality, yet it is specific enough in certain areas to offer guidance for ethical conduct in a variety of situations. It is intended to be universal without being platitudinous. On the other hand, it aims to be functional without being legalistic.
2. The Code calls for commitment to a distinctively Christian code of ethical behavior in our helping professions. Yet it recognizes that ethical behavior is certainly not the hallmark only of Christians; thus, there is no implication of judging persons of different faiths or value systems.
3. The Code is not a credo or doctrinal statement of CAPS. Article II of the CAPS Constitution and By-Laws contains the basis for our association:

    The basis of this organization is belief in God, the Father, who creates and sustains us; Jesus Christ, the Son, who redeems and rules us; and the Holy Spirit, who guides us personally and professionally, through God's inspired Word, the Bible, our infallible guide of faith and conduct, and through the communion of Christians.

4. The Code is not a position paper on major social issues. While CAPS has genuine interest in social issues, it has traditionally encouraged members to become involved personally, as led by God, rather than as prescribed by CAPS. Also, CAPS has traditionally encouraged the free exchange of ideas among members, rather than defining "truth" or a partisan viewpoint for its members.
5. All humans are created in the image of God. We are holistic in our being and thus most descriptions of our parts, such as mind, body, soul, spirit, personality, or whatever, are primarily to make it easier to discuss and evaluate our nature. Much of being created in the image of God is still a mystery to us. However, it does mean that we and

those persons we serve have basic dignity and worth, along with basic human rights and essential human responsibilities. Also, we are to glorify God in worship, service, and stewardship.

6. The family is the basic unit of our culture; it merits honor, encouragement, and protection. In addition, "family" to the Christian includes our "neighbor" (Luke 10:29–37). Thus, our "circle of love" embraces God, neighbor, and self (Luke 10:27). Not only that, we are to love our enemies (Matt. 5:43). Also, our influence, our activities in the helping professions, are to be "salt and light" in this world (Matt. 5:13, 14).

7. Scientific and humanistic activities in the helping professions are good, even excellent, but not good enough. While love without professional standards can become mere sentimentality, scientific observations and professional standards without love and Godly ethics can become mere clinical experiments. Thus, the Christian is called to maximize helping others by integrating the distinctives of Christian commitment—including prayer—with professional education, training, and, if appropriate, licensing.

8. The world as we know it is a temporal place of human existence with the ever-present contrasts or polarities such as good and evil, order and disorder, joy and sorrow, generosity and selfishness, love and apathy, abundance and scarcity. Further, we do not necessarily know the reasons for any particular situation, event, or relationship.

9. Exploiting or manipulating another person for our own or yet another's pleasure or aggrandizement is unethical and sinful.

10. Pretending to have expertise beyond our abilities or practicing beyond the scope of our licensure is unethical, very likely illegal, and does not value the person who needs help, nor does it glorify God.

11. Attempting to do for others what they are able and responsible to do for themselves, especially those persons who are seeking counsel, tends to create dependency and is thus unethical.

12. Some persons—such as children, for example—are more dependent than others and thus merit a greater degree of protection from persons who would thoughtlessly or selfishly take advantage of or manipulate them.

13. Each of us, whether helper or the person being helped, is a fallible human being who has limits that are universal in human nature yet unique in magnitude and proportion within each individual.

14. The helping professions are both art and science, with much to be learned. Also, each of us who serves, whether as professional or layperson, needs to be competent enough in what we do and of sufficient personal stability and integrity that what we do promotes healing rather than disorder and harm.

Articles of the Code of Ethics

Note: In the effort to avoid awkward and lengthy descriptions of persons we serve, the somewhat neutral word "client" is used. According to the perspective of members, words such as "peer," "parishioner," "communicant," "patient," "helpee," "counselee," or even "prisoner" may be used.

Also, the word "service" or "serving" is used frequently in the Code to describe what we do. Again, according to the perspective of members, words such as "helping ministries," "helping professions," "counseling," "ministering," or "pastoring," for example, may be substituted. Admittedly, no word is neutral, since language shapes (and reflects) our reality. Thus, the word "service" or its derivatives is meant to reflect Christ's statement that He came to serve, rather than to be served.

1. PERSONAL COMMITMENT AS A CHRISTIAN

1.1 I agree with the basis of CAPS, as quoted earlier in this Code, stated in the Constitution and By-Laws.

1.2 I commit my service, whether as professional or layperson, to God as a special calling.

1.3 I pledge to integrate all that I do in service with Christian values, principles, and guidelines.

1.4 I commit myself to Christ as Lord as well as Savior. Thus, direction and wisdom from God will be sought, while accepting responsibility for my own actions and statements.

1.5 I view my body as the temple of the Holy Spirit and will treat it lovingly and respectfully. Balance in my priorities will be prayerfully sought.

2. LOVING CONCERN FOR CLIENTS

2.1 Clients will be accepted regardless of race, religion, gender, income, education, ethnic background, value system, etc., unless such a factor would interfere appreciably with my ability to be of service.

2.2 I value human life, the sanctity of personhood, personal freedom and responsibility, and the privilege of free choice in matters of belief and action.

2.3 I will avoid exploiting or manipulating any client to satisfy my own needs.

2.4 I will abstain from undue invasion of privacy.

2.5 I will take appropriate actions to help, even protect, those persons who are relatively dependent on other persons for their survival and well being.

2.6 Sexual intimacy with any client will be scrupulously avoided.

3. CONFIDENTIALITY

3.1 I will demonstrate utmost respect for the confidentiality of the client and other persons in the helping relationship.

3.2 The limits of confidentiality, such as those based on civil laws, regulations, and judicial precedent, will be explained to the client.

3.3 I will carefully protect the identity of clients and their problems. Thus, I will avoid divulging information about clients, whether privately or publicly, unless I have informed consent of the client, given by express, written permission, and the release of such information would be appropriate to the situation.

3.4 All records of counseling will be handled in a way that protects the clients and the nature of their problems from disclosure.

4. COMPETENCY IN SERVICES PROVIDED

4.1 I pledge to be well-trained and competent in providing services.

4.2 I will refrain from implying that I have qualifications, experiences, and capabilities which are in fact lacking.

4.3 I will comply with applicable state and local laws and regulations regarding the helping professions.

4.4 I will avoid using any legal exemptions from counseling competency afforded in certain states to churches and other nonprofit organizations as a means of providing services that are beyond my training and expertise.

4.5 I will diligently pursue additional education, experience, professional consultation, and spiritual growth in order to improve my effectiveness in serving persons in need.

5. MY HUMAN LIMITATIONS

5.1 I will do my best to be aware of my human limitations and biases, and openly admit that I do not have scientific objectivity or spiritual maturity, insofar as my subjective viewpoint will permit.

5.2 I will avoid fostering any misconception a client could have that I am omnipotent, or that I have all the answers.

5.3 I will refer clients whom I am not capable of counseling, whether by lack of available time or expertise, or even because of subjective, personal reasons. The referral will be done compassionately, clearly, and completely, insofar as feasible.

5.4 I will resist efforts of any clients or colleagues to place demands for services on me that exceed my qualifications and/or the time available to minister, or that would impose unduly on my relationships with my own family.

6. Advertising and Promotional Activities

6.1 I will advertise or promote my services by Christian and professional standards, rather than commercial standards.

6.2 Personal aggrandizement will be omitted from advertising and promotional activities.

7. Research

7.1 Any research conducted will be done openly and will not jeopardize the welfare of any persons who are research, i.e., test subjects. Further, clients will not be used as publicly identifiable test subjects.

8. Unethical Conduct, Confrontation, and Malpractice

8.1 If I have sufficient reason to believe a Christian colleague in CAPS has been practicing or ministering in a way that is probably damaging to the client or the helping ministries, I will confront that person. The principles and procedures specified in Matthew 18:15–17 will be followed in confronting the person who appears to be behaving unethically. In addition, the more stringent actions against pastors specified in 1 Timothy 5:19–20 will be considered, if relevant.

8.2 In addition to the confrontation procedures based on Scriptural guidance, civil law will be followed if relevant or applicable.

8.3 If the CAPS Board becomes aware that a member has been accused of unethical conduct, the Ethics Committee (either standing or ad hoc) will investigate the situation and recommend ethical discipline, including expulsion from membership, if appropriate.

8.4 Since ethical concerns may be complex and/or have legal implications, the consultation provided will be primarily in helping think through a situation, without assuming responsibility for the case.

8.5 The value of malpractice insurance will be carefully considered, especially if a lawsuit—whether justified or not—would possibly drain financial resources of the ministry organization with which I am associated, or of my family.

9. GENERAL PRUDENTIAL RULE

9.1 Recognizing that no code of ethics is complete, I will make day-to-day decisions based on the criteria and principles stated at the beginning of this Code. Even more important, I will do my best to serve and live in a way that is congruent with the stated basic principles of this Code and with my faith as a Christian.[3]

Note: Two lengthy codes of ethics for Christian counselors are: American Association of Pastoral Counselors Code of Ethics[4] and Code of Ethics and Standards of Practice of the American Counseling Association.[5]

The Covenant and Code of Ethics for Chaplains of the Armed Forces

The Covenant

Having accepted God's Call to minister to people who serve in the Armed Forces of our country, I covenant to serve God and these people with God's help; to deepen my obedience to the commandments, to love the Lord our God with all my heart, soul, mind, and strength, and to love my neighbor as myself. In affirmation of this commitment, I will abide by the Code of Ethics for Chaplains of the Armed Forces, and I will faithfully support its purposes and ideals. As further affirmation of my commitment, I covenant with my colleagues in ministry that we will hold one another accountable for fulfillment of all public actions set forth in our Code of Ethics.

The Code of Ethics

I will hold in trust the traditions and practices of my religious body.

I will carefully adhere to whatever direction may be conveyed to me by my endorsing body for maintenance of my endorsement.

I understand, as a chaplain in the Armed Forces, that I must function in a pluralistic environment with chaplains of other religious bodies to provide for ministry to all military personnel and their families entrusted to my care.

I will seek to provide for pastoral care and ministry to persons of religious bodies other than my own within my area of responsibility with the same investment of myself as I give to members of my own religious body. I will work collegially with chaplains of religious bodies other than my own as together we seek to provide as full a ministry as possible to our people. I will respect the beliefs and traditions of my colleagues and those to whom I minister. When conducting services of worship that include persons of other than my religious body, I will draw upon those beliefs, principles, and practices that we have in common.

I will, if in a supervisory position, respect the practices and beliefs of each chaplain I supervise and exercise care not to require of them any service or practice that would be in violation of the faith practices of their particular religious body.

I will seek to support all colleagues in ministry by building constructive relationships wherever I serve, both with the staff where I work and with colleagues throughout the military environment.

I will maintain a disciplined ministry in such ways as keeping hours of prayer and devotion, endeavoring to maintain wholesome family relationships, and regularly engaging in educational and recreational activities for professional and personal development. I will seek to maintain good health habits.

I will recognize that my obligation is to provide ministry to all members of the Military Services, their families, and other authorized personnel. When on Active Duty, I will only accept added responsibility in civilian ministry if it does not interfere with the overall effectiveness of my primary military ministry.

I will defend my colleagues against unfair discrimination on the basis of gender, race, religion, or national origin.

I will hold in confidence any privileged communication received by me during the conduct of my ministry. I will not disclose confidential communications in private or in public.

I will not proselytize from other religious bodies, but I retain the right to evangelize those who are non-affiliated.

I will show personal love for God in my life and ministry, as I strive together with my colleagues to preserve the dignity, maintain the discipline, and promote the integrity of the profession to which we have been called.

I recognize the special power afforded me by my ministerial office. I will never use that power in ways that violate the personhood of another human being, religiously, emotionally, or sexually. I will use my pastoral office only for that which is best for the persons under my ministry.[6]

Appendix E

Sample Codes of Ethics

Pastor or Senior Minister Code

[Includes basic obligations for all ministers][1]
Preamble

As a minister of Jesus Christ, called by God to proclaim the gospel and gifted by the Spirit to pastor the church, I dedicate myself to conduct my ministry according to the ethical guidelines and principles set forth in this code of ethics, in order that my ministry may be acceptable to God, my service beneficial to the Christian community, and my life a witness to the world.

Responsibilities to Self

1. I will maintain my physical and emotional health through regular exercise, good eating habits, and the proper care of my body.
2. I will nurture my devotional life through a regular time of prayer, reading of Scripture, and meditation.
3. I will continue to grow intellectually through personal study, comprehensive reading, and attending growth conferences.
4. I will manage my time well by properly balancing personal obligations, church duties, and family responsibilities, and by observing a weekly day off and an annual vacation.

5. I will be honest and responsible in my finances by paying all debts on time, never seeking special gratuities or privileges, giving generously to worthwhile causes, and living a Christian lifestyle.
6. I will be truthful in my speech, never plagiarizing another's work, exaggerating the facts, misusing personal experiences, or communicating gossip.
7. I will seek to be Christlike in attitude and action toward all persons regardless of race, social class, religious beliefs, or position of influence within the church and community.

Responsibilities to Family

1. I will be fair to every member of my family, giving them the time, love, and consideration they need.
2. I will understand the unique role of my spouse, recognizing that his or her primary responsibility is as marital partner and parent to the children and secondarily as church worker and assistant to the pastor.
3. I will regard my children as a gift from God and seek to meet their individual needs without imposing undue expectations upon them.

Responsibilities to the Congregation

1. I will seek to be a servant-minister of the church by following the example of Christ in faith, love, wisdom, courage, and integrity.
2. I will faithfully discharge my time and energies as pastor, teacher, preacher, and administrator through proper work habits and reasonable schedules.
3. In my administrative and pastoral duties, I will be impartial and fair to all members.
4. In my preaching responsibilities, I will give adequate time to prayer and preparation so that my presentation will be biblically based, theologically correct, and clearly communicated.
5. In my pastoral counseling, I will maintain strict confidentiality, except in cases in which disclosure is necessary to prevent harm to persons and/or is required by law.
6. In my evangelistic responsibilities, I will seek to lead persons to salvation and to church membership without manipulating converts, proselytizing members of other churches, or demeaning other religious faiths.
7. In my visitation and counseling practices, I will never be alone with a person of another sex unless another church member is present nearby.

8. I will not charge fees to church members for weddings or funerals; for nonmembers I will establish policies based on ministry opportunities, time constraints, and theological beliefs.
9. As a full-time minister, I will not accept any other remunerative work without the expressed consent of the church.
10. In leaving a congregation, I will seek to strengthen the church through proper timing, verbal affirmation, and an appropriate closure of my ministry.

Responsibilities to Colleagues

1. I will endeavor to relate to all ministers, especially those with whom I serve in my church, as partners in the work of God, respecting their ministry and cooperating with them.
2. I will seek to serve my minister colleagues and their families with counsel, support, and personal assistance.
3. I will refuse to treat other ministers as competition in order to gain a church, receive an honor, or achieve statistical success.
4. I will refrain from speaking disparagingly about the person or work of any other minister, especially my predecessor or successor.
5. I will enhance the ministry of my successor by refusing to interfere in any way with the church I formerly served.
6. I will return to a former church field for professional services, such as weddings and funerals, only if invited by the resident pastor.
7. I will treat with respect and courtesy any predecessor who returns to my church field.
8. I will be thoughtful and respectful of all retired ministers and, upon my retirement, I will support and love my pastor.
9. I will be honest and kind in my recommendations of other ministers to church positions or other inquiries.
10. If aware of serious misconduct by a minister, I will contact responsible officials of that minister's church body and inform them of the incident.

Responsibilities to the Community

1. I will consider my primary responsibility to be pastor of my congregation and will never neglect ministerial duties in order to serve in the community.
2. I will accept reasonable responsibilities for community service, recognizing that the minister has a public ministry.

3. I will support public morality in the community through responsible prophetic witness and social action.
4. I will obey the laws of my government unless they require my disobedience to the law of God.
5. I will practice Christian citizenship without engaging in partisan
   politics or political activities that are unethical, unbiblical, or unwise.

Responsibilities to My Denomination

1. I will love, support, and cooperate with the faith community of
   which I am a part, recognizing the debt I owe to my denomination
   for its contribution to my life, my ministry, and my church.
2. I will work to improve my denomination in its efforts to expand
   and extend the kingdom of God.

Associate Minister Code (Education/Music/Youth/Etc.)

I will be supportive of and loyal to the senior pastor or, if unable to do so,
will seek another place of service.

I will be supportive of and loyal to my fellow staff ministers, never criticiz-
ing them or undermining their ministry.

I will recognize my role and responsibility to the church staff and will not
feel threatened or in competition with any other minister of the church.

I will maintain good relationships with other ministers of my special area
of ministry.

If single, I will be discreet in my dating practices, especially in relation to
members of my congregation.[2]

Pastoral Counselor Code

I will have a pastor/counselor to whom I can turn for counseling and
advice.

I will be aware of my own needs and vulnerabilities, never seeking to meet
my personal needs through my counselees.

I will recognize the power I hold over counselees and never take advantage
of their vulnerability through exploitation or manipulation.

I will never become sexually or romantically involved with a client or engage
in any form of erotic or romantic contact.

I will demonstrate unconditional acceptance and love toward all counselees, regardless of their standards, beliefs, attitudes, or actions.

If I am unable to benefit a client, I will refer him or her to another professional who can provide appropriate therapy.

I will maintain good relationships with other counselors and therapists, informing them and conferring with them about mutual concerns.

I will keep confidential all matters discussed in a counseling setting unless the information is hazardous for the client or another person or by law must be disclosed.

I will offer my assistance and services to fellow ministers and their families whenever needed.

I will support and contribute to the ministry of my church through personal counseling, seminars, lectures, workshops, and group therapy.

I will seek to support the policies and beliefs of my church without unduly imposing them on any counselee.[3]

Military Chaplain Code

I will be an ethical example of a Christian lifestyle in a military setting.

I will perform my service duties according to the military codes of conduct, recognizing that my ultimate allegiance is to God.

I will be truthful in my reports to my senior officers without divulging unnecessary confidential information.[4]

Notes

Introduction

1. Walker Percy, *The Thanatos Syndrome* (New York: Farrar, Straus & Giroux, 1987), 75.

2. James P. Wind, "Clergy Ethics in Modern Fiction," in *Clergy Ethics in a Changing Society: Mapping the Terrain,* ed. James P. Wind, Russell Burck, Paul F. Camenisch, and Dennis P. McCann (Louisville: Westminster John Knox, 1991), 99.

3. Glenna Whitley, "The Second Coming of Billy Weber," *D Magazine* (July 1989): 94.

4. Joy Jordan-Lake, "Conduct Unbecoming a Preacher," *Christianity Today,* 10 February 1992, 29.

5. Edward Leroy Long Jr., *A Survey of Recent Christian Ethics* (New York: Oxford University Press, 1982), 151.

6. Reprinted as J. Clark Hensley, *Preacher Behave! A Handbook of Ministerial Ethics,* rev. ed. (Clinton, Miss.: The Minister's Friend, 2001).

7. Karen Lebacqz, *Professional Ethics: Power and Paradox* (Nashville: Abingdon, 1985).

8. Darrell Reeck, *Ethics for the Professions: A Christian Perspective* (Minneapolis: Augsburg, 1982); and Dennis Campbell, *Doctors, Lawyers, and Ministers: Christian Ethics in Professional Practice* (Nashville: Abingdon, 1982).

9. See Gaylord Noyce, *Pastoral Ethics: Professional Responsibilities of the Clergy* (Nashville: Abingdon, 1988); Richard Bondi, *Leading God's People: Ethics for the Practice of Ministry* (Nashville: Abingdon, 1989); and Walter E. Wiest and Elwyn A. Smith, *Ethics in Ministry: A Guide for the Professional* (Minneapolis: Fortress, 1990).

10. See "Ministry Ethics," *Review and Expositor* (fall 1989): 505–73.

11. Wind, Burck, Camenisch, and McCann, *Clergy Ethics,* 13.

12. Another text appeared during this period compiled by two Assembly of God executives: T. Burton Pierce and Stanley M. Horton, eds., *Ministerial Ethics: A Guide for Spirit-Filled Leaders* (Springfield, Mo.: Gospel Publishing House, 1996), but most of the book discusses theology, church history, and social issues, dealing with the subject of the title only sparingly at the close of the book.

13. Richard M. Gula, *Ethics in Pastoral Ministry* (New York: Paulist Press, 1996).

14. William H. Willimon, *Calling and Character: Virtues of the Ordained Life* (Nashville: Abingdon, 2000). Willimon's more recent book, *Pastor: The Theology and Practice of Ordained Ministry* (Nashville: Abingdon, 2002), explores the vocation of ministry, including the distinct roles the pastor must fill.

15. Willimon admits prejudice in favor of "being over doing" (*Calling and Character,* 11–12) and insists that those of us who approach clergy ethics as dilemmas and situations give too little weight to character and virtue (166). As noted in chapter 2, ethicists such as Wil-

265

limon who focus exclusively on the minister's character fail to define or illustrate how a virtuous character acts in the complex moral choices of ministry.

16. James F. Kennan and Joseph Kotua Jr., eds. *Practice What You Preach: Virtue, Ethics, and Power in the Lives of Pastoral Ministers and Their Congregations* (Franklin, Wis.: Sheed & Ward, 1999).

17. See James E. Carter's book review in *Christian Ethics Today* 38 (February 2002): 29–30. Also available at www.ChristianEthics Today.com.

18. That school was the Southern Baptist Theological Seminary in Louisville, Kentucky. Southwestern Seminary in Fort Worth, Texas, had discontinued teaching a course previously offered but reestablished it in 1990.

19. Those two courses were taught by Richard Bondi of Chandler School of Theology and Walter Wiest of Pittsburgh Theological Seminary. The other school was Union Theological Seminary of Virginia.

20. See Nita Sue Kent, "One Choice at a Time," *The Baylor Line* (September 1991): 18–23, for a summary of efforts to teach ethics in schools of nursing, business, law, journalism, and other disciplines.

21. Joe E. Trull, "Newspaper Ethics and Theological Education," *Christian Ethics Today* 43 (February 2003): 2.

22. See Dallas Willard, *Renovation of the Heart: Putting on the Character of Christ* (Colorado Springs: NavPress, 2002); Kenneth Boa, *Conformed to His Image: Biblical and Practical Approaches to Spiritual Formation* (Grand Rapids: Zondervan, 2001); Urban T. Holmes II, *Spirituality for Ministry* (San Francisco: Harper & Row, 1982); and James Bryan Smith, Richard J. Foster, and Lynda L. Graybeal, *A Spiritual Formations Workbook* (San Francisco: Harpers, 1999).

23. "Report on the Task Force on Spiritual Development," American Association of Theological Schools, *Theological Education* 8 (spring 1972): 3.

24. See Evan Howard, "Three Temptations of Spiritual Formation," *Christianity Today,* 9 December 2002, 46–49; and Anne Davis and Wade Rowatt Jr., eds., *Formation for Christian*

Ministry, 3d ed. (Louisville: Review and Expositor, 1988).

25. Walker Percy, *The Second Coming* (New York: Farrar, Straus & Giroux, 1980), 93.

26. See Reeck, *Ethics for the Professions,* 38, where the author defines enablement as "the devotion of professional skills to meeting the needs of client groups and ultimately, to the common good." See also Patrick D. Miller, "Work and Faith," *Theology Today* 59 (October 2002): 350, where he notes, "The practice of a profession involves learning about another person or group in intimate ways. . . . [It is] full of dangers [and] knowing becomes a moral issue as matters of trust and confidence, judgment, and vulnerability join with the larger matter of how the knowledge that comes from experience is to meet and deal with the knowledge that comes from the one being served."

Chapter 1

1. Oliver Sacks, *The Man Who Mistook His Wife for a Hat* (New York: Summit Books, 1985).

2. I am indebted to James F. Drane, *Becoming a Good Doctor* (Kansas City: Sheed & Ward, 1988), 1, for the application of this story to ethics.

3. James M. Gustafson, "The Clergy in the United States," in *The Professions in America,* ed. Kenneth Lynn (Boston: Beacon Press, 1967), 70.

4. Ibid., 81.

5. Janet F. Fishburn and Neil Q. Hamilton, "Seminary Education Tested by Praxis," *Christian Century,* 1–8 February 1984, 108–12.

6. Gaylord Noyce, *Pastoral Ethics: Professional Responsibilities for the Clergy* (Nashville: Abingdon, 1988), 11.

7. Stanley Hauerwas and William H. Willimon, *Resident Aliens: Life in the Christian Colony* (Nashville: Abingdon, 1989), 113.

8. Ibid., 113–14.

9. William F. May, "Vocation, Career, and Profession" (paper presented at "A Consultation on Evangelicals and American Public Life," sponsored by the Institute for the Study of American Evangelicals, 17–19 November 1988), 3, 6.

10. Barbara Zikmund, "Changing Understandings of Ordination," in *The Presbyterian*

Predicament, ed. Milton Coulter, John Mulder, and Louis Weeks (Louisville: John Knox, 1990), 154.

11. John Piper, *Brothers, We Are NOT Professionals* (Nashville: Broadman & Holman, 2002).

12. "Minnesota Pastor Urges Colleagues to Stop Being Professionals," *Facts and Trends,* December 2002, 15.

13. Darrell Reeck, *Ethics for the Professions: A Christian Perspective* (Minneapolis: Augsburg, 1982), 33. The outline for this section and much content is gleaned from this seminal text.

14. James Luther Adams, "The Social Import of the Professions," *American Association of Theological Schools Bulletin* 23 (June 1958): 154.

15. Reeck, *Ethics for the Professions,* 35.

16. Anthony Russell, *The Clerical Profession* (London: SPCK, 1980), 6.

17. Ibid.

18. Kenneth S. Lynn, ed., *The Professions in America* (Boston: Beacon Press, 1967), xii.

19. Robert N. Bellah and William M. Sullivan, "The Professions and the Common Good: Vocation/Profession/Career," *Religion and Intellectual Life* 4 (spring 1987): 8.

20. "Expectations for Baptist Clergy a Source of Stress," *Baptist Messenger,* 31 October 1991, 6.

21. Dennis Campbell, *Doctors, Lawyers, Ministers: Christian Ethics in Professional Practice* (Nashville: Abingdon, 1982), 18–19.

22. Ibid., 20–21. Martin Marty notes, however, that other models have shaped the American clergy: (1) the public role in a congregational-territorial context (1492–1830s); (2) the congregational-denominational role; and (3) the emergent private-clientele expression. See Martin Marty, "The Clergy," in *The Professions in America,* ed. Nathan O. Hatch (Notre Dame, Ind.: University of Notre Dame Press, 1988), 76–77.

23. Reeck, *Ethics for the Professions,* 38.

24. Lisa Newton, "The Origin of Professionalism: Sociological Conclusions and Ethical Implications," *Business and Professional Ethics Journal* 1 (summer 1982): 3.

25. Adams, "Social Import of the Professions," 156.

26. Edmund D. Pellegrino, "Professional Ethics: Moral Decline or Paradigm Shift?" *Religion and Intellectual Life* 4 (spring 1987): 27.

27. Michael D. Bayles, *Professional Ethics,* 2d ed. (Belmont, Calif.: Wadsworth, 1989), 8–9.

28. Wilensky describes four structural attributes: (1) a full-time occupation, (2) a training school that transmits knowledge and skills, (3) a professional association that sets standards, and (4) the formation of a code of ethics. Hall describes five attitudinal attributes: (1) the use of the professional organization as a reference group, (2) a belief in service to the public, (3) a sense of calling to the field, (4) a belief in self-regulation, and (5) autonomy. Cited in Thomas M. Gannon, "Priest/Minister: Profession or Non-Profession?" *Review of Religious Research* 12 (winter 1971): 67.

29. Patrick D. Miller, "Work and Faith," *Theology Today* 59 (October 2002): 349.

30. Paul Camenisch has noted, however, that even professional characteristics such as "specialized skills" must be qualified for the clergy because ministers must often be a jack-of-all-trades, standards of admission to the profession are not uniform, and their skills are not consistently valued in the larger society. See Paul F. Camenisch, "Clergy Ethics and the Professional Ethics Model," in *Clergy Ethics in a Changing Society: Mapping the Terrain,* ed. James P. Wind, Russell Burck, Paul F. Camenisch, and Dennis P. McCann (Louisville: Westminster John Knox, 1991), 121–25.

31. Ibid., 68.

32. Ibid.

33. A. M. Carr-Saunders and P. A. Wilson, *The Professions* (New York: Oxford University Press, 1933), 290.

34. Adams, "Social Import of the Professions," 153.

35. Bayles, *Professional Ethics,* ix.

36. James Wind and Gil Rindle, *The Leadership Situation Facing American Congregations* (Bethesda, Md.: Alban Institute, 2001).

37. Max L. Stackhouse, *Public Theology and Political Economy* (Washington, D.C.: University Press of America, 1991), 172.

38. Pellegrino, "Professional Ethics," 21.

39. Nathan O. Hatch, "The Perils of Being a Professional," *Christianity Today*, 11 November 1991, 27.

40. Campbell, *Doctors, Lawyers, Ministers*, 31–36.

41. Ibid., 36.

42. Ibid., 38.

43. "Religious Index," *Baptist Message*, 23 January 2003, 2. The index is based on eight measurements of beliefs and practices. The highest score ever—746 of a possible 1,000—was recorded in 1956.

44. "The Clergy Receives High Ethical Marks," *Emerging Trends* 12 (March 1990): 1.

45. Tony Cartledge, *Biblical Recorder*, 25 January 2003, 2. In a Barna Research Group poll of non-Christians, respondents gave the highest favorable ranking to military officers (56 percent), followed by ministers (44 percent). Lawyers were near the bottom at 24 percent (*Baptist Standard*, 9 December 2002, 1).

46. James D. Glasse, *Profession: Minister* (Nashville: Abingdon, 1968), 13.

47. Ibid., 14–16.

48. James M. Gustafson, "An Analysis of the Problem of the Role of the Minister," *The Journal of Religion* 34 (July 1954): 187.

49. Martin E. Marty, "Clergy Ethics in America: The Ministers on Their Own," in *Clergy Ethics in a Changing Society*, 24.

50. Ibid., 24–35.

51. Gilbert L. Rendle, "Reclaiming Professional Jurisdiction," *Theology Today* 59 (October 2002): 419.

52. Reeck, *Ethics for the Professions*, 18.

53. Campbell, *Doctors, Lawyers, Ministers*, 24–25.

54. David L. Sills, ed., *International Encyclopedia of the Social Sciences* (New York: Macmillan, 1968), s.v. "professions."

55. Ibid.

56. Noyce, *Pastoral Ethics*, 198.

57. Peter Jarvis, "The Ministry: Occupation, Profession, or Status?" *Expository Times* 86 (June 1975): 264–66.

58. Ibid., 267.

59. Adams, "Social Import of the Professions," 162.

60. Ibid., 162–63.

61. Jacques Ellul, "Work and Calling," in *Callings*, ed. W. D. Campbell and J. Y. Holloway (New York: Paulist Press, 1974), 33.

62. Hauerwas and Willimon, *Resident Aliens*, 121.

63. Adams, "Social Import of the Professions," 163.

64. Glasse, *Profession*, 38.

65. Ibid., 38–43, where the author discusses each in detail.

66. Noyce, *Pastoral Ethics*, 21.

67. Ibid., 23–24.

68. Gaylord Noyce, "The Pastor Is (Also) a Professional," *Christian Century*, 2 November 1988, 976.

69. Glasse, *Profession*, 47.

70. Although the underlying assumption of this chapter seems to be that professionalism is a characteristic each minister develops, the reality is that social institutions, such as the church and education, play a significant role in determining ministerial professionalism, even though ultimately each minister must decide whether to accept that vocational identity.

71. Miller, "Work and Faith," 352, who also provided the illustration.

72. Camenisch, "Clergy Ethics and the Professional Ethics Model," 131.

Chapter 2

1. Lyman Abbott, *Henry Ward Beecher* (Hartford: American Publishing, 1887), 210.

2. Frederick Buechner, *Telling the Truth* (New York: Harper & Row, 1977), 2.

3. Ibid. In Edward Bok's Pulitzer Prize–winning autobiography, *The Americanization of Edward Bok*, a member of Beecher's church related what the pulpiteer told him years after the trial, in which the jury voted 9 to 3 in favor of Beecher. Said Beecher, "And the decision of the nine was in accord with the facts."

4. Michael Levin's article of 15 November 1989 was titled "Ethics Courses Useless" and was published in *Update* 6 (November 1990): 3, along with three typical responses from ethicists.

5. Ibid., 4–6.

6. See Bruce C. Birch and Larry L. Rasmussen, *Bible and Ethics in the Christian Life*, rev. ed. (Minneapolis: Augsburg, 1989), 43–62, for a discussion of these three elements.

7. T. B. Maston, *Why Live the Christian Life?* (Nashville: Broadman, 1974), 98.

8. See Richard Higgenson, *Dilemmas: A Christian Approach to Moral Decision Making* (Louisville: Westminster John Knox, 1988), 55–77, where he details the use of deontological rules and consequentialist principles for moral reasoning in both Testaments, as well as the use of story, imitation, key themes, and scale of values.

9. Birch and Rasmussen, *Bible and Ethics,* 14–16.

10. In addition to Birch and Rasmussen, see also Thomas Ogeltree, *The Use of the Bible in Christian Ethics* (Philadelphia: Fortress, 1983); H. Edward Everding Jr. and Dana Wilbanks, *Decision Making and the Bible* (Valley Forge, Pa.: Judson, 1975); and T. B. Maston, *Biblical Ethics* (Macon, Ga.: Mercer University Press, 1982).

11. Higgenson, *Dilemmas,* 76.

12. Birch and Rasmussen, *Bible and Ethics,* 42–65.

13. Albert Knudson, *The Principles of Christian Ethics* (New York: Abingdon, 1942), 39.

14. Stanley Hauerwas, *Character and the Christian Life* (San Antonio: Trinity University Press, 1975), 115.

15. William Willimon, *The Service of God* (Nashville: Abingdon, 1983), 28–29.

16. Sondra Ely Wheeler, "Virtue Ethics and the Sexual Formation of Clergy," in *Practice What You Preach: Virtue, Ethics, and Power,* ed. James F. Keenan, S.J., and Joseph Kotva Jr. (Franklin, Wis.: Sheed & Ward, 1999), 102–3.

17. D. Glen Saul, "The Ethics of Decision Making," in *Understanding Christian Ethics,* ed. William Tillman Jr. (Nashville: Broadman, 1988), 90.

18. Walter E. Wiest and Elwyn A. Smith, *Ethics in Ministry: A Guide for the Professional* (Minneapolis: Fortress, 1990), 182.

19. Stanley Hauerwas, *A Community of Character* (Notre Dame, Ind.: University of Notre Dame Press, 1981), 10.

20. Darrell Reeck, *Ethics for the Professions: A Christian Perspective* (Minneapolis: Augsburg, 1982), 43.

21. Richard M. Gula, *Ethics in Pastoral Ministry* (New York: Paulist Press, 1996), 33.

22. Daniel Taylor, "In Pursuit of Character," *Christianity Today,* 11 December 1995, 31.

23. Hauerwas, *Community of Character,* 111.

24. Birch and Rasmussen, *Bible and Ethics,* 46.

25. Reinhold Niebuhr, *The Nature and Destiny of Man* (New York: Charles Scribner's Sons, 1943).

26. Karen Lebacqz, *Professional Ethics: Power and Paradox* (Nashville: Abingdon, 1985), 76.

27. Ibid., 77–91.

28. Ibid., 114.

29. Lewis Smedes, "How the Bible Is Used in Moral Decision Making," lecture delivered at New Orleans Baptist Theological Seminary, 7 March 1971.

30. Gaylord Noyce, *Pastoral Ethics: Professional Responsibilities for the Clergy* (Nashville: Abingdon, 1988), 30–31.

31. Wiest and Smith, *Ethics in Ministry,* 21.

32. Ibid., 23.

33. Dennis P. McCann, "Costing Discipleship: Clergy Ethics in a Commercial Civilization," in *Clergy Ethics in a Changing Society: Mapping the Terrain,* ed. James P. Wind, Russell Burck, Paul F. Camenisch, and Dennis P. McCann (Louisville: Westminster John Knox, 1991), 157.

34. Lewis B. Smedes, *A Pretty Good Person* (San Francisco: Harper & Row, 1990), 3.

35. Ibid., 172.

36. William H. Willimon, *Calling and Character: Virtues of the Ordained Life* (Nashville: Abingdon, 2000), 21.

37. Nolan B. Harmon, *Ministerial Ethics and Etiquette,* rev. ed. (Nashville: Abingdon, 1978), 34.

38. Dudley Strain, *The Measure of a Minister* (St. Louis: Bethany Press, 1964), 21.

39. John B. Coburn, *Minister: Man-in-the-Middle* (New York: Macmillan, 1963), 159.

40. David K. Switzer, *Pastor, Preacher, Person: Developing a Pastoral Ministry in Depth* (Nashville: Abingdon, 1979), 16.

41. Lebacqz, *Professional Ethics,* 64. See also Henlee Barnette, "The Minister as a Moral Role-Model," *Review and Expositor* (fall 1989): 513.

42. Reeck, *Ethics for the Professions,* 47.

43. William Willimon seems to chide ethicists Wiest and Smith for "approaching clergy ethics as dilemmas and situations" (*Calling and Character,* 121); however, Willimon could receive equal criticism for a naivete that assumes ministers need to shape their character only to make good ethical decisions.

44. Richard Foster, *Money, Sex, and Power: The Challenge of the Disciplined Life* (San Francisco: Harper & Row, 1985), 15.

45. Ibid.

46. Wiest and Smith, *Ethics in Ministry,* 37–54.

47. Birch and Rasmussen, *Bible and Ethics,* 50.

48. Hauerwas, *Community of Character,* 92.

49. Stanley Hauerwas and William H. Willimon, *Resident Aliens: Life in the Christian Colony* (Nashville: Abingdon, 1989), 12.

50. Higgenson, *Dilemmas,* 107, who also notes that Niebuhr agreed that a more accurate title would be *The Not So Moral Man in His Less Moral Communities.*

51. Niebuhr, *Nature and Destiny of Man,* 248.

52. Reeck, *Ethics for the Professions,* 47.

53. L. H. Marshall, *The Challenge of New Testament Ethics* (London: Macmillan, 1960), 100.

54. John Macquarrie, ed., *Dictionary of Christian Ethics* (Philadelphia: Westminster, 1967), s.v. "Kant and Kantian Ethics."

55. W. D. Ross, *The Right and the Good* (Oxford: Oxford University Press, 1946), 19–21.

56. Lebacqz, *Professional Ethics,* 24.

57. Ibid., 75.

58. Maston, *Biblical Ethics,* viii, 168.

59. Higgenson, *Dilemmas,* 55–69.

60. Smedes, *A Pretty Good Person,* 85.

61. Birch and Rasmussen, *Bible and Ethics,* 59.

62. George Wharton Pepper, *A Voice from the Crowd* (New Haven: Yale University Press, 1915), 23.

63. Strain, *Measure of a Minister,* 50.

64. Lebacqz, *Professional Ethics,* 89.

65. Birch and Rasmussen, *Bible and Ethics,* 62.

66. Charles Swindoll, *Rise and Shine: A Wake-Up Call* (Portland, Ore.: Multnomah, 1989), 190.

67. Ibid., 191.

68. Hauerwas, *Community of Character,* 91.

69. Saul, "Ethics of Decision Making," 94. An example of narrative ethics written in a baptist theology is James McClendon, *Systematic Theology: Ethics* (Nashville: Abingdon, 1986).

70. Charles M. Sheldon, *In His Steps* (Chicago: Moody, 1956).

71. Hauerwas, *Community of Character,* 131.

72. T. B. Maston, *To Walk as He Walked* (Nashville: Broadman, 1985), 9–11.

73. Lebacqz, *Professional Ethics,* 103.

74. Reeck, *Ethics for the Professions,* 55.

75. Higgenson, *Dilemmas,* 230.

76. Fyodor Dostoevsky, *The Brothers Karamazov,* trans. Constance Garnett (Chicago: William Benton, 1952), 20.

Chapter 3

1. Theodore H. White, *Breach of Faith* (New York: Atheneum, 1975), 322.

2. Mark Wingfield, "Houston Pastor Spies Spiritual Warning in Enron's Downfall," *Baptist Standard,* 13 January 2003, 9.

3. Richard Foster, *Money, Sex, and Power: The Challenge of the Disciplined Life* (San Francisco: Harper & Row, 1985), 1.

4. David Aikman, "Interview: Preachers, Politics, and Temptation," *Time,* 28 May 1990, 13.

5. Walter E. Weist and Elwyn A. Smith, *Ethics in Ministry: A Guide for the Professional* (Minneapolis: Fortress, 1990), 97.

6. Kenneth Cooper, *The Aerobics Program for Total Well-Being* (New York: Bantam Books, 1982), 19.

7. Charles B. Bugg, "Professional Ethics among Ministers," *Review and Expositor* (fall 1989): 562–63.

8. Dean Merrill, *Clergy Couples in Crisis* (Carol Stream, Ill.: Leadership; Waco: Word, 1985), 9–10.

9. Glenn R. Putnam, *An Investigation of the Relationship of Marital Pressures to the Marital Satisfaction of the Wives of Southern Baptist Ministers* (Ed.D. diss., Mississippi State University, 1990), 44–46.

10. David and Vera Mace, *What's Happening to Clergy Marriages?* (Nashville: Abingdon, 1980), 24–25.

11. Martha G. Washam, "Preachers' Kids," *Your Church* (May/June 1987): 22.

12. J. Clark Hensley, *Preacher Behave!* (Jackson, Miss.: Dallas Printing Co., 1978), 9.

13. Mace, *What's Happening to Clergy Marriages?* 33.

14. Keith Miller, *Habitation of Dragons* (Waco: Word, 1970), 138–40.

15. Mace, *What's Happening to Clergy Marriages?* 33.

16. Helen Parmley, "Pastor's Pay in Area Leads U.S.," *Dallas Morning News,* 17 October 1987, 15-A.

17. David Briggs, "Clergy Salaries Lag Rate of Inflation," *Alexandria (La.) Daily Town Talk,* 21 March 1992, C-8. For the complete report, see the 1992 *Church Compensation Report* (Carol Stream, Ill.: Christianity Today, Inc., 1991).

18. James D. Berkley, "What Pastors Are Paid," *Leadership* (spring 1992): 89.

19. John C. LaRue Jr., "Seven Findings about Pastor Pay," *Christianity Today/Your Church,* March/April 2000, 88.

20. Matthew J. Price, "Fear of Falling: Male Clergy in Economic Crisis," *Christian Century,* 15–22 August 2001, 18.

21. Becky R. McMillan and Matthew J. Price, "'How Much Should We Pay the Pastor?' A Fresh Look at Clergy Salaries in the Twenty-First Century," *Pulpit and Pew: Research on Pastoral Leadership,* 2002; www.pulpitandpew. duke.edu/salarysummary.html.

22. James E. Carter, *A Sourcebook for Stewardship Sermons* (Grand Rapids: Baker, 1972), 110.

23. Foster, *Money, Sex, and Power,* 20–23.

24. Brenda Kent Paine, "NOBTS Graduates Told to 'Keep Your Vows,'" *Baptist Press,* 7 May 1991, 2.

25. Mary Foster, "Gorman's Suit against Swaggart Starts in NO," *Alexandria (La.) Daily Town Talk,* 9 July 1991, D-1.

26. Cited in Kenneth L. Woodward with Patricia King, "When a Pastor Turns Seducer," *Newsweek,* 28 August 1989, 48.

27. The Editors, "How Common Is Pastoral Indiscretion? Results of a *Leadership* Survey," *Leadership* (winter 1988): 12.

28. Richard A. Blackmon and Archibald D. Hart, "Personal Growth for Clergy," in *Clergy Assessment and Career Development,* ed. Richard A. Hunt, John E. Hinkle Jr., and H. Newton Maloney (Nashville: Abingdon, 1990), 39.

29. Cited in Joy Jordan-Lake, "Conduct Unbecoming a Preacher," *Christianity Today,* 10 February 1992, 6.

30. Woodward, "When a Pastor Turns Seducer," 49.

31. David Briggs, "Church Scandals Shed Light on Taboo Subject," *New Orleans Times-Picayune,* 24 May 1992, A-16.

32. Peter Rutter, "Sex in the Forbidden Zone," *Ministry* (January 1992): 6.

33. Woodward, "When a Pastor Turns Seducer," 48.

34. Ibid.

35. Briggs, "Church Scandals," A-16.

36. Blackmon and Hart, "Personal Growth for Clergy," 40.

37. Ibid.

38. Tim LaHaye, *If Ministers Fall, Can They Be Restored?* (Grand Rapids: Zondervan, 1990), 36–56.

39. Editors, "How Common Is Pastoral Indiscretion?" 12.

40. Woodward, "When a Pastor Turns Seducer," 49.

41. Editors, "How Common Is Pastoral Indiscretion?" 12.

42. Robyn Warner, "Are You Living a Double Life?" *Ministry* (November 1990): 11–12.

43. Karen Lebacqz and Ronald G. Barton, *Sex in the Parish* (Louisville: Westminster John Knox, 1991), 47–51.

44. Marie M. Fortune, *Is Nothing Sacred? When Sex Invades the Pastoral Relationship* (San Francisco: Harper & Row, 1989), 103–6.

45. David R. Brubaker, "Secret Sins in the Church Closet," *Christianity Today,* 10 February 1992, 30–32.

46. Lebacqz and Barton, *Sex in the Parish,* 104–5.

47. Fortune, *Is Nothing Sacred?* 106.

48. Blackmon and Hart, "Personal Growth for Clergy," 48.

49. Labacqz and Barton, *Sex in the Parish,* 107–8.

50. Quoted in Jordan-Lake, "Conduct Unbecoming a Preacher," 30–32.

51. Aikman, "Interview," 13. In 1948, during a citywide campaign in Modesto, California, the Graham team adopted what Cliff Barrows dubbed the Modesto Manifesto, which was a series of commitments to guide their future evangelistic work. They listed four items: money, the danger of sexual immorality, work with local churches, and publicity. Of the danger of sexual immorality Billy Graham wrote, "From that day on, I did not travel, meet, or eat alone with a woman other than my wife." See Billy Graham, *Just As I Am* (San Francisco: Harper, 1997), 127–29.

52. G. Lloyd Rediger, "Summary of Dr. Lloyd Rediger's Strategy for Prevention," *Church Management: The Clergy Journal* (May–June 1991): 24.

53. LaHaye, *If Ministers Fall,* 154–55.

54. Ibid., 171–84.

55. "Creating a Restoration Process: A Leadership Forum," *Leadership* (winter 1992): 122–34. Gordon MacDonald tells the story of his recovery and restoration to ministry following a moral failure in *Rebuilding Your Broken World* (Nashville: Oliver Nelson, 1988).

56. Dee Miller, a former missionary who suffered sexual abuse by a fellow missionary, has written two books about the subject: *How Little We Knew: Collusion and Confusion with Sexual Misconduct* (Lafayette, La.: Prescott Press, 1993); and a novel titled *The Truth about Malarkey* (Bloomington, Ind.: 1st Books, 2000). She has also founded a survivors' support group network and a web site devoted to advocacy: http://members.tripod.com/~NoColluding.

57. Ken Camp, "BGCT Will Provide Information on Verified Clergy Sexual Abusers," *Baptist Standard,* 2 October 2002, 6.

58. *Broken Trust: Confronting Clergy Sexual Misconduct* (Dallas: Christian Life Commission, Baptist General Convention of Texas, 2001), 27.

59. Quoted in Jordan-Lake, "Conduct Unbecoming a Preacher," 28.

60. "Where Judgment Begins: A Leadership Forum," *Leadership* (winter 2003): 26.

61. "Pastoring through the Ages," *Leadership Supplement,* 1.

Chapter 4

1. William F. May, "Images That Shape the Public Obligations of the Minister," in *Clergy Ethics in a Changing Society: Mapping the Terrain,* ed. James P. Wind, Russell Burck, Paul F. Camenisch, and Dennis P. McCann (Louisville: Westminster John Knox, 1991), 79–80.

2. Ibid., 80.

3. Terri Lackey, "'CEO' Pastors Forget Calling to be Servants," *Baptist Standard,* 18 March 1992, 12.

4. May, "Images That Shape the Public Obligations," 81.

5. Ibid.

6. Ibid.

7. Leonard Griffith, *We Have This Ministry* (Waco: Word, 1973), 48.

8. Ibid., 50–58.

9. Franklin M. Segler, "Theological Foundations for Ministry," *Southwestern Journal of Theology* (spring 1978): 7.

10. Herschel H. Hobbs, "The Role of the Pastor," *Baptist Standard,* 20 July 1988, 23.

11. Ibid., 27.

12. Segler, "Theological Foundations for Ministry," 5–6.

13. Charles Bugg, "Professional Ethics among Ministers," *Review and Expositor* (fall 1989): 565.

14. Felix Montgomery, "Authority in Ministry: Meaning and Sources," *Church Administration,* June 1990, 26.

15. Samuel Southard, *Pastoral Authority in Personal Relationships* (Nashville: Abingdon, 1969), 13–14.

16. Ibid., 14.

17. Ibid., 14–15.

18. Bugg, "Professional Ethics among Ministers," 565.

19. Ibid.

20. Montgomery, "Authority in Ministry," 28.

21. Ibid.

22. Karen Lebacqz, *Professional Ethics: Power and Paradox* (Nashville: Abingdon, 1985), 113.

23. Richard M. Gula, *Ethics in Pastoral Ministry* (New York: Paulist Press, 1996), 89.

24. John P. Kotter, *Power in Management* (New York: AMACOM, 1979), i.

25. Wayne Oates, "The Marks of a Christian Leader," *Southwestern Journal of Theology* (spring 1987): 19.

26. Richard Foster, *Money, Sex, and Power: The Challenge of the Disciplined Life* (San Francisco: Harper & Row, 1985), 178.

27. Marie M. Fortune, *Is Nothing Sacred? When Sex Invades the Pastoral Relationship* (San Francisco: Harper & Row, 1989), 102.

28. Foster, *Money, Sex, and Power,* 178.

29. Ibid., 196.

30. David C. Jacobson, *The Positive Use of the Minister's Role* (Philadelphia: Westminster, 1967), 107.

31. Richard M. Nixon, *Leaders* (New York: Warner Books, 1982), 4.

32. John C. Maxwell, *The Twenty-one Irrefutable Laws of Leadership* (Nashville: Thomas Nelson, 1998), xx.

33. Robert D. Dale, "Leadership-Followership: The Church's Challenge," *Southwestern Journal of Theology* (spring 1987): 23.

34. Philip M. Van Auken and Sharon G. Johnson, "Balanced Christian Leadership," *The Baptist Program,* November 1984, 13.

35. Dale, "Leadership-Followership," 23.

36. Raymond H. Bailey, "Ethics in Preaching," *Review and Expositor* (fall 1989): 533.

37. Harry Emerson Fosdick, *The Living of These Days* (New York: Harper & Brothers, 1956), 7.

38. Glenn W. Mollette, "Doing Pastoral Care through Preaching," *Proclaim* (April/May/June 1987): 41.

39. James Allen Reasons, "The Biblical Concept of Integrity and Professional Codes of Ethics in Ministerial Ethics" (Ph.D. diss., Southwestern Baptist Theological Seminary, Fort Worth, Texas, 1990), 14–15.

40. Ibid., 157.

41. Ron Sisk, "Preaching Ethically," EthicsDaily.com, 16 December 2002.

42. J. Clark Hensley, *Preacher Behave!* (Jackson, Miss.: Christian Action Commission, 1978), 57–58.

43. Nolan B. Harmon, *Ministerial Ethics and Etiquette* (1928; reprint, Nashville: Abingdon, 1987), 145.

44. Darrell Turner, "Third Pastor Accused of 'Lifting Another's Work,'" *Baptist Messenger,* 24 August 1989, 10.

45. Mike Clingenpeel, "Speak for Yourself, Preacher," EthicsDaily.com, 10 July 2002.

46. Nicholas K. Geranios, "Pastor Confuses Flock," *Alexandria (La.) Daily Town Talk,* 8 January 1992, A-3.

47. Bailey, "Ethics in Preaching," 536.

48. Segler, "Theological Foundations for Ministry," 16.

49. Walter E. Wiest and Elwyn A. Smith, *Ethics in Ministry: A Guide for the Professional* (Minneapolis: Fortress, 1990), 21.

50. Gaylord Noyce, *Pastoral Ethics: Professional Responsibilities for the Clergy* (Nashville: Abingdon, 1988), 53.

51. Segler, "Theological Foundations for Ministry," 18.

52. Lee A. Davis and Ernest D. Standerfer, *Christian Stewardship in Action* (Nashville: Convention Press, 1983), 13.

53. Noyce, *Pastoral Ethics,* 122.

54. Ibid., 123–25.

55. "Ministry Spends Most of Its Money on Overhead," Associated Press, 2 March 2003.

56. Wayne Oates, "Editor's Preface," in *An Introduction to Pastoral Counseling,* ed. Wayne Oates (Nashville: Broadman, 1959), vi.

57. Wayne Oates, *The Christian Pastor,* rev. ed. (Philadelphia: Westminster, 1964), 181–84.

58. Ibid., 184–219.

59. Noyce, *Pastoral Ethics,* 99.

60. The Editors, "How Common Is Pastoral Indiscretion? Results of a *Leadership* Survey," *Leadership* (winter 1988): 13.

61. Noyce, *Pastoral Ethics,* 92.

62. Gula, *Ethics in Pastoral Ministry,* 119.

63. Ibid., 117.

64. Noyce, *Pastoral Ethics,* 103–4.

65. Lynn R. Buzzard and Dan Hall, *Clergy Confidentiality* (Diamond Bar, Calif.: Christian Ministry Management Association, 1988), 4–5.

66. Ibid., 25.

67. Gula, *Ethics in Pastoral Ministry,* 132.

68. These topics are outlined in Wayne Oates, *Premarital Care and Counseling* (Nashville: Broadman, 1985), 22–34, an older but still helpful book on premarital care and counseling.

69. Harmon, *Ministerial Ethics and Etiquette,* 149.

70. James E. Carter, *Facing the Final Foe* (Nashville: Broadman, 1986), 30–33.

71. Wiest and Smith, *Ethics in Ministry,* 42.

72. Lyle Schaller, *The Pastor and the People* (Nashville: Abingdon, 1973), 32–44.

73. Ron Sisk, "Leaving Well," EthicsDaily.com, 23 September 2002.

74. Richard Bondi, *Leading God's People: Ethics for the Practice of Ministry* (Nashville: Abingdon, 1989), 102.

75. Morton F. Rose, "Ministerial Success," *Search* (fall 1985): 18.

76. William H. Willimon, *Calling and Character: Virtues of the Ordained Life* (Nashville: Abingdon, 2000), 22.

77. Martin Marty, "How Do You Spell Success?" *Context,* 15 November 1991, 3–4.

78. Kent and Barbara Hughes, *Liberating Ministry from the Success Syndrome* (Wheaton: Tyndale, 1987), 106.

79. Ibid., 106–7.

80. Robert Raines, *Success Is a Moving Target* (Waco: Word, 1975), 15.

81. Bondi, *Leading God's People,* 107.

82. William H. Willimon, "Leadership 101: Back to the Burning Bush," *Christian Century,* 24 April–1 May 2002, 8.

83. Jay Gillimore, "Measuring the Pastor's Success," *Ministry* (May 1990): 12–14.

Chapter 5

1. John Donne, *Devotions upon Emergent Occasions,* in *Handbook of Preaching Resources from Literataure,* ed. James D. Robertson (Grand Rapids: Baker, 1962), 87.

2. Norris Smith, "Forced Termination: Scope and Response," *Search* (fall 1990): 6.

3. Ibid.

4. Charles Willis, "Forced Terminations of Pastors, Staff Leveling Off, Survey Shows," *Facts and Trends* (October 2001): 8–9.

5. Smith, "Forced Termination," 6.

6. Ibid., 7.

7. Lee Morris, "Ethical Factors in Forced Termination," *Search* (fall 1990): 50–58.

8. "Inside Church Fights: An Interview with Speed Leas," *Leadership* (winter 1989): 15.

9. Edward B. Bratcher, *The Walk-on-Water Syndrome* (Waco: Word, 1984), 165.

10. *Quality in Southern Baptist Pastoral Ministry,* Summary and Conclusions, Phase One Research (Louisville: Southern Baptist Theological Seminary, n.d.), 16–17.

11. Smith, "Forced Termination," 7.

12. Brooks Faulkner, "Healthy Ministers," *Search* (fall 1990): 30–31.

13. Ibid., 32–34.

14. Ibid., 34–35.

15. Bratcher, *Walk-on-Water Syndrome,* 11.

16. William P. Tuck, "A Theology for Healthy Church Staff Relations," *Review and Expositor* (winter 1981): 5–6.

17. Charles A. Tidwell, "The Church Staff as a Ministering Team," *Southwestern Journal of Theology* (spring 1987): 29.

18. Ibid., 33.

19. Ibid., 12.

20. Hardy Clemons, "The Pastor and Staff as Ministry Team," *Review and Expositor* (winter 1990): 52–53.

21. Tuck, "Theology for Healthy Church Staff Relations," 20.

22. Henlee H. Barnette, "The Minister as a Moral Role-Model," *Review and Expositor* (fall 1989): 514.

23. "Church Staff Survey," November 1977, prepared by Research Services Department, the Sunday School Board of the Southern Baptist Convention (now LifeWay Christian Resources), 5, quoted in Brooks Faulkner, "Ethics and Staff Relations," *Review and Expositor* (fall 1989): 555.

24. Charles B. Bugg, "Professional Ethics among Ministers," *Review and Expositor* (fall 1989): 567.

25. Quoted in Nolan B. Harmon, *Ministerial Ethics and Etiquette* (Nashville: Abingdon, 1928), 66.

26. Ibid., 72.

27. James D. Berkley, "Turning Points: Eight Ethical Choices," *Leadership* (spring 1988): 38–39.

28. Cited in Gaylord Noyce, *Pastoral Ethics: Professional Responsibilities for Clergy* (Nashville: Abingdon, 1988), 137–38.

29. Ibid., 134.

30. Bugg, "Professional Ethics among Ministers," 569.

31. Noyce, *Pastoral Ethics,* 139.

32. Ibid.

33. Ernest T. Campbell, "Preaching out of Phase," *Campbell's Notebook* 12, no. 1 (January 1992): 1.

34. Richard Bondi, *Leading God's People: Ethics for the Practice of Ministry* (Nashville: Abingdon, 1989), 110.

35. Harmon, *Ministerial Ethics and Etiquette,* 80.

36. David C. Jacobsen, *The Positive Use of the Minister's Role* (Philadelphia: Westminster, 1967), 20.

37. Ibid., 21.

38. Ibid., 21–22.

39. Karen Lebacqz, *Professional Ethics: Power and Paradox* (Nashville: Abingdon, 1985), 71.

40. Jacobsen, *Positive Use of the Minister's Role,* 23.

41. Wayne Oates, *The Christian Pastor,* rev. ed. (Philadelphia: Westminster, 1964), 224.

42. Walter E. Wiest and Elwyn A. Smith, *Ethics in Ministry: A Guide for the Professional* (Minneapolis: Fortress, 1990), 176.

43. Howard Clinebell, *Basic Types of Pastoral Care and Counseling* (Nashville: Abingdon, 1984), 210–11.

44. Ibid., 210.

45. Barnette, "Minister as a Moral Role-Model," 510–13.

Chapter 6

1. Walker Percy, *The Thanatos Syndrome* (New York: Farrar, Straus & Giroux, 1987), 127–28.

2. James P. Wind, "Clergy Ethics in Modern Fiction," in *Clergy Ethics in a Changing Society: Mapping the Terrain,* ed. James P. Wind, Russell Burck, Paul F. Camenisch, and Dennis P. McCann (Louisville: Westminster John Knox, 1991), 102–4, uses Percy's novel to illustrate one of four clergy ethical situations that he calls "Ministry in the Extreme Case."

3. H. Richard Niebuhr, *Christ and Culture* (New York: Harper & Row, 1951).

4. See T. B. Maston, *Why Live the Christian Life?* (Nashville: Broadman, 1974), 174–87, for a discussion of this "Tension Strategy."

5. Walter E. Wiest and Elwyn A. Smith, *Ethics in Ministry: A Guide for the Professional* (Minneapolis: Fortress, 1990), 144.

6. See John Yoder, *The Politics of Jesus* (Grand Rapids: Eerdmans, 1972) for the proposal that Jesus' public ministry was primarily a political statement.

7. R. E. O. White, *Christian Ethics* (Atlanta: John Knox, 1981), 58–59.

8. Wiest and Smith, *Ethics in Ministry,* 172–73.

9. Gaylord Noyce, *Pastoral Ethics: Professional Responsibilities for the Clergy* (Nashville: Abingdon, 1988), 168.

10. See Walter Rauschenbusch, *Christianizing the Social Order* (New York: Macmillan, 1912). Charles Sheldon's novel *In His Steps* (Chicago: Advance Publishing, 1899) reflects the idealism of that era from an evangelical viewpoint.

11. Martin Luther King Jr., *Why We Can't Wait* (New York: NAL, 1988), 76–95.

12. Richard Bondi, *Leading God's People: Ethics for the Practice of Ministry* (Nashville: Abingdon, 1989), 73.

13. Ibid., 73–74.

14. Oliver S. Thomas, "Church and State: Matthew 22:15–22," *Theological Educator* (fall 1987): 35–43.

15. *Light* (July 1984): 6.

16. Noyce, *Pastoral Ethics,* 166.

17. Cited in Henlee H. Barnette, "The Minister as a Moral Role-Model," *Review and Expositor* (fall 1989): 514.

18. Richard V. Pierard, "One Nation under God: Judgment or Jingoism?" in *Christian Social Ethics,* ed. Perry C. Cotham (Grand Rapids: Baker, 1979), 81.

19. Terry Muck, "Holy Indignation," *Christianity Today,* 21 October 1988, 14–15.

20. Ibid.

21. Stephan Charles Mott, *Biblical Ethics and Social Change* (New York: Oxford University Press, 1982), 161–65.

22. Noyce, *Pastoral Ethics,* 164.

23. IRS investigations of Jimmy Swaggart Ministries led to a ruling that the evangelist's endorsement of Pat Robertson for president in a 1986 church service and a later publication endorsement violated the Internal Revenue Code.

24. "IRS Issues Election-Year Warning," *Report from the Capital,* 25 July 2000, 2; and Glenn Brown, "Electioneering Off Limits to Churches," *Baptist Message,* 5 March 1992, 2.

25. Richard John Neuhaus, *The Naked Public Square: Religion and Democracy in America,* 2d ed. (Grand Rapids: Eerdmans, 1984), ix.

26. Paul Simmons, "The Pastor as Prophet: How Naked the Public Square?" *Review and Expositor* (fall 1989): 519.

27. Cecil Sherman, "Preaching on Ethical Issues," *Light* (December 1981): 9–10.

28. Don B. Harbuck, "Preaching on Ethical Issues in the Context of the Pastor's Total Ministry," *Light* (December 1981): 11–16.

29. Charles Swindoll, "Discipleship and Ethics," speech delivered at the Christian Life Commission Seminar, Nashville, Tennessee, May 1983.

30. Quoted in Mott, *Biblical Ethics,* 57.

31. Ernst Troeltsch, *The Social Teachings of the Christian Churches,* 2 vols. (Chicago: University of Chicago Press, 1960), 112.

32. Noyce, *Pastoral Ethics,*168.

33. Bondi, *Leading God's People,* 17.

34. See, for example, "To Meet Aids with Grace and Truth," a statement adopted by the 200th General Assembly of the Presbyterian Church—U.S.A.

35. Noyce, *Pastoral Ethics,* 157–62.

36. Oliver Thomas, "Clergy Malpractice after *Nally v. Grace Community Church:* Where Do We Go from Here?" (paper delivered to the University of Virginia Law School, 1991), 2, and the basis for much of the material in this section.

37. *Destafano,* 729 P.2d 290 (Quinn, C. J., concurring).

38. Oliver Thomas, "State Court Upholds Filing of Clergy Malpractice Suits," *Baptist Message,* 9 November 1989, 2.

39. Thomas, "Clergy Malpractice," 14–16.

40. *Hester v. Barnett,* 723 S.W.2d 544, 555 (1987).

41. *Destafono v. Grabrian,* 763 F.2d 275 (Colo. 1988), and *Erickson v. Christenson,* 99 Or. App. 104, P.2d (1989), in which the court ruled that "the harm to plaintiff stemmed from Christenson's misuse of his position of trust, not from the seduction as such."

42. Thomas, "Clergy Malpractice," 16–29.

43. "Church Sued in Abuse Case," *Austin American-Statesman,* 6 May 1999, B-5.

44. Thomas, "Clergy Malpractice," 29–34.

45. *Guinn v. Church of Christ of Collinsville,* 775 P.2d 878, 883 (Okla. 1989).

46. *Gorman v. Swaggart,* 524 So.2d 915 (La. App. 1988).

47. Thomas, "Clergy Malpractice," 34–52.

48. Ibid., 47–52.

49. *Guinn v. Church of Christ of Collinsville,* 775 P.2d 766 (Okla. 1989).

50. *Hester,* 723 S.W.2d 544 (Mo. App. 1987).

51. Jacqueline Kersh, "Attorney Cites Measures to Cut Church Liability," *Baptist Press Release,* 31 May 1989.

52. Because legal responsibilities that apply to the clergy vary from state to state, a minister should be familiar with the laws in his or her locale.

53. John Oman, *Concerning the Ministry* (New York: Harper & Brothers, 1937), 9.

Chapter 7

1. Marie M. Fortune, *Is Nothing Sacred? When Sex Invades the Pastoral Relationship* (San Francisco: Harper & Row, 1989).

2. Cited in Joy Jordan-Lake, "Conduct Unbecoming a Preacher," *Christianity Today,* 10 February 1992, 26.

3. "Religion Newswriters Pick Their Top Stories of 2002," *Baptist Message,* 2 January 2003, 4.

4. Laurie Goodstein, "Church Abuse Crisis Spans Nation, Study Finds," *Austin American-Statesman,* 12 January 2003, A-15. The survey, the most complete compilation of data on the problem available, contains the names and histories of 1,205 accused priests and 4,268 people who have claimed publicly that they were abused by priests.

5. "Clergy Ratings at Lowest Point Ever," *Christianity Today,* February 2003, 21.

6. Cited in Teresa Watanabe, "Problem of Clergy Abuse Extends to All Denominations," *Austin American-Statesman,* 31 March 2002, A-13.

7. Ibid, A-15.

8. Richard Land, president of the Southern Baptists' ethics commission, states that autono-

mous churches "probably did not adopt written policies because it was obvious that sexual misconduct was wrong" (ibid.).

9. When Dee Ann Miller first told church officials she was assaulted by a fellow Southern Baptist missionary in Africa, two leaders replied that it was partly her fault. Read her story in *How Little We Knew: Collusion and Confusion with Sexual Misconduct* (Lafayette, La.: Prescott Press, 1993); her novel *The Truth about Malarkey* (Bloomington, Ind.: 1st Books, 2000); or visit her web site at http://members.tripod.com/~NoColluding.

10. Peter Rutter, *Sex in the Forbidden Zone: When Men in Power—Therapists, Doctors, Clergy, Teachers, and Others—Betray Women's Trust* (Los Angeles: Jeremy P. Tarcher, 1986), 15–16.

11. Ibid., 15.

12. Stanley J. Grenz and Roy D. Bell, *Betrayal of Trust: Confronting and Preventing Clergy Sexual Misconduct*, 2d ed. (Grand Rapids: Baker, 2001), 19.

13. Tom Economus, "Buzz-Words That Put Victims over the Edge!" *Missing Link* (spring/summer 1998): 1.

14. Rutter, *Sex in the Forbidden Zone*, 17.

15. Thomas S. Giles, "Coping with Sexual Misconduct in the Church," *Christianity Today*, 11 January 1993, 49.

16. David Rice, *Shattered Vows: Exodus from the Priesthood* (Belfast: Blackstaff, 1990), 3.

17. Dee Miller, "The Kingdom Is Not Served by Self-Serving Secrecy," *Baptists Today*, 4 May 1995, 7.

18. Richard A. Blackmon and Archibald D. Hart, "Personal Growth for Clergy," in *Clergy Assessment and Career Development*, ed. Richard A. Hunt, John E. Hinkle Jr., and H. Newton Maloney (Nashville: Abingdon, 1990), 39.

19. Richard Allen Blackmon, "The Hazards of Ministry" (Ph.D. diss., Fuller Theological Seminary, 1994).

20. The Editors, "How Common Is Pastoral Indiscretion? Results of a *Leadership* Survey," *Leadership* (winter 1988): 12.

21. Jeff T. Seat, "The Prevalence and Contributing Factors of Sexual Misconduct among Southern Baptist Pastors in Six Southern States," *Journal of Pastoral Care* (winter 1993): 363–64.

22. See "No Longer Silent," *Christian Century*, 4 April 2001, 7, which reports a study in 1993 by a consortium of eight major missionary organizations randomly surveying twelve hundred former missionary children. Of more than six hundred responding, 6.8 percent experienced sexual abuse during primary school, and 4 percent said they were sexually abused during grades seven through twelve.

23. Quoted in Gerald L. Zelizer, "Sex Scandals Rock Trust in All Religions' Leaders," *USA Today*, 23 April 2002, 11A.

24. Blackmon and Hart, "Personal Growth for Clergy," 39. A national survey by Nanette Gartrell (1986) identified 7 percent of male psychiatrists and 3 percent of female psychiatrists who admitted to sexual involvement with patients.

25. G. Lloyd Rediger, "Clergy Moral Malfeasance," *Church Management—The Clergy Journal* (May–June 1991): 37–38.

26. This is partly due to the fact that most ministers are male but also due to the nature of sexual abuse: "In a U.S. survey, 80% of professional sexual abuse cases involved a male therapist and a female client" (from a study cited in Carl Sherman, "Behind Closed Doors: Therapist-Client Sex," *Psychology Today* [May–June 1993]: 13).

27. Grenz and Bell develop these two aspects of clergy sexual abuse in chapters 3 and 4 of *Betrayal of Trust*.

28. Ibid., 83.

29. John D. Vogelsang, "From Denial to Hope: A Systemic Response to Clergy Sexual Abuse," *Journal of Religion and Health* (fall 1993): 197.

30. Rutter, *Sex in the Forbidden Zone*, 124.

31. Karen Lebacqz and Ronald G. Barton, *Sex in the Parish* (Louisville: Westminster John Knox, 1991), 199. Sexual contact during or after any counseling relationship is considered grossly unethical by all counseling associations, such as the American Association of Christian Counselors, the American Association of Pastoral Counselors, and the National Association of Social Workers.

32. Recent Roman Catholic Church scandals concerning priests and children have underscored an important distinction between pedophiles (sexual desire for children) and

ephebophiles (desire for post-pubescent adolescent boys), the target of roughly 80 percent of abusing priests (Jennifer Daw, *Monitor on Psychology* [June 2002]).

33. See Grenz and Bell, *Betrayal of Trust,* 203 n. 4, which lists the sources of the seven profiles.

34. Ibid., 42–47.

35. Fortune, *Is Nothing Sacred?* 47.

36. Ibid., 156.

37. One of the authors was the "after pastor" in this incident.

38. Cited in Greg Warner, "Sexual Misconduct by Ministers—A Cause for Concern," *Baptist Message,* 17 February 1994, 5.

39. Grenz and Bell, *Betrayal of Trust,* 27.

40. Quoted in Herbert S. Strean, *Therapists Who Have Sex with Their Patients: Treatment and Recovery* (New York: Brunner/Mazel, 1993), 4.

41. Fortune, *Is Nothing Sacred?* 103–6.

42. David R. Brubaker, "Secret Sins in the Church Closet," *Christianity Today,* 10 February 1992, 30–32.

43. Lebacqz and Barton, *Sex in the Parish,* 224–25.

44. See Allen Roy Johnston, "Wounded Churches: Causes and Long Term Curative Suggestions for Congregations and After-pastors," a published D.Min. project with an extensive bibliography that records the author's seventeen-year history in a severely wounded congregation (60 Lyle Lane, Selah, WA 98942).

45. Annette Lawson, *Adultery: An Analysis of Love and Betrayal* (New York: Basic Books, 1988), 221.

46. Grenz and Bell, *Betrayal of Trust,* 33.

47. College of Physicians and Surgeons of Ontario, *The Preliminary Report of the Task Force on Sexual Abuse of Patients* (1991), 12.

48. Pamela Cooper-White, "Soul-Stealing: Power and Relations in Pastoral Sexual Abuse," *Christian Century,* 20 February 1991, 197.

49. Jack Balswick and John Thoburn, "How Ministers Deal with Sexual Temptation," *Pastoral Psychology* (1991): 285.

50. Dee Miller, "How Could She?" (unpublished article [1998]).

51. Survivor advocate Dee Miller writes, "The demons are not the perpetrators. They aren't the colluders, and certainly not the sur-vivors. I've named the collective demons in an acronym—DIM thinking—Denial, Ignorance, and Minimization" ("Moving beyond Our Fears" [unpublished article (1998)]).

52. Cited in Greg Warner, "With Sexual Misconduct, All Suffer in Blame Game," *Associated Baptist Press,* 23 December 1993, 6–8.

53. Ibid.

54. Grenz and Bell, *Betrayal of Trust,* 134.

55. Warner, "With Sexual Misconduct," 4.

56. Rutter, *Sex in the Forbidden Zone,* 223.

57. Lebacqz and Barton, *Sex in the Parish,* 107–8.

58. Ibid., 65.

59. Fortune, *Is Nothing Sacred?* 106–7, 148–53.

60. Grenz and Bell, *Betrayal of Trust,* 145.

61. Balswick and Thoburn, "How Ministers Deal with Sexual Temptation," 280, 270.

62. For an explanation of accountability groups, see *Broken Trust: Confronting Clergy Sexual Misconduct* (Dallas: Christian Life Commission, Baptist General Convention of Texas, 2001), 28.

63. See Barbara A. Williams, "Clergy Sexual Misconduct: A Primer for Denominational Church Leaders," American Baptist Churches in the USA (spring 1995); Peter Rogness, "Making the Church a Safe Place," *The Lutheran: ELCA* (June 2002); and the United Methodist Church's extensive program in Donald C. Houts, *Clergy Sexual Ethics: A Workshop Guide* (Decatur, Ga.: Journal of Pastoral Care Publications, 1991).

64. Fortune, *Is Nothing Sacred?* 106.

65. Ray Furr, "Churches Can Prevent Sexual Abuse by Screening Staff and Volunteers," EthicsDaily.com, 12 April 2002.

66. Marie Fortune closes her text with a model of procedure developed by the American Lutheran Church for responding to complaints of unethical behavior by clergy (*Is Nothing Sacred?* 135–53).

67. The Baptist General Convention of Texas now maintains a file that records the congregational history of sexual incidents in churches. A case is placed in this file only when a minister (1) confesses to the abuse or sexual misconduct, (2) the minister is legally convicted of sexual misconduct, or (3) "substantial

evidence" points to the minister's guilt (*Baptist Standard,* 22 April 2002, 5).

68. For a full discussion of the pros and cons of a code of ethics for ministers, see chapter 8 as well as numerous sample denominational and ministerial codes in the appendices.

69. A motion for a committee to be formed for this purpose was approved at the 2002 Baptist General Convention meeting in Waco, Texas.

70. Grenz and Bell, *Betrayal of Trust,* 115–18.

71. Fortune, *Is Nothing Sacred?* 66.

72. Grenz and Bell, *Betrayal of Trust,* 118.

73. "Convention Resolution Addresses Sexual Integrity for Spiritual Leaders," *Baptist Press,* 12 June 2002.

74. Nancy R. Heisy, "Another Look at Matthew 18," *The Mennonite,* 27 October 1992, 466–67.

75. Fortune, *Is Nothing Sacred?* 99.

76. Grenz and Bell, *Betrayal of Trust,* 156.

77. Toby A. Druin, "Ridding the Ministry of Sexual Predators," *Baptist Standard,* 30 September 1998, 4.

Chapter 8

1. Dennis Campbell, *Doctors, Lawyers, Ministers: Christian Ethics in Professional Practice* (Nashville: Abingdon, 1982), 23.

2. Nolan B. Harmon, *Ministerial Ethics and Etiquette,* rev. ed. (Nashville: Abingdon, 1979), 201–8, listed Congregational, Disciples, Methodist, Presbyterian, and Unitarian codes of ethics.

3. See the National Capital Presbytery Code of Ethics in William H. Willimon, *Calling and Character: Virtues of the Ordained Life* (Nashville: Abingdon, 2000), 151–64.

4. Arthur H. Becker, "Professional Ethics for Ministry," *Trinity Seminary Review* 9 (fall 1987): 69.

5. James Allen Reasons, "The Biblical Concept of Integrity and Professional Codes of Ethics in Ministerial Ethics" (Ph.D. diss., Southwestern Baptist Theological Seminary, Fort Worth, Texas, 1990), 1.

6. James M. Aldurf, review of *Is Nothing Sacred? When Sex Invades the Pastoral Relationship,* by Marie Fortune, *Christianity Today,* 16 July 1990, 53.

7. Seminary professors Walter E. Wiest and Elwyn A. Smith state that such codes are "inherently legalistic" and "will not do" (*Ethics in Ministry: A Guide for the Professional* [Minneapolis: Fortress, 1990], 12).

8. Reasons, "Biblical Concept of Integrity," 4.

9. Amatai Etzioni, "Money, Power, and Fame," *Newsweek,* 18 September 1989, 10.

10. Alasdair MacIntyre, *A Short History of Ethics* (New York: Macmillan, 1966), 266.

11. Jane A. Boyajian, ed., *Ethical Issues in the Practice of Ministry* (Minneapolis: United Theological Seminary, 1984), 82.

12. Michael D. Bayles, *Professional Ethics,* 2d ed. (Belmont, Calif.: Wadsworth, 1989), 197.

13. Karen Lebacqz, *Professional Ethics: Power and Paradox* (Nashville: Abingdon, 1985), 66.

14. Lisa Newton, "The Origin of Professionalism: Sociological Conclusions and Ethical Implications," *Business and Professional Ethics Journal* 1 (summer 1982): 40.

15. Lebacqz, *Professional Ethics,* 18.

16. Bayles, *Professional Ethics,* 84.

17. Darrell Reeck, *Ethics for the Professions: A Christian Perspective* (Minneapolis: Augsburg, 1982), 64.

18. Reasons, "Biblical Concept of Integrity," 12–13.

19. Campbell, *Doctors, Lawyers, Ministers,* 23. Darrell Reeck also notes many "unspoken purposes," such as to give an air of professionalism, to enhance public relations, and to enable bureaucritization (*Ethics for the Professions,* 64).

20. Lebacqz, *Professional Ethics,* 68.

21. William F. May, "Code and Covenant or Philanthropy and Contract?" *Hastings Center Report* 5 (December 1975): 29–38.

22. A. M. Carr-Saunders and P. A. Wilson, *The Professions* (New York: Oxford University Press, 1933), 421.

23. Reasons, "Biblical Concept of Integrity," 17.

24. C. S. Calian, *Today's Pastor in Tomorrow's World* (New York: Hawthorne Books, 1977), 104–5.

25. Bayles, *Professional Ethics,* 177.

26. Ibid., 166–67.

27. Lebacqz, *Professional Ethics,* 68.

28. Bayles, *Professional Ethics,* 185.

29. May, "Code and Covenant," 38.

30. Reasons, "Biblical Concept of Integrity," 46–54, provides a detailed discussion of this topic.

31. Lebacqz has made a significant contribution by focusing on the importance of roles for professional relationships (*Professional Ethics,* 135).

32. Lisa H. Newton, "A Professional Ethic: A Proposal in Context," in *Matters of Life and Death,* ed. John E. Thomas (Toronto: Samuel Stevens, 1978), 264.

33. Gaylord Noyce, *Pastoral Ethics: Professional Responsibilities for the Clergy* (Nashville: Abingdon, 1988), 198.

34. Susan Bryant, "'Didn't Mean It' Is No Excuse," *Richmond Times-Herald,* 24 February 1992, B5.

35. James D. Berkley, "Turning Points: Eight Ethical Choices," *Leadership* 9 (spring 1988): 32.

36. Z. N. Morrell, *Flowers and Fruits in the Wilderness,* 3d ed. (St. Louis: Commercial Printing, 1882), 33.

37. Boyajian, *Ethical Issues,* 89.

38. Nolan B. Harmon, *Ministerial Ethics and Etiquette* (Nashville: Abingdon, 1928).

39. "Focus on the Family Now Promoting 'Shepherd's Covenant' for Pastors," *Baptist Standard,* 24 February 2003, 8.

40. *Richmond Times-Dispatch,* 19 October 1991, B10.

41. Boyajian, *Ethical Issues,* 85.

42. Paul F. Camenisch, "Clergy Ethics and the Professional Ethics Model," in *Clergy Ethics in a Changing Society: Mapping the Terrain,* ed. James P. Wind, Russell Burck, Paul F. Camenisch, and Dennis P. McCann (Louisville: Westminster John Knox, 1991), 125.

43. Minnesota State Statue 148A requires all employers of counselors to make an inquiry of previous employers for the last five years to determine if there have been any occurrences of illegal sexual contact.

44. Boyajian, *Ethical Issues,* 79.

45. Henlee H. Barnette, "The Minister as a Moral Role-Model," *Review and Expositor* (fall 1989): 505–16.

46. W. Ward Gasque, "God's Assistant Watchdog," *Christianity Today,* 5 November 1990, 19.

47. Archibald D. Hart, "Being Moral Isn't Always Enough," *Leadership* 9 (spring 1988): 25.

48. Boyajian, *Ethical Issues,* 90.

49. Harmon, *Ministerial Ethics and Etiquette,* 202. Hereafter, references to codes will indicate their location in the appendices.

50. Noyce, *Pastoral Ethics,* 193. As previously noted, however, a minister's multiplicity of roles makes competency in all areas virtually impossible.

51. See appendix II in the 1993 edition of this text.

52. Hart, "Being Moral Isn't Always Enough," 26.

53. "Policy on Sexual Ethics in the Pastoral Relationship as Recommended to the Board of Directors of the Potomac Association," unpublished document of the UCC in Virginia.

54. Becker, "Professional Ethics for Ministry," 70.

55. Lebacqz, *Professional Ethics,* 68.

56. Richard A. Hunt, John E. Hinkle Jr., and H. Newton Maloney, eds., *Clergy Assessment and Career Development* (Nashville: Abingdon, 1990), 40–41.

57. M. Pabst Battin, "Professional Ethics and the Practice of Religion: A Philosopher's View," in *Ethical Issues,* 17–20.

58. Margaret Battin, *Ethics in the Sanctuary: Examining the Practices of Organized Religion* (New Haven: Yale University Press, 1990), 3–4.

59. Hart, "Being Moral Isn't Always Enough," 27–29, focuses on four principles: accountability, confidentiality, responsibility, and integrity.

60. Reasons, "Biblical Concept of Integrity," 134–38.

61. Becker, "Professional Ethics for Ministry," 75.

62. Becker notes a Lutheran Council recommendation not to divulge "unless it is reasonably anticipated that such persons may do great harm to themselves or others." He also suggests that pastors ought never to agree to *secretiveness,* only to confidentiality (ibid., 74).

63. "Report for the Task Force on Ministerial Ethics: Eastern Oklahoma Presbytery," adopted by Presbytery, 13 February 1990. Portions of this code are in the 1993 edition of this book, appendix II.

64. See "When a Pastoral Colleague Falls," *Leadership* 11 (winter 1991): 102–11.

65. "NRB Moves Slowly to Enforce Ethics Code," *Christianity Today,* 9 March 1992, 59.

66. Robert Spanier, "Anti-Board Sentiment Rouses Mass. Physicians," *American College of Physicians Observer* 9 (December 1989): 7.

67. Rudolph W. Nemser, "Guidelines for the Unitarian Universalist Ministry: A History," in *Ethical Issues,* 70–75, which explains the function of these *Guidelines.*

68. Rev. Wayne Arnason of Charlottesville, Virginia, in an interview by the author on 14 February 1992, and UUMA *Guidelines,* 28.

69. Ron Sisk, "More Groups Embrace Ethics Code for Ministers," EthicsDaily.com, 3 March 2003.

70. Hunt, Hinkle, and Maloney, *Clergy Assessment and Career Development,* 40.

71. Pamela Cooper-White, "Soul-Stealing: Power Relations in Pastoral Sexual Abuse," *Christian Century,* 19 February 1991, 199.

72. H. Newton Maloney, "Codes of Ethics: A Comparison," *Journal of Psychology and Christianity* 5 (fall 1986): 94.

73. Jane Clapp, *Professional Ethics and Insignia* (Metuchen, N.J.: Scarecrow Press, 1974); and Rena A. Gorlin, ed., *Codes of Professional Responsibility,* 2d ed. (Washington, D.C.: Bureau of National Affairs, 1990).

74. Thomas Schaffer, "Work and Faith," *Theology Today* 59 (October 2002): 351–52.

75. Reeck, *Ethics for the Professions,* 61–62.

76. Arthur L. Caplan, "Cracking Codes," *The Hastings Center Report* 8 (August 1978): 18.

77. Reasons, "Biblical Concept of Integrity," 40–41.

78. Reeck, *Ethics for the Professions,* 61.

79. C. S. Lewis, *Mere Christianity* (New York: Macmillan, 1960), 71.

80. Lewis Smedes, *A Pretty Good Person* (San Francisco: Harper & Row, 1990), 86.

81. Reeck, *Ethics for the Professions,* 66.

82. James D. Berkley discusses eight areas of ethical concern for pastors who construct their own codes: beliefs, service, morality, competence, compensation, colleagues, confidentiality, and friendships ("Turning Points," 32–41).

83. Smedes, *Pretty Good Person,* 86.

84. Reeck, *Ethics for the Professions,* 69.

85. Ibid., 72.

86. Joy Jordan-Lake, "Conduct Unbecoming a Preacher," *Christianity Today,* 10 February 1992, 30.

87. On November 11, 2002, Joe E. Trull made a motion at the Baptist General Convention of Texas meeting in Waco that a representative committee be appointed to study and develop by 2004 a "Code of Ethics for Baptist Ministers which could serve as a model for ministers, churches, and Baptist institutions to utilize, adapt, and adopt if they so choose as guidelines which reflect basic ethical obligations for ministry, define the ministerial profession, and serve as a support to protect the individual minister." The motion passed, and the committee is at work as this edition is published.

88. Richard Spann, *The Ministry* (New York: Abingdon-Cokesbury Press, 1959), 44–48.

Appendix A

1. This model is adapted from Stanley J. Grenz and Roy D. Bell, *Betrayal of Trust: Confronting and Preventing Clergy Sexual Misconduct* (Grand Rapids: Baker, 2001), 162–74. Originally published in *Broken Trust: Confronting Clergy Sexual Misconduct* (Dallas: Christian Life Commission, Baptist General Convention of Texas, 2001), 25–26.

Appendix B

1. Nolan B. Harmon, *Ministerial Ethics and Etiquette,* rev. ed. (Nashville: Abingdon, 1983), 201, states that the code was adopted by the New Haven, Connecticut, Association for Congregational Ministers and published in *Church Administration* by Cokesbury Press in 1931.

2. Harmon states that this code was adopted "by a group of Methodist ministers meeting in conference at Rockford Illinois," and it was

published in *Christian Century,* 16 December 1926 (ibid., 204).

3. Harmon notes that this code was adopted by the New York Presbytery and quoted in an article by William H. Leach in *The Methodist Quarterly Review* (July 1927) (ibid., 205).

4. Harmon indicates that this code was adopted by the Unitarian Ministerial Union and quoted in *Church Management* (August 1926) (ibid., 206).

Appendix C

1. Comparing this contemporary Disciples Code with the one printed in Nolan B. Harmon, *Ministerial Ethics and Etiquette,* rev. ed. (Nashville: Abingdon, 1983), 202–4, reveals only one word change: "Kingdom of God" to "Realm of God."

2. "My Ministerial Code of Ethics" (Indianapolis: Department of Homeland Ministries—Christian Church [Disciples of Christ], 1990). The foreword written by an executive states, "Since its publication in 1944, more than 30,000 copies of the code have been distributed. . . . With each successive reprint, a general committee was given the possibilities of change in the code. When all the suggestions were received, it was determined that they were sufficient only to effect editorial changes. The code has stood well the test of time and is commended to all ministers as a high code of professional conduct."

3. As published in the *Guidelines: Unitarian Universalist Ministers Association* (Boston: UUMA, 1988), 11–14.

4. Provided by the First Congregational Church, Chesterfield, Virginia, affiliated with the United Church of Christ. Similarities to the Disciples Code are quite obvious.

5. Provided by Harley D. Hunt, executive director of the Ministers Council, American Baptist Churches, USA, and dated May 1991. Also available is "A Process for Review of Ministerial Standing" adopted by the National Commission on the Ministry, January 18, 1991, which defines the procedures for handling allegations and enforcing the code.

6. Sexual exploitation is defined as but not limited to all forms of overt and covert seduction, speech, gestures, and behavior. Harassment is defined as but not limited to repeated unwelcome comments, gestures, or physical contacts of a sexual nature.

7. *Ethics in Ministry Relations—1992,* approved by the 1992 Annual Conference of the Church of the Brethren, Elgin, Illinois, September 1992. The twenty-three-page document also includes an excellent section titled "A Theology of Ministerial Ethics" (4–9) and one titled "Process for Dealing with Allegations of Sexual Misconduct" (11–18).

8. Richard M. Gula, *Ethics in Pastoral Ministry* (New York: Paulist Press, 1996), 142–52.

9. "Report from the Task Force on Ministerial Ethics," Eastern Oklahoma Presbytery.

10. In the appendix of William H. Willimon, *Calling and Character: Virtues of the Ordained Life* (Nashville: Abingdon, 2000), 151–64.

Appendix D

1. "Policy on Sexual Ethics in the Pastoral Relationship as Recommended to the Board of Directors of the Potomac Association," unpublished copy of the Potomac Association Church and Ministry Committee of the Central Atlantic Conference of the United Church of Christ, provided by Rev. Jerry Moore, St. John's United Church of Christ, Richmond, Virginia, February 1992.

2. Published in *Broken Trust: Confronting Clergy Sexual Misconduct* (Dallas: Christian Life Commission, Baptist General Convention of Texas, 2001), after approval by the annual meeting of the BGCT in 1999.

3. Published in *The Journal of Psychology and Christianity* 5 (fall 1985): 86–90; includes an analysis and responses to the code by members.

4. Randolph K. Sanders, ed. *Christian Counseling Ethics* (Downers Grove, Ill.: InterVarsity, 1997), 352–60.

5. Ibid., 365–90.

6. Printed with permission of the National Conference on Ministry to the Armed Forces.

Appendix E

1. These sample codes are generic examples of ministerial codes, and they have been edited to include the most significant emphases, both principles and specific guidelines, in each

category. To write a personal code of ethics, a minister should evaluate his or her own ministry obligations in light of the discussions in the text, then refer to these sample codes as broad statements of possibilities for a personal code of ethics.

2. The sample codes of the associate ministers and others that follow include only those obligations, in addition to the senior minister code, that uniquely apply to each special ministerial role.

3. See appendix D for the code of the Christian Association of Psychologists and Counselors, which, although it has many obvious weaknesses, does deal with the primary issues facing pastoral counselors.

4. See appendix D for the Covenant and Code of Ethics for Chaplains of the Armed Forces. These statements have been suggested by military chaplains as possible additions to that code.

Index